DIFFERENTIATED INSTRUCTION GUIDE

FOR

INCLUSIVE TEACHING

Anne M. Moll, Ed.D.

DUDE PUBLISHING
A Division of
National Professional Resources, Inc.
Port Chester, New York

Moll, Anne M., 1959-
    Differentiated instruction guide for inclusive
teaching / Anne M. Moll.
    p. cm.
    Includes bibliographical references.
    ISBN 1-887943-64-1

    1. Children with disabilities--Education--United
States. 2. Individualized instruction--United States.
3. Inclusive education--United States.   I. Title.

LC4031.M64 2003   371.9'04394
                               QBI03-200327

Cover, Book Design, & Production by Andrea Cerone,
National Professional Resources, Inc.,
Port Chester, NY

Dude Publishing
A Division of National Professional Resources, Inc.
25 South Regent Street
Port Chester, New York 10573
Toll free: (800) 453-7461
Phone: (914) 937-8879

Visit our web site: www.nprinc.com

Printed in the United States of America

ISBN 1-887943-64-1

Dedication

To my mother, the wind of grace beneath my wings; without you I would be lost.

To my father, for lighting the path of education with your laughter, support, and faith in me.

To my husband, for your encouragement and unconditional love.

To my friends, for not just saying I should, but for never calling me crazy when I did.

To Maverick and Bailey, for reminding me to take time to play!

Table of Contents

Appendices

Foreword

When the author and publisher of this book discussed its title, there was a concern that the use of the word "inclusive" would lead potential readers to believe that its content offerings were only for special education teachers. Most certainly, the word "inclusion" has become linked with the movement to educate students with disabilities in general education classrooms - where there is an increasing amount of evidence that these students achieve better than in more segregated special classes. For some teachers and schools, however, the word "inclusion" has become a focal point of debate and concern as they struggle with the many local, state, and federal demands for accountability and improved student outcomes. The difference between "inclusion" and "inclusive" goes well beyond one being a noun and the other an adjective. "Inclusive" is exactly the descriptor we want every classroom to attain. Simply put, an inclusive classroom is one that is welcoming and pedagogically capable of educating the naturally diverse population of students who arrive at its door.

Differentiated instruction is the very foundation upon which teachers can create such classrooms. Developed with an appreciation that our nation's classrooms are becoming increasingly diverse, differentiated instruction provides teachers with a set of strategies to identify and teach to the unique combinations of individual strengths and needs that each child brings to learning. Educational strengths and needs arise from the child's ethnicity, culture, talents, family, disability(ies), prior learning opportunities, and/or community. As today's classroom is an amalgam of the individual strengths and needs of each enrolled child, today's teachers are in critical need of the very strategies that differentiated instruction provide.

Dr. Anne Moll has made a significant contribution to meeting this need. Grounded in her more than 20 years of teaching and serving as a teacher educator, *Differentiated Instruction Guide for Inclusive Teaching,* is a step-by-step, practical, how-to guide for teachers in developing and refining inclusive, high-performing classrooms. Throughout, Dr. Moll serves as a patient coach to her readers; offering case studies, reflective exercises, and tools that produce ready success and gratification. Through her Essential Curricular Questions and Essential Student Questions, Dr. Moll steers teachers in (1) determining the critical instructional requirements of the curriculum, (2) identifying strategies for engaging each child in the intended learning, and (3) implementing lesson plans that meaningfully engage all students - regardless of his/her individual strengths and needs - in effective learning. It is hard to imagine our nation's schools achieving the lofty purposes of the *Individuals with Disabilities Education Act* or the *No Child Left Behind Act of 2001* without every teacher understanding and practicing the principles of differentiated instruction. This book makes the "gift of differentiated instruction" more accessible to every teacher.

David P. Riley, Ph.D.
Executive Director, Urban Special Education Leadership
Collaborative Education Development Center, Inc.
Newton, Massachusetts

I believe all teachers should have a vision of their purpose in the lives of children. That vision should be rooted in what they believe and serve as the foundation for all actions they take. It should be the one thing that brings them back to center when times are troublesome, and gives them hope for the future. This is mine.

<u>My Daily Canon</u>

We must hold ourselves accountable for the very best education for each and every child.

We must value and measure the success of every child.

Words and actions alone are not enough; we must adjust the structures and functions of our schools and represent these changes in all philosophical, actual, and symbolic practices.

This is no simple task. It is an experience that will take us a while to recover from, once it is over.

But the changes to our lives, and the lives of all children who come to our schools as ambassadors of the future, will be richer, and most importantly — **honorable**.

Anne M. Moll, Ed. D.
3/12/91

Federal Laws and Their Implications for Differentiated Instruction

Given the increasingly diverse nature of today's schools, teachers carry an enormous responsibility of ensuring that every child has the opportunity to grow and learn in school environments that offer fair and equitable experiences. Add to this the stress of following federally mandated laws that often feel unmanageable to teachers as they go about their daily work and you have a recipe for trouble...unless there is a systematic method for creating a classroom that naturally meets diverse learner needs.

A brief look at the primary federal laws that impact classrooms, and their implications, is in order. These laws, whose very mandates necessitate the use of differentiated instruction, are the Elementary & Secondary Education Act 2002, (often referred to *as No Child Left Behind (NCLB)* and the *Individuals with Disabilities Education Act 2005 (IDEA).* Each of these has very specific and detailed components that drive classroom practices. However, taken together, they contain common elements that have implications for the use of differentiated instruction. These elements are presented below in the form of a "To Do" list, implying they are tasks that teachers are expected to address within their classrooms.

Teachers' "To Do" List

Across both laws, there are eight major implications for teachers. Teachers are expected to:
- ensure each student has equitable access to curriculum, instructional opportunities, & materials;
- provide challenging academic content;
- present quality instructional time;
- address the needs of students who are low-achieving or not making educational progress;
- deliver instruction that meets the unique needs of all students;
- improve student performance on traditional assessments;
- close the achievement gap between high- and low-achieving students without harming the achievement of high achieving students; and
- efficiently use resources.

Review of this "To Do" list emphasizes the need to provide quality instructional time, with challenging content, using equitable instruction and materials. It also suggests that teachers must understand their content and know which instructional strategies typically work well in teaching the content to students. Addressing the unique needs of all learners- including those who are gifted, low-achieving, and disabled- implies that teachers must understand how students learn differently and know how to match the students' learning styles to instructional strategies. The need to improve student performance across traditional assessments and yet meet non-traditional needs implies that teachers must know how to teach using more non-traditional methods while simultaneously connecting the learning to traditional assessment methods.

Both NCLB and IDEA require that students engage in learning the same curriculum (standards-based) and participate in the same assessment system (standardized, nationally based) so teachers have limited flexibility in those areas. However, there is great flexibility available in the choice of instructional methods, materials, and experiences that teachers can use to help students experience success.

Too often, as teachers strive to meet the demands of the laws, they fall prey to three common missteps that make differentiated instruction appear to be ineffective.

1. <u>Choosing a "Pop Culture" strategy to change student learning</u>. Teachers may grab at the most popular or most commercialized strategy as their great hope of "fixing" students' problems without systematically analyzing whether or not the strategy is a good fit for the learning needs. When the strategy does not work, they simply say, "See, differentiation did not work!" and they go back to the old methods of teaching.

2. <u>Making decisions without data</u>. Under extreme pressure to get results, teachers may choose a strategy to implement without really knowing what problems the students are experiencing. Often strategies are chosen from a "101 ways…" list where the decision is based on the generic characteristics of an educational label instead of the "real time" problem in the classroom.

3. <u>Changing strategies too quickly</u>. Teachers may feel the need to see changes happen quickly, so it is not unusual for a teacher to try a strategy for one week, see minimal results and drop the strategy for something else.

It is important to note that the culture of the school and school district may actually support these missteps. For example, teachers may be given mandated curriculum packages to implement, regardless of the fit between the methodology and individual student needs.

To meet the demands of the laws, and more importantly, to help all students reach their greatest potential, teachers will have to engage in differentiated instruction. They will have to avoid the missteps mentioned above by implementing a specific, systematic method for determining what and when to differentiate. Teachers will need to use specific, time sensitive data (what is currently happening in the classroom) to make instructional decisions. Finally, research supports that changing behaviors takes time and repeated exposure to new methods and techniques. Teachers will have to be patient and give strategies time to work.

This book has been designed to help teachers avoid these missteps in differentiating instruction by outlining a specific, developmental process for approaching the design, implementation and evaluation of instruction. In the pages that follow, the **D**ifferentiated **I**nstruction **G**uide for **I**nclusive **T**eaching (**DIGIT**) process will guide teachers toward effective instruction that will increase student learning and lead toward narrowing the achievement gap. Concurrently, such instruction will respond to both the spirit and the letter of NCLB and IDEA.

Introduction and Overview

There is no question that today's classrooms come complete with a multitude of diversity issues that teachers must address, including gender, race, ethnicity, religion, economics, family culture, sexual orientation, giftedness, and disability. This multidimensional reality creates an environment that requires teachers to develop learning experiences that speak to the diversity. Such responsibility can sometimes feel unmanageable. This book should help you, the teacher, learn to manage that responsibility, using realistic, simple actions to differentiate instruction in the classroom.

Unwrapping the Gift of Differentiated Instruction

The greatest gift you can give yourself as a teacher is that of differentiated instruction. Differentiated instruction brings to center the professional paradox of creatively meeting the unique needs of a diverse student population while employing an increasingly standards-based curriculum under litigative and regulated circumstances. Differentiated instruction facilitates your use of a standards-based curriculum to meet the unique needs of students in the classroom within the legal and ethical principles of today's schools. What will a teacher find inside the differentiated instruction gift? Knowledge. Power. Promise.

Knowledge. Given that virtually every classroom in any school has students with unique needs and abilities, teachers *need to know three pivotal things: (1) how to embed national standards for curricular areas into everyday learning events, (2) federal and local laws that define how to serve a diverse population of students, and (3) how to design instruction to meet the unique needs of the diverse student population.* Many teachers feel that teaching to the requirements of the national standards-based curriculum creates an environment in which individual differences cannot be addressed. They struggle with the apparent paradox of teaching content or teaching children. However, differentiated instruction brings this paradox to center line because it **is** the design of instruction to meet the unique needs of students, using the national standards-based curriculum within the regulations of today's classroom. By learning how to differentiate curriculum, teachers give themselves the pivotal knowledge to thrive in today's classroom.

Power. Knowledge generates power. Knowing how to differentiate instruction sheds light on the fact that teachers do not have to choose between teaching national standards, following regulations, or teaching to the unique abilities of students. Differentiated instruction gives teachers the power over their own classroom in that they can meet high standards, follow regulations, and actually *teach* children. Such power allows teachers to generate instruction that is intentional, purposeful, and effective. When teachers have such power, learning becomes the focal point of the classroom. By making learning the focal point of the classroom, teachers commit to a positive experience for students.

Promise. Committing to differentiated instruction offers the gift of promise for students' present and future well being. When teachers use differentiated instruction, students have the opportunity to engage in purposeful learning designed to meet their specific talents and needs. Teachers who generate such a meaningful environment are in essence promising each student that they are of great importance every day. Employing differentiated instruction suggests that the teacher really does believe that each student can learn. When students feel valued and are engaged in challenging learning experiences, the likelihood that they will remain in school, continue to learn, and become successful citizens increases exponentially. Thus, differentiated instruction offers the promise of a brighter future.

Differentiated instruction then is the gift of learning wrapped up in individual needs-based instruction, using standards-based curriculum and assessment, and following laws and regulations. It is the gift that gives a teacher the knowledge to design instruction and the power to see it through. It offers students the promise of a positive today and a bright tomorrow. When a teacher puts together the knowledge, power, and promise of differentiated instruction, there is nothing that can stop the learning.

This book is designed as an interactive guide to help teachers unwrap the gift of differentiated instruction. The contents are based upon my 23 years of teaching experience, specific research-based practices, empirical evidence, and practical advice collected through those years working with other teachers, parents, administrators, and students. It is my hope that you will find this book useful as you develop your own gift in differentiating instruction.

About this Book

The premise.

The premise for differentiated instruction as it is defined within this book is twofold: (1) ALL students can benefit from instruction that is based on national standards-based curriculum and wrapped around the students' unique needs, and (2) ALL teachers should use differentiated instruction within their classrooms to create purposeful learning.

Based upon this premise, the *outcome* of differentiated instruction is higher levels of achievement for all students regardless of the educational label used to define them (e.g., gifted, at-risk, disabled, or non-disabled). The *process* for developing, implementing, and assessing differentiated instruction is appropriate for all teachers, regardless of the content, grade level, age, or "type" of student they teach.

The process outlined in this book can be used by an individual, a group of teachers, or other professional service providers. It can be used at any level from preschool through university. Teachers who may particularly benefit from this process include those who serve students considered to be:
- typical learners,
- gifted and talented,

- at-risk for failure,
- disabled, or
- developmentally delayed.

In other words, any teacher can benefit from using this process to enhance the learning of any student.

Even though the process unveiled in this book can be used by any teacher, the examples used in this book focus primarily on meeting the unique challenges of students with diverse needs in both the general education setting and other learning environments (e.g., resource or self contained classrooms). These examples will be particularly helpful for the following:

- general education teachers whose students have diverse learning abilities;
- general and special education teachers who work collaboratively to serve students in inclusive learning environments;
- special education teachers who serve students with disabilities in separate environments, and need support in identifying curriculum for each;
- other professional service personnel who integrate their services with the general education curriculum (e.g., physical therapists, occupational therapists, speech language pathologists);
- instructional supervisors who work to support teachers in schools;
- parents who want to be actively involved in the instructional decisions of their child;
- members of the Multidisciplinary Team (MDT) before and during the development of an Individual Education Program (IEP).

The process.

Included in the book is a step-by-step decision making process for developing, implementing, and assessing instruction that is differentiated for the levels of learners presented in any teaching situation. To facilitate your learning, the book provides specific questions and forms for each step of the process. As when learning any new process you may find yourself revisiting the chapters, reviewing the steps, and using the forms quite often in the beginning. The first few times you use this particular process you may find it somewhat time consuming and mentally challenging. However, after the first few times you will find that the steps become a natural part of your overall thinking process and the forms become more of a mental construct than a physical crutch as you plan, implement, and evaluate instruction. Teachers who currently use this process say that as you become familiar with the process the amount of time to get from beginning to end is less than 30 minutes. Most teachers can live with that!

There are seven basic steps in the differentiating process. These steps are outlined in **Exhibit i.1** on the following page, and in **BLM 1.** Within the chapters of the book, each step is defined with specific examples, and one continuous case study is applied to all the steps. You will be asked to work through each step using your own curriculum and case study.

Exhibit i.1 Process for Differentiated Instruction

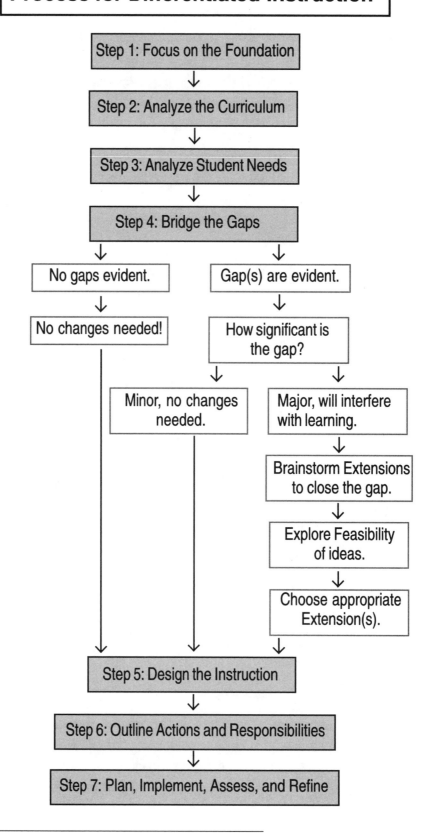

Chapter 1 provides the background on why differentiated instruction is such a critical skill for today's teacher. It details the concept of _access to the curriculum_ for all students and the implications for differentiating instruction. It provides a clear definition of what _access_ means, specific reasons for ensuring access for students (particularly those with disabilities), and a definition of fairness in relationship to differentiation. At the end of the chapter, there are scenarios to test your understanding of access to the curriculum in relationship to differentiated instruction.

Chapter 2 details Step 1 of the process: _Focus on the Foundation_. It describes the foundation for differentiation as four interconnected elements that are critical for access to the curriculum for all students. The chapter includes a description of each element, compares the implementation of each element in a non-differentiated classroom to implementation in a differentiated environment, and explains the significant difference in learning outcomes when differentiated instruction is used for all students. The four elements are presented in a pyramid format offering a visual continuum of change from a non-differentiated environment (the base of the pyramid) to one which meets the unique needs of all learners (the apex of the pyramid). This foundation should be the starting place each time you begin the process of differentiating instruction.

Once you have an understanding of the foundation of differentiated instruction the actual work can begin. Chapter 3 engages you in _Step 2: Analyze the Curriculum_ by posing a series of questions related to the content, instructional methods, and assessment of your own teaching environment. Fourteen Essential Curricular Questions (ECQ) are posed and explained in relationship to their importance for differentiating instruction and their impact on students with disabilities. By answering these questions, you will have analyzed the curriculum and have a clear picture of the way you normally teach and how instruction is typically provided.

In Chapter 4 you will complete _Step 3: Analyze Student Needs_ by answering corresponding questions related to the unique needs of students for whom you must differentiate instruction. These Essential Student Questions (ESQ) focus on the uniqueness of the students in relationship to the content, instructional methods, and assessment typically provided in a non-differentiated classroom. By the end of this step in the process you will have outlined the strengths and places where students might face challenges given a non-differentiated learning environment.

Step 4: Bridge the Gaps is presented in Chapter 5. Here you will identify areas in which students need differentiation and choose specific methods for addressing those needs. This step requires that you compare the two sets of questions to determine where instruction will meet the students' needs and where gaps exist between the instruction and students' needs. To bridge the gap, you will brainstorm ideas for differentiation, explore the feasibility of the ideas, and identify one or a series of changes to make. By completing this step you will have a clear picture of what can remain the same in your original instructional plan and what needs to be changed to meet the needs of the students.

Once the gap analysis is complete you can begin developing a specific differentiated instructional lesson plan. Using _Step 5: Design the Instruction_ in Chapter 6, you will apply the information gathered thus far to the components of an effective instructional lesson. This chapter describes each component, discusses its importance in the development of a differentiated lesson, and challenges the teacher to create a lesson plan outline using these components and the information collected in Steps 1 - 4.

Step 6: Outline the Actions and Responsibilities is the last step before actually using the differentiated instruction lesson in your classroom. Chapter 7 guides you through the process of completing Step 6 by describing the finishing touches of a differentiated lesson, exploring their importance for effective implementation of a differentiated lesson plan, and guiding you toward completion of the plan. When this step is complete, you will know exactly what actions to take when implementing instruction and who will be responsible for seeing the instruction through.

Steps 5 and 6 join together to create a specific differentiated lesson plan based upon the foundations of differentiation, specific curriculum, and unique students needs. At this point, you will have a complete differentiated plan ready to use in your own teaching situation.

Chapter 8 pulls together the differentiated instruction process, and describes how to avoid common pitfalls and use the process for improving both student and teacher performance as part of *Step 7: Plan, Implement, Assess, and Refine.* From this data collection and analysis you will have collected new information about the curriculum, the students, and your abilities to differentiate instruction. This new information will loop you back to the beginning of the differentiation process as you once again begin planning for instruction.

Chapter 9 includes a summary as well as details of six research-based stories that support the premise and intended outcomes of Differentiated Instruction; each case relates how teachers are using the structured **D**ifferentiated **I**nstruction **G**uide for **I**nclusive **T**eaching process, known as **DIGIT** model, at different grade levels to identify strategies that will bridge the gap between defined student needs and the curriculum; impressive academic performance results are presented.

The tools.

Specific tools are provided in Chapters 2 - 7 to help you differentiate instruction. These tools have been developed by the author and used by her and hundreds of classroom teachers in urban, suburban, and rural schools. The tools draw upon research-based and practical best practices and guide the actual development of plans that work in the diverse classroom.

Each tool comes in the form of a Black Line Master (BLM), also commonly know as Reproducible, which can be copied and used repeatedly until the process of differentiation becomes so natural that the support of the tool is no longer necessary. These reproducible masters are in a separate section at the end of the text.

There are, in each chapter, _work areas_ for you to stop, use the tools provided, and apply the new knowledge to your own teaching situation. These _work areas_ are meant to be working and reflective spots, a place to stop, think about what is already known, apply what is being presented, and develop new questions. They are marked with this icon:

The tools provided in this book include:
- Process for Differentiated Instruction
- Differentiated Instruction Pyramid
- Essential Curricular Questions
- Essential Student Questions
- Gap Analysis for Differentiation
- Extensions for Learning
- Feasibility Worksheet
- Differentiated Lesson Plan Guide Part 1
- Differentiated Lesson Plan Guide Part 2

The Case Study: Nicholas

To show continuity between the steps of differentiation, each step of the process has been applied to one case study. This case study is not meant to be seen as the perfect example of a differentiated lesson, but as an example of how two teachers worked toward creating a lesson that would meet their needs in teaching a particular grade level, the needs of the general population of the classroom, and the specific needs of Nicholas.

The Language.

For the purposes of continuity and ease of reading, you will find that the word "she" is used when referring to teachers and the word "he" is used for students. This in no way is meant to discount those wonderful male teachers and female students in the real world. However, using a single word flows better than reading those "she and he" and "he/she" combinations.

The Research.

If the major premise for using Differentiated Instruction is that ALL children can learn and the outcome is higher levels of achievement for every child, the research-based cases in Chapter 9 support both this premise and the intended outcome. In each of the six cases presented, teachers:

- used the process for differentiation known as **DIGIT** (**D**ifferentiated **I**nstruction **G**uide for **I**nclusive **T**eaching), to identify possible gaps in instruction and student learning;
- identified and implemented specific Extensions to bridge those gaps through differentiated instruction;
- collected instructional data that indicated higher levels of achievement, not just for students targeted for differentiated instruction, but for all students in their classrooms.

In each case, the teams reported positive academic results, with several teams documenting *__significant impact__* on student academic outcomes. An analysis of the **Points to Ponder**, which follows each case presentation, provides some important themes relevant to the myths of differentiation and the reality of implementation. Let's review these!

Myth 1

In differentiated instruction, content is "dumbed down" and tests always have to be modified.

Fact 1

The teachers did NOT change their content or their test methods/types. They continued to use the typical tests given for these units: No "dumbing down" of the curriculum, no use of tests that had been modified.

Myth 2

You have to change the student before you can get any positive results.

Fact 2

The teachers *changed their own behaviors* and this, in turn, changed the students' performance. They did not "fix" the students' problems but rather gave students the tools to use for learning. **Every** team reported that they changed their own behaviors (e.g., planning, teaching, interacting with students), which in turn changed student performance. This detail, that differentiated instruction is the method for improving student performance without "fixing" the child, is critical for teams' to understand. More simply stated, teachers became more aware that what they chose to do and use in the classroom did, in fact, impact student performance.

This set of data might be the most important for the project, in that is it **positive proof** that differentiated instruction and collaborative efforts of teachers improve student performance.

Myth 3

Differentiated instruction only works for students with problems, and will hurt the performance of non-disabled students.

Fact 3

The students who were targeted for differentiated instruction did improve when the Extensions were provided. In addition, in each case, the overall performance of the entire class improved by using the Extensions. The differentiated instruction helped close the performance gaps of the targeted students and also increased the class' performance. No child got left behind!

Myth 4

Teachers lose instructional time when they have to differentiate.

Fact 4

In five of the six research cases, teachers felt that using the Extension actually increased their instructional time. Only one teacher indicated that the instructional time stayed about the same when using the Extension. None of the teachers reported a loss of instructional time when implementing the Extensions.

Myth 5

Differentiation is costly and difficult to implement in a general education classroom.

Fact 5

In each research case, the Extensions chosen <u>did not cost anything</u>. The teachers all reported the Extensions were easy to implement. The only down side some teachers noted was the amount of time they initially needed to plan the implementation of the strategy. All teachers indicated in their reports that the planning time decreased significantly after they used the strategy more than once.

Myth 6

There is really no way to tell if differentiating makes a difference in students' scores.

Fact 6

The teachers were able to <u>collect important data</u> with relative ease. They reported that once they had identified specifically what they wanted to change, the collection of data became much easier. In addition, the teachers all indicated that the data they collected was useful in changing their instructional practices. By knowing if student performance was increasing, the teachers could determine whether or not to keep or change an Extension.

Myth 7

There is no research-based method for deciding how to differentiate instruction.

Fact 7

In each research case, the teachers <u>used the **DIGIT**</u> (**D**ifferentiated **I**nstruction **G**uide for **I**nclusive **T**eaching) process to identify specific gaps and choose methods for differentiating instruction. These cases demonstrate that a very specific process does indeed exist that can help teachers identify what and how to differentiate instruction so that all children learn.

Looking over the results of these research cases, one can see that differentiating instruction is indeed the gift of knowledge, power, and promise which helps the teacher meet those shared goals of NCLB and IDEA, as outlined in the list of "To Do's" from page _____ of this book. In each research case, teachers reported they were able to:

- meet the needs of low-achieving children;
- provide individualized instruction that meets the unique needs of students;
- close the achievement gap between high- and low-achieving children without harming the achievement of high achieving children;
- efficiently use resources;
- expose students to challenging academic content;
- improve student performance on traditional assessment systems; and
- increase quality instructional time.

The use of the **DIGIT** process helped teachers avoid making classic missteps. These teachers did not choose a "Pop Culture" strategy simply because it was in vogue. They collected data that helped them make specific instructional decisions. Instead of just "knowing" whether some strategy was working or not, they had hard facts to help them determine what to do next. Finally, they took time to analyze the teaching, content, and student needs before they chose a specific Extension to implement. The teachers gave the Extension/strategy time to work. In several of the research cases, if the teacher had given up on a strategy after the first week, significant academic and behavioral gains would likely have been lost.

Chapter 1

Access to the General Curriculum and Differentiated Instruction

It is unlikely that there is another nation in the world that has more diversity in ethnicity, cultural heritage, and ability within its public schools than the United States. People of many faiths, races, cultures, heritages, and abilities make up our neighborhoods and the classrooms in our public schools. Today's public schools must do more than "value" diversity; schools must use the general curriculum and instruction to support the differences in students, including those with educational disabilities.

While the inclusion of students with educational disabilities into the general education classroom with access to the general education curriculum has been required since 1975, when P.L. 94-142, the Education for All Handicapped Act was passed, emphasis on using the general curriculum as the primary curriculum for all students with disabilities had not been formally addressed until reauthorizations of the law in 1990 and 1997. Now referred to as the Individuals with Disabilities Education Act (IDEA), the law heavily emphasizes that students with educational disabilities participate in the general education curriculum. In addition to the IDEA emphasis on participation in the general education curriculum, the reauthorization of the Elementary and Secondary Education Act (P.L. 107-110), also known as No Child Left Behind Act (NCLB), clearly requires that all students make progress in the general education curriculum, thus supporting the need for students with disabilities to participate and make progress in that curriculum.

General education curriculum, according to the law, includes what each state educational entity has outlined for its students in a normal school environment and includes academic, extracurricular, and non academic activities. Gartner and Lipsky (2002) provide an educator-friendly description of what the law requires related to serving students with disabilities in the general education setting. To emphasize its importance to differentiated instruction, their description can be summarized in five major points.

1. Students with disabilities must have beneficial access to the general curriculum, not a separate curriculum.

2. A team, including someone familiar with the general education curriculum, must design the educational program and write the Individualized Education Program (IEP) for a student with a disability.

3. Supplementary aids and services (tools or support by personnel) must be available for the student with disabilities to benefit from involvement in the general curriculum (e. g., student needs braille version of content texts to be successful in the classroom).

4. The Individualized Education Program must be provided in the regular classroom environment unless specific justification is documented indicating otherwise.

5. Students with disabilities must be tested with necessary modifications provided, using the same state and district wide assessments as peers without disabilities.

These five points, taken in combination, outline why differentiated instruction is critical for today's classroom. Students with disabilities must be working toward progress in the content considered important for all students. Therefore, even if the student is in a more restrictive environment than the regular classroom, the special education teacher must *know* the content and be able to design instruction that helps the student progress. To remove a student from the regular classroom there must be significant evidence that the student cannot progress, even when modifications, aids and services are provided. Given this, teachers must understand how to modify instruction and assessment, use the aids to enhance learning, and utilize the services of other adults within the regular classroom for a significant period of time before the student can be moved to a more restrictive environment. The law requires that the regular education teacher be involved in the development of the IEP, so he or she must not only know the curriculum, but have visions of how to modify without losing the integrity of the content. Finally, the fact that students must be included in state and district assessments suggests that teachers must understand how the students learn, how they can show what they know, and what modifications to the assessment will remove barriers without compromising the test.

In keeping with the law, to develop a learning environment where students progress in the general curriculum using modifications, aids, and services of other adults, the regular education teacher and special education teacher must know how to differentiate instruction and assessment for individual students. Teachers are directed to create environments that support a barrier-free learning environment where students with disabilities have access to the general education curriculum - which in essence is what differentiation is all about.

As issues of access to the general education curriculum are discussed, it must be remembered that this topic is of great significance to many students who are not classified with disabilities. Given the ever-increasing heterogeneity of our classrooms and the ever-widening range of student needs and abilities, the processes and strategies presented in this book have extremely broad application to every teacher and every learning environment.

What do we mean when we refer to *general education curriculum?*

The easiest way to answer this question is to pose some questions.

- What content is required for most students at your grade level?

- In what different environments do students learn?

- What other activities do students engage in during their school career?

- What behaviors are expected of students across environments?

Anything listed in your reflection above could be considered general curriculum if it applies to all or most of the students. Often educators mistake the general curriculum as just content. However, the actual curriculum of a school reflects its overall expectations of students' for participation in school, kindergarten through graduation. The general education curriculum comprises a **body of knowledge, processes, and set of skills often generalized into the term *content*, and behaviors for life long success, learned in a range of environments.**

The *content* is the information and special skills believed to be most important for students to master to ensure success in their lives as adults. Content varies to some degree by the region of country, but there is a basic set of core content that spans nearly every public school in the United States that includes: mathematics, reading, writing, English, social studies, science, history, music, art, physical education and health, vocational skills, and technology. (For a web page that lists links to all national content standards try: http://www.education-world.com/standards/national/index.shtml.)

The *environment* refers to the settings in which learning occurs. In schools there are a wide variety of settings in which students learn including, but not limited to, the classroom, library, media center, outdoors, science labs, and the community.

The *behavior* aspect of curriculum refers to the often unwritten expectations of the student within the learning environment including, but not limited to, social skills, cooperative work, organization, class participation, and study skills. Included in those expectations are behaviors requiring the student to develop skills outside of the classroom that lead to successful transition into the social world after graduation. These skills are often developed in extracurricular activities.

Extracurricular activities refer to those activities offered for students during their school careers that build their capacities to use what they know and build their skills for their life in the community including civic duties, recreation, and leisure. For example, special groups, clubs, and organizations are typically offered in conjunction with the school (e.g., Boy and Girl Scouts, Future Farmers of America, Governor's Cup). This area is often overlooked in its importance for building the skills of students for future success.

The primary focus of this book is on differentiating the *content* students should learn. Throughout discussion of the process on how to differentiate instruction and assessment for students with disabilities, issues related to the environment, behaviors and extracurricular activities will be discussed because content cannot be separated from these other areas.

What does "access" to the general curriculum mean?

Let's start with another question.

• When you hear the word access, what comes to mind?

Did you put words or phrases such as: open, get in, use, go on the internet, entrance ramp, or road? Good. You are on your way to understanding access to curriculum.

Access simply means a ***barrier-free opportunity to learn and use materials, resources, and events in natural settings.*** Barrier-free can be defined as *without any unnatural or arbitrary obstacles*. Opportunity simply means having a *chance to use* something. Barrier-free opportunity does not mean complete access 100% of the time. Temporary obstacles spring up in every situation in life. Getting access to the internet means you get on-line and can use the resources, but sometimes the site you desire is unavailable. Using the ramp to the interstate allows you to drive to a specific destination without the hassle of multiple street lights and stop signs, but sometimes there is an accident which blocks traffic. Barrier-free opportunity *does* mean having the same chance as others, under natural circumstances.

Access to the general curriculum means students have a barrier-free opportunity to learn the knowledge, skills, procedures, and behaviors deemed important by a school through the use of materials, resources, and events in appropriate settings. To be barrier-free schools must create learning environments that knock down arbitrary or unnatural obstacles. For example, prior to Brown v. Topeka Board of Education (1954), arbitrary obstacles were in place that prevented students of African American heritage from using materials, resources, events, and settings that were natural for students of Euro-American background. The heritage and color of the students' skin were arbitrary barriers used to prevent them from benefiting from a sound public education in American schools. These students did not have access to the general education curriculum because they could not use or benefit from the resources, materials, events, and settings for learning. The 1956 ruling gave African American students access to the general education curriculum in America's public schools by legally breaking down the barrier of skin color and heritage.

Access to the general curriculum then, means barrier-free opportunities to participate in activities, use materials, and benefit from services provided for other individuals in a school environment.

What does "access" to the general curriculum mean for students with disabilities?

For decades, just as students of African American decent were denied access to the general education curriculum, students with disabilities were arbitrarily prevented from participating in the same curriculum as their peers without disabilities. Now, Federal laws (IDEA and Section 504 of the Rehabilitation Act of 1973) make it very clear that students with disabilities cannot be denied access to the general education curriculum based on arbitrary reasons. (For more information on IDEA go to the web page: http://www.ed.gov/offices/OSERS/Policy/IDEA/; for more information on Section 504 go to http://www.wsc.edu/frc/disable.html.)

For example, a student with a disability in *reading written words* is not necessarily disabled in the area of science, social studies, or math. If the teacher only provides information in written format to students, the method through which information is presented provides a barrier and interferes with the student having access to the content. Therefore, if the teacher only uses print to teach the content of the science class, the student who cannot read those words is being denied access to the science. It becomes the teacher's responsibility to make sure that the student can get the information in a different format such as books on tape, lecture, pictures, or voice command computer programs.

As another example, consider the student with autism who has difficulty with transitions from one activity to another. This student is not necessarily disabled in a content area, but rather in the routines and procedures associated with that content. This is the student who tends to "go off" when the teacher unexpectedly or quickly changes gears. The quick or unexpected transition sets the child in motion, requiring 15 minutes of cool down time before the student can rejoin the group. By then the teacher has covered content that the student may not ever have the chance to get again. The routine, or lack of a transition routine, becomes a form of denying access for the student with autism because the technique the teacher uses prevents student from learning. The teacher can open access by simply using some type of routine or procedure for warning the student that a change is about to occur - such as a laminated schedule, writing the change on the board and drawing the student's attention to it before announcing it to the class. By changing the technique, the aspect of the disability that might interfere with getting the content has been circumvented.

What about the student who has violent behavior - how does access apply to him? If the student is in a self-contained setting where the main priority is getting the behaviors under control so he can reenter the general classroom, it does not make sense to arbitrarily place him back into a general classroom just in the name of inclusion. What makes sense, and is required, is that during the time the student is in the self contained setting working on behaviors, he is also working on the same *content* that is being taught in the general setting so that when the student does re-enter the general classroom setting, he is not further behind.

One important point should be made here. While this book focuses primarily on access to the content, there is typically confusion about the environment for learning. Access to the curriculum does not always mean that learning will occur in the general education classroom. For some students, because of their particular learning or behavior goals, the general education classroom may not be the most appropriate environment. The student might need a more specialized environment for learning, such as a special classroom. Even though the student is not located in the general classroom, he has the right to learn the same content as his peers without disabilities. The student must have use of whatever books and tools are used in the general education classroom, thereby guaranteeing that even if the location changes, the other aspects of access to the curriculum do not.

A second important point to make is that providing access <u>does **not** mean doing the work for the student</u>; it means removing basic barriers so that the student can do the work himself. Being able to get on-line with the internet does not automatically mean you know how to use the resources. Entering the interstate using a ramp does not take care of your need to be able to drive safely. Using the wheelchair ramp to enter the restaurant does not order and eat the food for you. However, if you did not have access to the internet, could you send e-mail? If you did not have an on ramp for the interstate, could you use it to get to a new destination? The answer is, of course, NO. These tools and methods give the opportunity to participate in various life activities. Gaining access to the general education curriculum is about that same thing - gaining access to information so that individual students can participate in life activities.

For the student with disabilities, access means opportunity to use and learn the same knowledge, skills, procedures, and behaviors deemed important by a school for students without disabilities. This includes the use of materials, resources, events, and settings. Access does not mandate setting, but the further students work from the general education environment, the less natural and more restrictive their opportunities are for progressing in content as compared to their peers without disabilities. The biggest difference between access to the curriculum for students with disabilities and their non-disabled peers is that the student with the disability may need to use methods, tools, or techniques that are not typically used by students without disabilities.

Why must I provide access to students with disabilities?

There are at least six good, and one really great, reason.

Reason #1 - We do NOT have a choice! That was easy, wasn't it? Federal law requires that students with disabilities have access and opportunities to learn using the general curriculum, regardless of *where* they learn. Three laws that mandate students with disabilities have opportunities to learn using the general curriculum are the Individuals with Disabilities Act (IDEA), Section 504 of the Rehabilitation Act, and NCLB. Each provides protections for the student, guaranteeing access to and participation in the same types of learning opportunities as his peers without disabilities. These laws specify that teachers must remove any external barriers to learning through modifications and adaptations for the student with a disability.

Reason #2 - We can't afford not to! It is a necessity to have students with disabilities working with the same curriculum as their peers primarily because we want our children to grow up to live fulfilling lives and contribute to the success of our society. The old system is not preparing students with disabilities for such a life. There is consistent evidence over the decades that proves that students with disabilities have been denied access to the general education curriculum, leading to very poor performance in school and in life. Just a few examples of the sobering data are that students with disabilities have nearly double the dropout rate of their peers without disabilities, lower graduation rates with less than 45% graduating with diplomas, and the highest unemployment rates of any population subgroup (Algozzine, Christenson, & Ysseldyke, 1982; Allington & McGill-Franzen, 1989; Lipsky & Gartner, 1989; Lipsky & Gartner, 1994; Moll, 1996; Pugach & Johnson, 1989; Wang, Reynolds, & Walberg, 1986).

With such dismal outcomes it is clear that students with disabilities are not contributing to the economy or becoming purposeful members of the community to the degree that is considered desirable by our society. Remember, students who do not become employed, become the responsibility of society and need support from the system (e.g., welfare). We want all of our students to become contributing members of society in the best way they are capable.

Reason # 3 - It is a professional and ethical requirement. As professionals, teachers are trained to help children grow, learn, and become thriving citizens using the general curriculum as the base for that learning. The National Board of Professional Teacher Standards (NBPTS) outlines 5 essential standards for teachers: (1) *Teachers are committed to students and their learning. (2) Teachers know the subjects they teach and how to teach those subjects to students. (3) Teachers are responsible for managing and monitoring student learning. (4) Teachers think systematically about their practice and learn from experience. (5) Teachers are members of learning communities. (For complete information on these standards visit www.nbpts.org.)*

Essential components of professional behavior from these five standards that relate directly to teaching students with disabilities include:

- acting on the belief that all students can learn;
- making knowledge accessible to all students;
- treating students equitably, recognizing individual differences;
- adjusting practices based on observation and knowledge of their students' interests, abilities, skills, knowledge, family circumstances, and peer relationships;
- developing students' cognitive capacity;
- fostering students' self-esteem, motivation, character, civic responsibility and their respect for individual, cultural, religious and racial differences; and
- understanding where difficulties are likely to arise and modifying their practice accordingly.

These national standards do not say teachers believe that *some* students can learn, it emphasizes believing that _all_ can learn. All of these professional behaviors speak to treating students with disabilities as students who can learn when the teacher creates the appropriate learning environment. To deny some students access to curriculum and opportunities to learn would be, in essence, a form of malpractice.

Reason # 4 - It only makes sense. When we pull students with disabilities away from the general curriculum and teach them in a separate, unrelated curriculum, we are actually adding to or compounding the disability and pushing them further behind their peers in content knowledge, ability to compete in today's economy, capacity to develop a social and personal life, and be a contributing member of society. If we want students with disabilities to be as close as possible to "normal" (although I would argue there is no such thing as normal), why would we want to teach them something that we do not teach the "normal" student?

Reason #5 - It WORKS! Students with disabilities who are educated using the general curriculum, even when in a more exclusive environment (such as a self contained setting) do better academically and socially, retain information longer, and experience greater success in post secondary life (e.g., jobs, college, social connections). Enough said. (Baker, 1994; Baker, Wang, & Walberg, 1995; Carlberg & Kavale, 1980; Moll, 1996; Wang & Baker,1986).

Reason #6 - It does NOT hurt a school's statewide or national test scores! In the past, students with disabilities were often excluded from taking national or state mandated tests for two reasons. One reason was that educators did not necessarily believe the students could learn the general curriculum and thus used other, more watered-down curriculum to teach. With students getting a watered-down version of curriculum it made no sense to have them take a test on content to which they were not exposed.

Second, in direct relationship to, or caused by the first reason, schools did not like the potential for the students with disabilities "pulling their overall school scores down". The concern over students with disabilities hurting school scores has been disproved in at least one state. Kentucky public schools have included all students with disabilities in their statewide assessment and accountability practices since 1990. Disaggregated data from the Kentucky Department of Education each year shows that students with disabilities do NOT pull the overall scores of a school down if the students have access to the general curriculum (KDE, 2002).

It only makes sense that students with disabilities will score higher on such statewide assessments when they are exposed to the curriculum that is tested!

Reason #7 - It is FAIR.... the "Great" answer! Would it be fair to ask a person who wears glasses or contacts to remove them and perform a dangerous task? Absolutely not. The person with glasses or contacts needs them to function in their day–to-day life. Would it be fair to ask a surgeon to conduct neurosurgery with a butter knife? Definitely not. The butter knife would not allow her to perform the surgery adequately. The glasses/contacts and the scalpel/laser serve as *tools* for the individual to function in his daily life.

Is it fair then to ask students with disabilities to function without the tools they need in their daily lives? To deny students with disabilities the opportunity to learn the same content using similar materials and environments is to deny them access to the tools they need for daily life. We cannot expect students with disabilities to be successful in life if we do not give them the chance to learn what it is that will make them successful. Differentiated instruction is teaching the student to use different tools to complete similar tasks. It provides the opportunity to be successful without any barriers and without putting up barriers for others.

How do we ensure fairness as we give students with disabilities access to the curriculum?

As with the other questions, let's start with a question for you:

* What things (tools, methods, supports) do you need every day to complete your role as a teacher, parent, friend, spouse?

Did you list items like: car, cell phone, food, glasses, money, secretary, or assistant? These are all things that allow you to function in your job/life role. These things do not do the work for you, but help you get your work done, or remove barriers so you can get your work done. These tools and services provide you with access to the content of your life. You still must have the knowledge of what to do and how to use those tools to get it done. So tools and knowledge are both very important. Is it fair that you get to use a cell phone and someone else only uses a land based line? Then why would it not be fair for a student with a disability to use a tool, such as a calculator, to complete math problems while another student uses memorized facts? The only time it might not be fair is if we were testing their *speed* of calculating or ability to *memorize,* not their ability to correctly compute a number.

Teachers often have legitimate questions about the fairness of access to the curriculum for students with disabilities using accommodations and adaptations. It is important to realize that the accommodations and adaptations provided for students with disabilities are nothing more than tools — similar to the ones you use to get your job done every day.

Every day in general classrooms we provide tools in the form of materials, methods, and supports for students to access the curriculum. Materials include text books, calculators, computers, rulers, televisions, newspapers, paper. Typical teaching methods include visual, auditory, and hands-on (kinesthetic). Supports include knowledgeable teachers, assistants, counselors, or peers. Teachers make accommodations for students without disabilities every day through simple actions like allowing one student to have five extra minutes to finish a project or letting a student use markers to color a picture instead of crayons. The issue of fairness seems to come up when the accommodation (e.g., longer time or using a different tool) is <u>required</u> for the student with a disability. Fairness is about giving a student the chance to learn, when without such modifications the student with a disability would not get that chance. Why do we question the fairness of a student with a disability using a different type of tool that helps him overcome a barrier to the content? Access to the curriculum for students with disabilities is simply providing a barrier-free opportunity for the student to use the content for learning.

Do we really believe students with disabilities can master general education curriculum?

Yes.

Students with disabilities are students first and disabled second. Very few disabilities create such an obstacle for students that they cannot learn from the general education curriculum. In most cases the disability interferes with *how* or *the degree* to which students learn, not necessarily their ability to learn content. When we remove barriers to learning for students with disabilities, the sky is the limit. The following is just one example of how student success can change when access to the curriculum is provided.

> James was a student identified as having a specific learning disability in the area of reading. He struggled with sight words and comprehension. His reading skills were well below his same age peers. So, during several content teaching times (science, social studies, and math) James was pulled out of the general classroom to work on sight word and reading comprehension. The special education teacher used a special reading program to work on these skills. While James was in the resource room practicing reading, the other students were learning the science, social studies, and math. As one might

predict, not only did James continue struggle with reading problems, but his grades in science, social studies, and math began to decline.

In this case, James was being denied access to the science, math, and social studies content in three ways: (1) the primary barrier to learning was reading which the general teacher used as the primary learning tool; (2) he was not in the regular room when content was discussed, thus preventing him from even hearing the information, and (3) the special education teacher did not use the content he was missing to work on reading skills. He was working on isolated reading skills in a separate environment during the time he could have been comprehending the content because of the discussion format in the general classroom environment.

Using the process for differentiation outlined in this book, James' teachers developed ideas for differentiating the instructional plan to remove some of the barriers. The teachers identified several ways to remove the barriers and equip James with the tools to be successful. They agreed to let him stay in the classes for the content, to audio tape his text book, and to use the content from the classroom as the basis for teaching him reading skills in the special education environment. James was in the resource room during language arts reading time only.

By changing these three things, or removing those barriers, James was able to learn the content and apply it in his real life after graduation, particularly the science! James never did learn to read beyond a second grade level, but today he is a physician with a family practice. He learned how to use different tools to access knowledge and show what he knows. To this day, in his professional work, James employs a personal assistant who puts everything he needs to read on audio tape and transcribes his audio taped notes to written reports.

We must recognize that the range of capabilities of students with disabilities is unfathomable. Students will learn if we design instruction and assessment experiences to be barrier-free.

What does "access" look like?

To create access we must remove barriers and sometimes add supports. To create access to the curriculum, we as educators have to take down the barriers that impede learning, just as the engineer has to remove the barrier of the curb on a side-walk to allow a person in a wheel chair or walker to have access to a restaurant or store. The modifications and adaptations that are outlined on a student's IEP provide the guidelines for access to the curriculum. Access to the curriculum means considering more than one way to reach the content, just as we have more than one way to reach a destination - some of us use side roads, alleys, the interstate or a combination of all of these. Think of modifications and adaptations for students with disabilities as the on-ramp for their learning.

Let's try a few examples to see if you can determine when access is provided or denied.

Scene 1: Miguel is a student who has difficulty writing words down on paper, but can verbally tell what he knows in great detail. He has an IEP which includes specially designed instruction that calls for him to (1) receive support for information provided orally (e.g., use a peer note taker, tape lectures) and (2) to provide responses to questions/activities/tests/papers using a verbal to print format (e.g., use a scribe, tape the material, use the voice to text software on the computer).

The history teacher says Miguel needs to be in a special education classroom because in the history class there is a lot of lecture with note taking and research papers are required. The teacher does not think that Miguel can be successful in the class and will not be able to pass history class.

By moving him to a special education environment for the reasons stated by the teacher, would we be denying Miguel access to the curriculum?

Scene 2: Sherri is a student who has shown violent behaviors and has difficulty working in a large group for long periods of time. She is currently in a special education classroom for all instructional areas. In the special education classroom the teacher uses workbooks and materials that are at least 10 years old and were given to him by general education teachers who said they did not use them any more. The special education teacher says he is more concerned about getting Sherri's behaviors under control than about her learning content, so he does very little instruction, and allows her to sit and do worksheets all day as long as she behaves.

Is Sherri being denied access to the curriculum?

Scene 3: Vance is a student who has auditory processing problems that lead to difficulty learning new math concepts when working in groups of two or more. He has difficulty filtering out the noises and other distractions caused by student movement in a large group. However, once he learns the basics of the math concepts he can apply the concepts in small and large groups with relative ease. Vance is in the general education classroom for math, but the special education teacher works with him in a resource room setting each week as new concepts are taught in the general classroom. When a new concept is being introduced to the math class, Vance is pulled to the resource room. The special education teacher uses the same textbook, materials, and methods as the general education teacher, but spends more time using concrete examples and manipulatives than the teacher does in the general classroom setting. Once he *has grasped the concept in the resource room. Vance returns to the general classroom to participate in all related math activities.*

Is Vance being denied access to the curriculum?

✓ Check Your Answers

Miguel: By moving Miguel to a special education environment for the reasons stated by the teacher (his teaching methodology), we <u>would</u> be denying the student access to the curriculum. Because of the teaching methodology, not the ability of the student to learn, the teacher wants the student removed. The teaching methodology is an arbitrary barrier that <u>can be changed or modified to meet the student's needs</u>. We deny access to Miguel by removing him from the environment where the content is taught to peers without disabilities. In addition, we would be overriding the specially designed instruction outlined on the IEP. If the IEP says the student can use a tape recorder or peer note taker, the teacher cannot deny the use of such items in the general education classroom.

In Miguel's' case the history teacher must differentiate his instructional methodology and assessment techniques to address the student's needs. The teacher could differentiate in a variety of ways simply by paying attention to the IEP which calls for peer or scribes, audio taping, or interviews. None of these methods would prevent Miguel from staying in the general education setting.

Sherri: In this case, Sherri should be in a more restrictive environment until she gets her behaviors under control. However, the fact that the special education teacher is not teaching Sherri any content and is using materials that are outdated and not used by the general education teachers is in fact denying her access to the same curriculum as her peers without disabilities.

The special education teacher has the responsibility to teach Sherri content within the special education environment. That content must be the same as what her peers are learning.

Vance: Vance does indeed have access to the curriculum. He learns the content (math) in two settings, both settings use the same materials and methods. Vance's problems with auditory processing in large group settings is overcome by providing him a small group, distraction-free zone until he learns the concepts.

How did you do? Did you get all three examples correct? Hopefully through these questions and exercises you have grown to understand more about access to the curriculum and differentiated instruction. In the next chapters you will have the opportunity to use a case study (or provide your own case study) to walk step-by-step through the decision making process for differentiating instruction. Remember that while the majority of the examples used in the book are focused on students with disabilities, the process for differentiation could be used to meet the unique needs of any student.

Chapter 2

Elements for Differentiation

Chapter 2 starts the teacher on the journey towards differentiation by focusing on the first step in the differentiation process—*Step 1: Focus on the Foundation.* See **BLM 1, Process for Differentiated Instruction.** Please remember that all Black Line Masters (**BLM**) are found after the Epilogue, beginning on page 159.

This foundation is based upon the Differentiated Instruction Pyramid which offers a visual framework of where typical classrooms currently operate and where instruction must move to improve student performance. (**BLM 2** provides a completed, three dimensional version of the pyramid used in this chapter. You might want to cut the pyramid out, assemble it, and use it as a reference as you work through this chapter. If you prefer to build your pyramid by writing the information down on the pyramid as you learn about it, use **BLM 3**.) This chapter describes and provides concrete examples of the four elements of the pyramid that help the teacher put in perspective ideas that address specific needs of students in accessing the general education curriculum. Attending to the most important elements of differentiation is the first step in the differentiation process. The four elements are:

- Content Requirements,
- Student Influences,
- Instruction Components, and
- Assessment Techniques.

This pyramid model was developed by the author and is being presented here for the first time. The pyramid model is meant to be a guide for all teachers as they design instruction for elementary, middle, or secondary schools. The elements of the model are based on sound practices, research, and common sense. This pyramid model and the process for designing and implementing differentiated instruction explained in the chapters that follow are significantly important for <u>all</u> students.

The Elements for Differentiating Instruction

The ultimate goal for every school is to develop students into competent citizens with strategies for living in the context of their community. Unfortunately, the number one component missing from instruction and assessment is often the connection between content and context. Students are not experiencing the content in such a way that it lends itself to use in the context of their lives. Pressures for high test scores often put schools at odds with good teaching and assessment. Teachers feel forced to focus on <u>what</u> is important to know. However, to thrive in society, students must also know <u>when, where, how, and why</u> to utilize the knowledge and skills. Learning in context requires the analysis of the multiple dimensions of the student, the knowledge and skills needed for living, and the environment of learning. To teach so that students learn in context, the classroom must be reasonably differentiated by considering the elements of the pyramid.

A master teacher will have a difficult time separating the following four elements because she will see that each is highly dependent upon the other for success. However, it is important to outline them separately in this chapter to emphasize the impact each has on differentiating instruction.

Content Requirements: the standards for applying knowledge, skills, and specific concepts of various disciplines including, but not limited to, math, science, language arts, social studies, art, music, physical education, history, and social skills. All students who attend public schools are expected to work toward mastery of the content outlined by national, state, and local school standards. Students with disabilities are no exception. While not all students with disabilities will master all content (neither will all students without disabilities), each student must have the opportunity to work toward mastery of that content within the context of their abilities and life-long goals. Emphasizing instructional design that supports students with disabilities accomplishing life long goals requires that the teacher focus on the context (why, when, where, and how) of content, instead of just the coverage (what) of content.

Student Influences: the strengths, needs, and motivations of an individual that impact learning. Every student brings a unique perspective to the classroom. Students come with different personalities, strengths, weaknesses, interests, fears, beliefs, and dreams. Students with disabilities are no different. Each student brings the ability to learn into the classroom, no matter how "severe" the disability appears. Instead of being hindered by the disability, students must have the opportunity to use their abilities to learn. In differentiated instruction, the teacher must focus on what each student <u>can do</u> and what they dream of doing, not on what they cannot accomplish.

Instructional Components: the methods, materials, procedures, and environments used for teaching and learning. No two students in any classroom learn the same way. The teacher must vary, in a purposeful way, the methods, materials, procedures, and environments of learning to reach every student in the classroom. This is true in teaching students with disabilities. There is no single instructional method that works for all students with disabilities. The good news is that many instructional practices work for both students with disabilities and their non-disabled peers. In differentiated instruction, the teacher must focus on creating a combination of schemas that will reach all students in the classroom instead of using one method.

Assessment Techniques: the methods and styles of collecting specific formative (ongoing) and summative (final/end) data to determine student learning and progress toward goals. No single content test will tell a teacher everything he or she wants to know about the student's learning. At a minimum, the teacher must attend to content, mental processes, and social skills. Often, in a general education setting, the focus of assessment is placed primarily on content, while mental processes and social skills are considered of secondary importance. However, research shows that for students with disabilities it is not that the actual content is too difficult to learn, but that mental processes or social skills interfere with learning the content. In differentiated instruction the assessment is focused equally on all three aspects, requiring the teacher to develop reasonable methods for measuring content knowledge, the mental processes for learning the content, and the social skills required when using the content in context.

In the following chapters of this book, a series of questions are offered to help the teacher address the four elements of differentiated instruction. However, before attending to the questions, it is important to discuss the change in teaching practices required for differentiated instruction. The pyramid offers a visual reminder of the essence of differentiating instruction.

Each side of the pyramid represents one of the four elements, with the four elements ultimately coming together at the top to indicate that they are all interconnected. At the top of the pyramid are research based best practices. At the base are well intended, but ineffective practices. To differentiate instruction for students with disabilities it is necessary to examine the current practices in classrooms (the bottom of the pyramid) and reframe them in a manner that focuses on life-long learning (the top of the pyramid).

Let's Get Started!!

Make a copy of the **Differentiated Instruction Pyramid, BLM 2** or **3**. Use **BLM 2** if you would like to see the pyramid already completed. Use **BLM 3** if you would like to create your own pyramid by filling in each side as your read about the elements in the following sections.

Content Requirements: The Details

To differentiate instruction, content must be considered within the context of the student's life. Instead of asking what should be taught, the teacher asks how the content will be used by the student in real life. To differentiate instruction, the teacher must move her practices from being classroom-based to society-focused. **Exhibit 2.1** shows the three levels of Content Requirements: Classroom, Community and Societal-Based Content.

Exhibit 2.1 Content Requirements

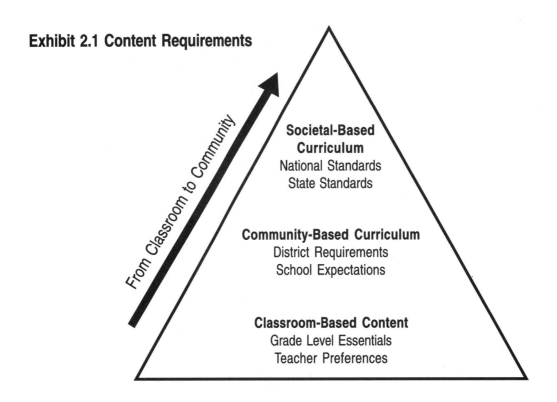

From Classroom to Community

Societal-Based Curriculum
National Standards
State Standards

Community-Based Curriculum
District Requirements
School Expectations

Classroom-Based Content
Grade Level Essentials
Teacher Preferences

Classroom-Based Content

In a typical classroom the content taught is influenced by the expectations for a particular grade or age level and the preferences of the teacher at that grade for what seems most important to teach. For example, the fifth grade language arts teacher uses fifth grade textbooks and fifth grade scope and sequences for teaching reading. The teacher uses specific stories from a grade level anthology and uses the pre-identified vocabulary as a basis for teaching decoding, spelling, and creating meaning. Here, the learning is limited to a specific set of questions and answers from specific stories and a limited set of vocabulary words.

When a teacher uses only the lowest level of the pyramid for determining content, she bases the teaching on just the content for that grade level, makes few if any connections to previously learned content, and no connections to how the content impacts future learning or life skills.

When the content is taught in such a limited fashion, students make few, if any, connections to the context or reason for learning it. In empirical evidence collected by Moll in 2001, data from interviews with 50 "A" level algebra students from ten different schools showed that 75% of the students indicated that the reason they were learning algebra was "because the teacher has to teach it and we have to pass a test." The importance of algebra in their daily lives was not perceived by these students as the primary reason for learning it. These classrooms were stuck at the bottom of the pyramid, in classroom or grade level driven content.

Community-Based Content

The classroom in transition toward differentiated instruction will attend to the fact that content is influenced by the student's community. These expectations are outlined by school and district standards and policies. Here the teacher must look beyond the typical grade level textbook and work local expectations into the learning environment. For example, in agricultural areas, teachers are expected to work activities into their instruction that build the skills students use to participate in Future Farmers of America; in some mountainous regions curriculum includes winter survival skills (e.g., avalanches); and in some urban areas curriculum emphasizes technology as a primary mode of research and communication. By attending to the local influences and desires, the teacher helps the students make connections from the content to their life at home and in the community. This connection may be critical for some students who are unable to see this relationship on thier own.

Societal-Based Content

In a differentiated classroom, the national and state standards for learning have the highest level of influence on the content. This level of the pyramid is influenced by a broader set of expectations including what each state believes is important and the essential skills deemed necessary to live in a global society.

At this level of instruction the teacher must address the complexity of preparing a student for success as a citizen in family, local community, national, and international societies. Instruction has to focus on content and skills that facilitate students' participation in a complex world. The teacher bases the teaching on content and skills for citizenship, helps the student make connections to previously learned content and identifies how the content connects to future learning or life skills.

Exhibit 2.2, on the following page, is a chart comparing classroom focused content and society focused content.

The teacher can use the National Reading Standard for teaching reading (listed in **Exhibit 2.2** under Society) to differentiated learning. By using this standard, the teacher can teach reading skills within context. Instead of using one book and one set of vocabulary words, the teacher can use a variety of texts and use vocabulary words that the students do not know from those texts. For example, if the teacher has students whose reading levels range from third to seventh grade, the

Exhibit 2.2 Classroom vs. Societal-Based Content

Classroom driven content: reading	Society focused content: reading
Goals: Decide words with blends, diphthongs Identify major parts of a story Identify author's intent	Goals: Apply a wide range of strategies to comprehend, interpret, evaluate, and appreciate texts and non-text prints (literary, informational, practical/workplace, and persuasive) to reach personal goals, understand human experiences, create products, and develop ideas
Outcome: learn to read isolated content	Outcome: learn to read content in context
Reading skills: learn isolated rules	Reading skills: learn strategies for decoding, making meaning, and using information across different texts
Resources: preselected books	Resources: variety of texts
Vocabulary: predetermined	Vocabulary: based on the type of text and purpose for reading, words likely to find in real world, based on student need

teacher and students can identify vocabulary words appropriate for their level from the reading materials instead of being locked into using one set of vocabulary words for all the different levels.

In the classroom where societal goals are important, the focus is on learning *strategies* for reading, not simply on reading a story or word. The reading standard used for instruction identifies important types of texts with which students should be comfortable and requires that the student develop skills to use what they read for real life purposes. The vocabulary set is completely open to the types of print students choose, thus creating the opportunity to develop a broader vocabulary than ones found in a typical grade level text book.

By using the societal focus, or national standards for planning and designing instruction, the teacher has flexibility to use a variety of materials that interest the students and connect to their lives. The teacher creates an environment where students:

- develop life-long strategies using content knowledge,
- learn to apply those strategies to different situations,
- create a broader understanding of the content skills than any single school textbook could provide, and
- choose learning content in the context that is of the most interest and use to them in their lives.

Why is this important for student with disabilities?

Students with disabilities may come into a grade level without the knowledge, skills, or behaviors that are expected of their peers without disabilities. Teachers who remain locked into teaching the grade level curriculum will find their instruction leaves these students behind. In a classroom where the teacher focuses on life-long use of skills, the student with a disability can progress at an appropriate speed and still work within the context of the classroom.

Students with disabilities may have difficulty handling information at a particular mental processing level (e.g., abstract concepts) but can learn when concrete examples are provided. If teachers remain locked into grade level curriculum, they will not feel able to provide instruction in formats that the student might need.

For example, one general education teacher helped her students with moderate mental disabilities understand the more abstract concepts of linear equations algebra by working the equation out in real life. To teach the distributive property formula $\underline{a(b+c) = (ab) + (ac)}$ the teacher used pizzas and demonstrated the formula by using $\underline{2(b+c) = (2 \text{ barbecue pizzas}) + (2 \text{ cheese}}$ $\underline{\text{pizzas})}$. She had the students manipulate the pizzas first into each side of the equation, then put the symbols right on the pizzas and had the student manipulate each one again. Eventually the students were able to manipulate the symbols without the pizza!

While the intention of using the pizzas to teach the concept was for those students with moderate mental disabilities to learn in a concrete fashion, many of the other students in the room told the teacher they finally understood the abstract concept once they could see it at work! In this case, the teacher did not give up teaching the abstract concepts, she merely embedded the concepts in concrete learning first and allowed some students to show they understood the concepts using concrete examples instead of solving formulas only using symbols.

In a classroom-focused curriculum, the teacher would stick to the textbook-generated grade level expectations (abstract) as the *only way* to teach and measure a student's performance. However, at the society-focused level, the teacher used the standards for algebra, but was not locked into the abstract level of instruction, nor the prescribed examples in a sixth grade textbook. If that teacher had required that the students only learn and complete abstract math, the students with moderate mental disabilities would have failed the course and, in turn, been less successful in real life situations requiring similar problem solving.

Student Influences: The Details

To differentiate instruction, the teacher must take into consideration what is influencing the student as a learner. This side of the pyramid outlines what teachers should consider about the student as they design and implement instruction. **Exhibit 2.3**, on the following page, shows the three levels of Student Influence: Cornerstones, Transitions, and Personal Connections.

Cornerstones

The bottom level of the pyramid on this side represents the cornerstones a student needs for survival in school. The Cornerstones level of the pyramid validates that students need basic skills and life skills to participate in school. Basic skills in a typical classroom are considered the ability to read, write letters, and calculate numbers. Life skills extend beyond the basics to a wider range of skills such as the ability to communicate, negotiate, transport oneself around the community, or be a member of a group.

In a typical classroom, the skill often becomes more important than the student. Teachers focus on the teaching and rote use of those skills. The acquisition of the skill becomes the end instead of the means for learning. The student remains passive, involved in skill development with little understanding of how those skills might be important.

Transitions

The middle level of the pyramid requires that the teacher apply basic skills to a variety of settings where students will use the information. There are two important components to this level: generalization and problem solving. Here it becomes the teacher's role to help the students learn techniques for converting basic skills in isolation to useful strategies. The teacher focuses on helping the students apply what is known to various situations. The skill remains important but the *use* of the skill takes on a greater emphasis. The students become less passive, potentially seeing how those skills might be important.

Exhibit 2.3 Student Influences

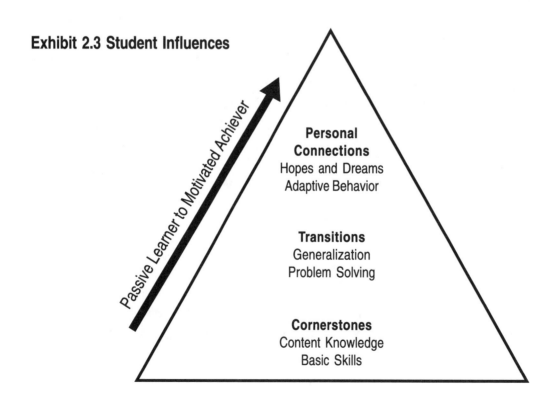

Personal Connections

In the differentiated classroom, the emphasis is on what motivates students and how learning will help them adapt to different environments in their life. Perhaps the single most motivating factor for students is realizing their own hopes and dreams. If the learning is directly connected to what the students dream of becoming or doing (long or short term), the depth of understanding increases and is sustained much longer than when learning is disconnected from the students' own desires.

If connecting to students' hopes and dreams is the single most motivating factor for success in the classroom, developing adaptive behavior skills is the single most important factor for success in the work force. The National Skills Standards Board (NSSB) is developing a national set of skills and standards for working in a global society. The single most important skill on their list is adaptive behavior, or the ability to adjust appropriately to the expectations and rules of new environments. Without adaptive behavior skills, students will have a difficult time acquiring their hopes and dreams.

Exhibit 2.4 provides a comparison of a classroom where student influences are left at the bottom of the pyramid to a differentiated classroom where personal connections are the primary focus.

Exhibit 2.4 Cornerstones vs Personal Connections

Cornerstones: Basic skills	Personal Connections: Hopes and Dreams
goal: pass the test	goal: desire to take a field trip
memorize addition and subtraction facts; use percentages	use a variety of mathematical processes for daily life
teacher chooses book and workbook activities	students develop strategies to earn money using most financially sound method; use an accounting system to tract progress toward earning money for trip
activities: practice, drill	activities: sell items, earn, add, calculate interest, subtract, market items
end: pass or fail the test	end: earn enough money to take the trip, and then take it!

When a teacher works from the top level of the pyramid she sees the students as the most important focus and creates opportunities for them to use information in a variety of settings in their own lives. Each student becomes a motivated investigator when he has the opportunity to improve the chances of making a dream come true.

Why is this important for students with disabilities?

Creating a learning environment where students make connections to their own life is important to students with disabilities for several reasons. First, students with disabilities are people who have dreams and desires just like their peers without disabilities. They have as much of a right to learn the skills to help them attain those dreams as any other person.

Second, many students with disabilities have trouble developing skills in a random fashion and generalizing them to new environments. When skills are connected to their lives, they have an easier time learning, remembering, and using the skills in multiple ways.

Third, it often takes students with disabilities longer than their non-disabled peers to learn and apply skills. When the focus of instruction is on their life after school (e.g., independent living, holding a job) from an early age, these students are ensured they have time to learn the skills.

Fourth, some students with disabilities may not learn all the basic skills even when the learning is connected to their personal lives. If teachers stay at the bottom of the pyramid, the same skill will be taught from kindergarten through high school, with little or no progression in learning. If, instead, teachers move to the top of the pyramid and consider what students want to do upon graduation, they can go beyond the skills the students cannot learn by circumventing or compensating for the skill.

Instruction Components: The Details

To differentiate instruction, the methods, materials, procedures, and environments must focus on genuine learning experiences. Typical teaching methods have focused on isolated learning experiences that result in rote memorization of information for passing a test. To be successful in life, students must experience learning in a situation that is as close to real life as possible. This side of the pyramid is about the considerations for instruction that lead to life-long learning. **Exhibit 2.5** shows the three levels of Instruction Components: Isolated Exercises, Scaffolded Instruction, and Genuine Experiences.

Isolated Exercises

In a typical classroom, the teacher often designs or uses predesigned activities or lessons in isolation. Instruction is based on separate, disconnected ideas by "covering the material." Typically, this type of instruction is single-dimension (only taught one way), using one type of material (usually a workbook), one method for solving the problem, taught in a traditional setting (at tables or desks), and is disconnected from any previous or future learning (not what they did yesterday and not planned for tomorrow). Such isolated instruction prevents students from making connections across ideas and content, and lessens the likelihood that they will be able to use the content or skills in real life experiences.

Exhibit 2.5 Instruction Components

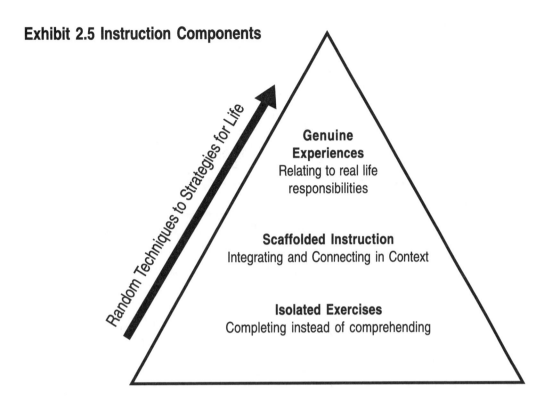

Scaffolded Instruction

The classroom in transition toward differentiated instruction will begin focusing on learning experiences that support students integrating and connecting content and skills. Designing instruction at this level requires that the teacher create scaffolded experiences in which the framework for using knowledge and skills is evident. At this level, instruction begins to integrate learning from various content areas and connect the learning to real life events where the learning will be used.

Genuine Experiences

In a differentiated classroom, the teacher plans for and uses learning experiences that really put the student to the test in the most life-like situation possible. This level of instruction focuses on the end result—life after graduation—and requires the teacher to develop authentic experiences in which students can apply what they have learned in situations that have real life consequences.

Exhibit 2.6, on the following page, provides a comparison of instruction using isolated exercises and genuine experiences.

In a differentiated classroom, students are given the opportunity to identify how the learning applies to their own life. Instruction is multi-dimensional (taught in a variety of ways), using many different materials, allowing for multiple methods to solve a problem, taught in any appropriate setting, and is connected to previous and future learning. By designing instruction in this fashion the teacher creates true-to-life opportunities for students.

Exhibit 2.6 Isolated Exercises vs Genuine Experiences

Isolated Exercises	Genuine Experiences
Goal: students learn to use research tools for information - warranties, newspaper, labels, web pages	Goal: students use a variety of resources, methods and tools to gather ideas and information and to communicate learning for a specific purpose
Time frame: warranties - 1 week; newspapers - 1 week; labels - 1 week; web pages - 2 weeks	Time frame: 5 weeks
Products: 1 report for each source	Product/Procedure: students research and change one important issue in their own lives; report on outcome
Topics: predetermined by teacher	Topics: student chooses
Lessons: one for each source	Lessons: how to read different types of resources, compare information, conduct research and create change
Example: report on warranty of a used car	Example: Report sent to the state legislature on sewer overflow into natural creeks during heavy rains based on government reports, local sewer district reports, interviews with engineers, doctors, biologist, and citizens of the city. Requested response.

Why is this important for students with disabilities?

Within the instruction element of the pyramid, there are four important considerations for students with disabilities: methods, materials, procedures, and environments.

Methods. Students with disabilities do not always learn through traditional methods (e.g., lecture, reading). To create authentic experiences for students with disabilities, the teacher must plan from the beginning to use multiple methods to teach content and skills. For example, using books on tape, text to voice, and picture walks for the student who does not read at grade level.

Materials. Students with disabilities do not always learn using traditional materials (e.g., workbooks, white board). To create authentic experiences for students with disabilities, the teacher must incorporate materials that reflect real life. For example, teaching money using real coins and bills instead of pictures of coins and bills.

Procedures. Students with disabilities do not always internalize the specific procedures used to learn or problem solve, and may need to use a different technique or a concrete method for addressing problems. For example, a student might need polaroid pictures of himself executing each step of the scientific process.

Environments. Some students with disabilities will need environments other than the traditional classroom setting to learn and generalize new content and skills. For example, a student may need to ride the bus instead of reading a map to determine how to get from one place to another.

Students with disabilities may not easily make connections from the classroom to real life. They may learn a skill in isolation, but not comprehend how to use that skill in the real world or they may not learn a skill in isolation at all and need the real world application to understand why the skill is important. If the teacher focuses on students' mastering the lesson instead of the knowledge, the student may never learn or use the skills and content. Students with disabilities need learning to be real and as close to what they will have to do in life as possible.

Assessment Techniques: The Details

In a differentiated classroom, no single content test or style of test is used as the sole measure of a student's learning. The teacher attends to content in light of the context, mental processes, and social skills of the student. By combining these, the teacher has a more detailed picture of what the student knows and is able to do. Authentic assessment moves the focus of testing from situation specific learner to independent problem solver. **Exhibit 2.7** shows the three levels of Assessment Techniques: Situation Specific Tests, Supported Performances, and Authentic Assessment.

Exhibit 2.7 Assessment Techniques

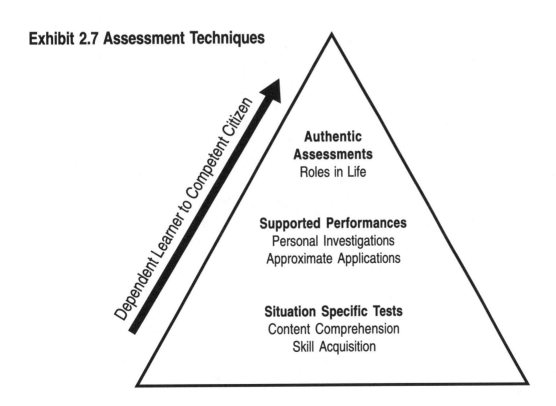

Authentic Assessments
Roles in Life

Supported Performances
Personal Investigations
Approximate Applications

Situation Specific Tests
Content Comprehension
Skill Acquisition

Dependent Learner to Competent Citizen

Situation Specific Tests

In a typical classroom assessment techniques focus on content comprehension and skill acquisition. The tests are based on the classroom curriculum concepts taught under isolated circumstances. In this case the assessment is intended primarily to determine if the student understands and can perform the skill. Traditional paper and pencil tests, worksheets, and board work are examples of this level of assessment.

When assessment is kept at the bottom level, the teacher knows little more than how well the students can feed back what they have learned. The students are not required to apply the skills to new situations or actually use the skills to problem solve.

Supported Performances

At the middle level are those assessment techniques that allow the students to begin choosing how they investigate and apply skills and knowledge to show what they know. Here the teacher opens the door for students to demonstrate, under supportive circumstances, what they know and can do. At this level the teacher uses assessments in which students conduct personal investigations (they design what they want to know) and approximate applications (close to real life, but still in the school setting). For example, using personal investigations instead of lecture, the teacher allows the students to investigate the causes of World War II and report on those causes. The teacher guides the investigation by requiring the students to delve into the dates, names and locations of importance during the war.

At this level of assessment, the teacher gives the students the opportunity to apply and analyze new learning. Students are guided toward using skills in particular ways under particular circumstances. Each student approximates the skills and knowledge needed for use in life.

Authentic Assessments

The ultimate goal for all teachers is to develop in students the skills needed to be as independent as possible when they leave school. The ultimate assessment of what students know comes when they fulfill their life roles (e.g., brother, mother, employer, taxpayer, friend, parishioner). All of these roles involve using knowledge and skills in a complex and independent level. At this level, the teacher focuses on the processes the student uses to think through a problem and solve it, as well as the social skills involved that will prepare the student for real life consequences.

The ultimate goal is to develop assessment that is as close to real life as possible. At this level, the student uses content and skills to investigate and participate successfully in various life activities. The teacher develops assessments that will demonstrate whether the student is developing skills to become a competent member of society.

Exhibit 2.8 provides a comparison of situation specific tests and authentic assessments.

Exhibit 2.8 Situation-Specific Tests vs Authentic Assessment

Situation-Specific Tests	Authentic Assessments
Type: paper and pencil	Type: presentation at community meeting
Topic: World War II	Topic: Impact of WWII and other wars on acquisition of land and resources for government use
Assessment: 20 Multiple choice, 5 essay	Assessment: By researching causes and outcomes of wars in history, students will research, report, and propose alternative solutions to the proposed acquisition of private land for a new airport at the Community Action Meeting

Why is this important for student with disabilities?

As mentioned in Chapter 1, the post-secondary outcomes for students with disabilities have been bleak in the past. Students have not come out of school prepared to join the work force or enter post-secondary education to the same degree as their peers without disabilities. In many cases, the problem has not been the students' content knowledge, but their mental processing, and social skills.

Students with disabilities often need multiple opportunities to work through similar problems in different situations. Sometimes a subtle difference in an event can throw a student off course for completing an activity. The more opportunities students have to practice skills in real situations, the better able they will be to address subtle changes once out of school.

For example, Boris is a student with a learning disability in math who uses a calculator for problems requiring addition, multiplication, subtraction and division. Boris can complete problems using a calculator in the classroom. However, the teacher has the responsibility to provide opportunities for Boris to use this skill in real life. Boris should be challenged to use the calculator to solve problems he will face as adult. For example, he should use the calculator at the book store to add his purchases, or at the grocery store to purchase food for a class party. By providing these opportunities, the teacher can intervene when necessary to improve his skills (e.g., watch him use the calculator, analyze what errors he might be making and reteach those skills).

Students with disabilities need opportunities during their school careers to learn and practice skills they will need in their life. Creating assessments that allow students with disabilities to use the information in real life situations provides opportunities for the teachers to intervene, improve, and hone the students' skills.

How does the Differentiated Instruction Pyramid help a teacher with differentiating instruction?

The pyramid represents the foundation for differentiation in that it proposes what must be taken into consideration when deciding how to differentiate. In essence, to differentiate instruction, the teacher must:

- teach content in relationship to how, when, why, and where students will use it in their world, both currently and in their future;
- develop the skills of the student, using the content as the backdrop for reaching personal goals or dreams;
- design instruction that provides a variety of paths and tools for students to reach learning goals; and
- evaluate student progress from various perspectives to gain a complete picture of the student's capabilities in real life.

When placed side-by-side, or in a 3-D format, the critical elements for differentiation align. The sides, when put together, create a continuous circle of considerations that a teacher must keep in mind when examining instruction and the students who need differentiated experiences. Students who need differentiated instruction require the teacher to analyze the purpose, intent, and long range outcomes of instruction. Such analysis should move the teacher from less effective practices at the bottom of the pyramid, to the top of the pyramid where the focus is on effective instruction and assessment for all students, including those with disabilities.

This is the first step in the process for differentiation: thinking about and planning for instruction that meets the top of the Differentiated Instruction Pyramid. In the next chapter, you will explore the second step of the decision making process that leads to the creation of differentiated instruction based on the essential elements found at the top of the pyramid. As you work through this step, and those that follow it, keep the model of the pyramid by your side as a reference. It will remind you to focus on the essential aspects of instruction and assessment that make learning exciting and purposeful for all students.

Chapter 3

Essential Curricular Questions

The second step in developing differentiated instruction is to analyze the curriculum. Often, within the curriculum and environment lie the barriers to learning. No matter what learning environment the teacher is in (general classroom, resource, collaborative, self contained) there are questions that must be asked about the instructional situation. The answers to these questions provide guidance to creating an accessible curriculum as required by federal law.

The questions posed in *Step 2: Analyze the Curriculum* offer the teacher a thinking process for the development, implementation, and assessment of accessible curriculum. The questions are organized around three of the four sides of the pyramid discussed in Chapter 2: Content, Instruction, and Assessment.

By answering the questions in this chapter teachers get a picture of what "normally" happens in an instructional environment when teaching a particular content area. Once teachers have a picture of "normal" they can begin to identify the gaps that explain why some students "get it" and others do not.

Eventually, teachers will not be able to separate the questions on curriculum posed in this chapter from those relating to students posed in the next chapter because the two are highly intertwined. However, when first beginning to use this process teachers need to look at their curriculum and learning environment separate from student-specific issues. Looking at the curriculum and learning environment in this fashion allows teachers to get a clear vision of what typically happens or what the teacher wants to happen. Once this vision is established, teachers can then begin to analyze where barriers might exist for individual or groups of students.

Let's Get Started!!

Make a copy of **BLM 4, Essential Curricular Questions.** As we address each question, a case study is provided to give an idea of how to respond to the questions. **BLM 5** is the completed case study for the Essential Curricular Questions. However, please use your own teaching situation and **BLM 4** to build a picture of what normally happens when your teach and assess.

When you see this hard hat symbol it means you should stop reading and start working on your answers.

Question 1: What is the content to be taught?

Identify the specific content for the unit or series of lessons to be taught. Sources for this information should be based upon national standards and local requirements. Answers should be as specific as possible, identifying the level as well as the content.

What this answer should include:	Examples:
• specific concepts, topics	• political causes of the civil war
• processes	• five-step writing process
• skills	• renaming fractions
• steps	• scientific inquiry steps

Why answer this question?

If the teacher cannot identify what should be taught, then it is very unlikely the students will ever understand it either. Knowing what you are going to teach is critical for student learning. Knowing what is to be taught also outlines what should be assessed.

Case Study:

Content - Mathematics. Topic - Measures of Central Tendency.
Level - mean, median, and mode using two-digit numbers.

In the case study that will be used for this chapter, the teacher wants to teach *calculating mean, median, and mode from a set of two-digit data*. We know there are three concepts to be learned and applied (mean, median, mode) and we know that the data will come from two-digit numbers (not one-digit, not three-digit, thus giving us the level of math skill). The teacher's answer to Question 1 would look like this:

Q 1	What is the content to be taught?	introduce calculating mean, median, and mode using two-digit number sets

---

On **BLM 4,** for Question 1, choose one topic or content area. Identify the concept, skill, process, or steps that you will teach. Write those in the space next to Question 1.

Question 2: How will the student use the content in real life?

Identify how the content is typically used in a person's everyday life during school years or after graduation.

What this answer should include:	**Examples:**
• future use in school	• reading harder text books; learning how to make graphs
• daily living	• purchases; paychecks; business reports
• job/life goal related	• artist; engineer; poet; physicist

Why answer this question?

If the teacher cannot connect the content to what is or will be important for the student as they work toward their life goals, the students will never understand why it is important to learn the content. If students see the connection between the learning and their lives, they are more likely to learn it and use it competently over time.

Case Study

Using the *calculating mean, median, and mode from a set of two-digit data* example, the teacher should be able to identify why students should learn this content. Within the school, students learn about mean, median, and mode so they can progress in mathematics and scientific studies such as statistical analysis. Mean, median and mode are also used in a variety of ways in our everyday life including recreational activities, daily living, and job related activities. The teacher's answer to Question 2 would look like this:

Q 2	How will the student use the content in real life?	statistics; stock market; sports scores (aka batting averages); voting outcomes; weather patterns; shopping

 On **BLM 4,** identify the real life connections in school and life to the content you expect to teach. Write those in the space next to Question 2.

Question 3: What background knowledge is important for this content?

Identify the specific background knowledge students should have prior to this learning experience. Answers should be as specific as possible and include information related to the content, skills, behaviors, or experiences they should have had before this learning event.

What this answer should include:	Examples:
• prior knowledge	• knowing addition of single-digit numbers
• skills	• using a ruler
• behaviors	• working in a small group
• experiences	• seen an elevator working (from a lesson on pulley systems), been to the zoo (from a lesson requiring students to write about and draw a polar bear)

Why answer this question?

If the teacher does not identify the foundation expected of students, the best planned and implemented instruction will flop. When the teacher overestimates what knowledge the students bring to the learning, the students will be frustrated and perhaps unable to acquire the knowledge.

Case Study

When the teacher plans to teach *calculating mean, median, and mode from a set of two-digit data,* the background knowledge might include: addition, subtraction, multiplication, and division of double-digit numbers; rank ordering numbers from least to most; simple counting; number recognition; and use of a calculator. The teacher's answer to Question 3 would look like this:

Q 3	What background knowledge is needed for this content?	addition of double-digit numbers, rank ordering number sets; numbers up to 1,000; use of calculator

 On **BLM 4,** identify the background knowledge needed for the content you plan to teach. Write it in the space next to Question 3.

Question 4: What is the language of instruction for this content?

Identify the terminology and directional words that are used for this content. The language of instruction is more than just the vocabulary words you teach the students. It is the language you use to get the students to do what you want of them.

What this answer should include:	**Examples:**
• directional approach	• explain, write, show, argue
• vocabulary implicating process	• write a persuasive piece, combine in beaker
• vocabulary indicating projects	• research, create a model, develop a picture

Why answer this question?

The teacher must attend to specific words that are used which, if not understood, will make a significant difference in student performance. This language of instruction is NOT about vocabulary so much as it IS about capacity to use procedures, follow directions, complete assignments, and use the vocabulary of the content in CONTEXT. Consider the words *solve, equate, sum, show your work.* When these words are used in math, they imply very specific techniques (e.g., *show* in math means put numbers on paper in step by step fashion), while in other content areas they mean very different behaviors (e.g., *show* in language arts writing class means write sentences that tell what you are thinking).

If the teacher does not identify the *context* for these content specific words it is likely that students, particularly those with specific learning problems, will misinterpret the meaning and not complete the activities appropriately.

Case Study

In the case study we know the vocabulary would at least include these three words: mean, median, and mode. In addition, the language of instruction is going to include words like: rank order, average, and compute. The teacher's answer to Question 4 would look like this:

Q 4	What is the language of instruction for this content?	order; rank; add; subtract; sum; count; graph; categorize; average; show work; divide; explain

 On the **BLM 4** identify the language of instruction for your content area. Write it in the space next to Question 4.

Question 5: What reading and writing skills are necessary for the written materials used?

Identify the reading level and specific types of skills necessary. Identify the writing skills and types necessary for the content. Answers should be as specific as possible, providing a picture of what the student should do when reading the information.

What this answer should include:	Examples:
• reading level of materials[1]	• second grade; fifth month
• skills for reading for meaning	• skimming; decoding
• genre of the reading	• fantasy; historical; fiction; opinion; scientific
• writing level	• simple sentences; compound sentences
• skills for writing	• grammar; tense; subject-verb agreement
• genre of the writing	• transactive; fiction; biographical

Why answer this question?

It is important to recognize what types of reading skills are expected. For example, in reading Shakespeare, the student must not only read each word, but also translate the language into modern day understanding. However, when reading a local newspaper the language is typically written using common daily language and needs little translation. If reading techniques are expected but students are not able to use them effectively it will inhibit their ability to acquire knowledge or complete activities.

It is equally important to identify the writing skills expected. If writing is the primary method for assessing what students know during and after instruction and students are not able to use writing as their best mode to communicate knowledge, the teacher will not get a true picture of what was learned.

Case Study

Using the content *calculating mean, median, and mode from a set of two-digit data*, the teacher will be using definitions from the text and word problems. The students will need to: be able to read the words in the text and problems, decipher word problems, and decode number words. The teacher's answer to Question 5 would look like this:

Q 5	What reading and writing skills are necessary or expected?	read directions; read numeric symbols for meaning (worth); decipher word problems; read 7th grade level terms; - write numbers 0 - 1000; write short answers using vocabulary

 Using **BLM 4,** identify the reading and writing skills required. Write them in the space next to Question 5.

---

[1] Don't know how to determine the real reading level of your materials? Go to Appendix for a reference or to the web site: www.cdc.gov/od/ads/fry.htm

---

Question 6: How do I normally present this content to the students?

Outline how <u>you</u> present or show information to the students. Answers here include anything that connects to the five senses. For example, in math, information is usually represented numerically (symbols), with pictures (e.g., graphs, number lines, formulas), while in language arts, information is usually represented in words and pictures.

<u>**What this answer should include:**</u>

- visual aids
- auditory aids
- kinesthetic aids

<u>**Examples:**</u>

- pictures; symbols; objects
- lecture; tapes; music
- manipulatives; textures; actions

Why answer this question?

The teacher must be aware of how she presents information to students. All students do not learn using just one format. If a teacher only provides information one way, it is likely that she is leaving many students behind. For example, if the teacher uses only lecture to share information, those students who learn better through pictures, reading, or acting out their learning will not be very successful.

Case Study

To show *calculating mean, median, and mode from a set of two-digit data* the teacher typically uses some lecture and demonstrates the calculations with an overhead calculator and the white board. The teacher's answer to Question 6 would look like this:

Q 6	How do you normally teach this content?	mini-lecture; demonstrate with overhead calculators; demonstration of steps for each concept on board or overhead

 Using **BLM 4,** identify how <u>you</u> demonstrate the new concepts or procedures for the content. Write it in the space next to Question 6.

Question 7: What learning strategies are used to teach this content?

Identify the approach or physical and mental processes used to grasp information and solve problems. Answers here should include techniques or strategies to acquire and use the content. For example, if the curriculum is focusing on political concepts behind the civil war, and the teacher tells the students to "research different views" or read historical documents to find answers, the students must understand what strategy should be used to accomplish the task (e.g., research = searching-reading-analyzing and compiling information).

What this answer should include:	Examples:
• techniques	• scientific inquiry steps; outlining; venn diagrams; highlighting
• approach	• note taking; skimming; C.O.P.S.; reading for detail

Why answer this question?

Often the learning strategies that a teacher uses are unspoken or not actually taught to the student. The students must understand that the teacher expects them to use the same strategy to acquire the knowledge and likely use that strategy to prepare for assessment of the knowledge. For example, the teacher uses a venn diagram to teach the similarities and differences between WWI and WWII. It is likely the teacher will expect the students to create the same venn diagram in their notes and use that type of diagram-comparison strategy in an upcoming test. If the students recognize this strategy as an integral part of their learning and assessment, they are more likely to use and benefit from it. If the students do not understand the importance of such strategies, they will miss out on critical components of the learning situation.

Case Study

In the process of teaching *calculating mean, median, and mode from a set of two-digit data*, the students are required to graph, rank order highest to lowest, manipulate data, input data and check answers. The teacher also requires the students to take notes during class and copy information from the board. Each of these is a technique or approach to the learning. The teacher's answer to Question 7 would look like this:

Q 7	What types of learning strategies are part of this content?	ranking highest to lowest; manipulating data; checking for accuracy; note taking; discovery

 Using **BLM 4,** identify learning strategies that are important for this content. Write it in the space next to Question 7.

Question 8: What activities will engage and immerse the learner?

Consider two issues: (1) what activities are usually part of the teaching and (2) what activities would attract the students to the content. Describe the activity in detail and explain why the students would like to do it (e.g., how it connects to their own lives).

What this answer should include:	Examples:
• type of activity	• addition – count money from a school fund raiser; history - research school rule that they would like to have changed and write a persuasive essay to change the rule
• age/grade level interests	• kindergartners love songs; fifth graders enjoy games; high schoolers like social justice

Why answer this question?

When a teacher identifies the activities that match students' interests, she creates a "hook" that pulls them into the learning. When students are interested in the content they are more likely to learn, retain, and use the information in the future.

Case Study

In general, seventh grade students may not be too interested in learning to *calculate mean, median, and mode from a set of two-digit data* as a pure math skill, but they are very interested in fairness, consumerism, and comparing themselves to others. The teacher can use this information to create activities that catch the students' attention and help them understand why the concepts are important. The teacher's answer to Question 8 would look like this:

Q 8	What activities will engage the learner?	seventh graders are interested in social issues, fairness, consumerism so activities like graphing income levels of different jobs, collecting personal data for comparison; comparing items at different shops or restaurants by using mean, median, mode might get them more interested in the topic.

 Using **BLM 4,** identify activities that will engage the learner. Write them in the space next to Question 8.

Question 9: What adaptive behaviors are expected during instruction?

Adaptive behavior refers to a student's ability to change his or her focus and interactions as called for by the environment. For example, an adult is expected to adapt his or her behavior to different situations (e.g., behavior at a family reunion vs. an office meeting). In this case, the teacher must identify: the types of transitions, or changes in activities, including persons, pace, and level of intensity that occur during typical instruction, and the types of behavioral interactions expected.

What this answer should include:	**Examples:**
• groupings	• independent; small or large group
• time frames	• change tasks every 15 minutes; work on one project for 45 minutes
• interactions	• no talking; sharing materials; cooperative learning
• behaviors	• follow directions; listening to others; raise your hand; stay in seat

Why answer this question?

In school students are expected to adapt behaviors continually without much fanfare. On an average, students are expected to change from one activity to another (e.g., small to large group) or one environment to another (e.g., playground to classroom) every twenty minutes. Sometimes teachers do not realize how often and the degree of adaptation students are asked to make. The speed, frequency, and degree of adaptation can impact a student's ability to learn. If the teacher is not aware of these expectations conflict may arise within the classroom and the teacher might not understand why.

Case Study

When teaching *calculating mean, median, and mode from a set of two-digit data*, the teacher has the students watch her complete a problem. They then transition to working on their own problem, and then must work together sharing calculators to solve a group problem. The teacher's answer to Question 9 would look like this:

Q 9	What adaptive behaviors are expected during instruction?	independent work; small group cooperative learning; movement around the room and to the library to collect data; change from teacher demonstration to student work every 10 minutes; raise hand to ask for help

 Using **BLM 4,** identify the adaptive behaviors expected during instruction. Write them in the space next to Question 9.

Question 10: What class management systems do I use?

Identify those techniques that you use to keep the order and the flow of learning in place, keep the students safe, and facilitate the learning. These are not inherently instructional in nature but they are essential to keep everything running smoothly so that instruction can occur.

What this answer should include:	Examples:
• methods of gaining attention	• raising hand; counting backward from 5; clapping
• methods for handling papers	• teacher hands out; assigned student; materials special boxes for homework
• ways of answering during class	• raised hand; hold up flag; signs
• time frame for preparing/closing	• last 5 minutes to clean up after a lesson
• behaviors prepare/participate	• sign-in sheets; have paper, pencil, textbook at desk before bell; in seat at all times; always raise hand to ask or answer question
• normal class routines	• start every class with a DOL (daily oral language); journal entry; lecture-try-discuss; assignments written in agenda

Why should you answer this question?

Each and every teacher uses some forms or systems to manage the classroom. These systems set up a consistent learning environment for students and help the teacher feel some order to the learning process. Often teachers forget how integral the management system is to the smooth functioning of a classroom. Some students may not understand or know how to follow a particular management system and must be explicitly taught how to use the system. By identifying the systems used before teaching begins, the teacher will be more likely to determine when a student is having difficulty understanding or using the management system and address the issue before it becomes a major problem.

Case Study

The teacher working on *calculating mean, median, and mode from a set of two-digit data* identifies what she sees as important procedures for getting the work done and keeping things under control in the classroom. The teacher's answer to Question 10 would look like this:

Q 10	What procedures and routines are used/expected?	at the beginning of class pick up math packet with calculator; bring book, paper and pencil to class; check in at the door using chart; raise hand to answer questions; one student collects and distributes papers; turn lights off for attention

 Identify the procedures and routines needed to participate in the learning. Write them in the space next to Question 10 on **BLM 4.**

Question 11: What physical and sensory skills will students need?

Identify which senses the student will use during the learning and assessment, and outline what physical skills are needed by the student to participate in the learning. Senses include vision, hearing, touch, taste, smell. Physical skills include fine (e.g., holding a pencil) and gross (e.g., walking) motor skills.

<u>What this answer should include:</u>	<u>Examples:</u>
• gross motor skills	• raising hands; clapping; running; hopping; walking
• fine motor skills	• holding a pencil; using paint brush; cutting; turning pages
• visual skills	• reading the white board
• auditory skills	• listening to lecture for details
• tactile skills	• ability to tolerate different textures
• olfactory	• smelling the difference between two chemical compounds
• taste	• identifying the difference between bitter and sweet

Why answer this question?

Not all students respond to learning using the same senses. It is important for the teacher to be aware of what is required so that she can balance the use of various senses in the learning. In addition, not all students have the same degree of skill in each of the physical and sensory areas. To use only one sense or physical skill for teaching a particular content would prevent some students from learning.

Case Study

The teacher working on *calculating mean, median, and mode from a set of two-digit data* identifies what physical and sensory skills are required in the instruction. The teacher's answer to Question 11 would look like this:

Q 11	What physical or sensory skills are involved in the learning?	punching numbers on a calculator; viewing information from paper, board, books; listening to directions; writing using a pencil; talking with peers; standing to write on the board

 Using the **BLM 4,** identify the physical or sensory skills needed for learning. Write them in the space next to Question 11.

Question 12: What materials or services do the students use for learning?

Identify the materials (e.g., tools) or services (e.g., internet, librarian) that will be used during instruction. Materials include any apparatus, manipulatives, or physical items that are used for instruction and learning. Services include actions provided by people or technology that assist with learning.

<u>What this answer should include:</u>	<u>Examples:</u>
• materials	• crayons; computer; beakers; chart paper; counters; protractor; graphing calculator; dictionary
• services	• e-mail; internet; physician's advice; counseling; mentoring; speech language pathologist

Why answer this question?

The materials and services used to teach content are important because they help students search, manipulate, and problem solve. The teacher must be aware of the materials and services because some students may have difficulty using one type of tool, but not another. Knowing which materials are commonly used gives the teacher a chance to plan ahead for students who may need a different tool or service to learn the content.

Case Study

The teacher working on *calculating mean, median, and mode from a set of two-digit data* identifies the calculator, pencils and paper as the primary tools used in the instruction and indicates that the student will be doing some research using the internet. The teacher's answer to Question 12 would look like this:

Q 12 What materials or services do the students use?	calculator, paper and pencil, internet sites

 Using the **BLM 4,** identify the materials or services that will be used for learning. Write them in the space next to Question 12.

Question 13: Where will the learning occur?

Identify the typical place or setting where learning occurs and also implicate where the content would be used in the real world. In the best of worlds students would have the opportunity to practice skills in school and then go out and use them in the world before they leave school.

<u>**What this answer should include:**</u>

- setting or location

<u>**Examples:**</u>

- library; technology lab; science lab; lunch room; art room; local restaurant

Why answer this question?

Often teachers ask students to learn information completely out of context. While some students can learn information out of context and generalize to other environments, MOST students need at least some connection to the real world. By knowing where learning typically occurs and how it is connected to real world environments, the teacher can prepare instruction to mimic, if not be, real world.

Case Study

The teacher working on *calculating mean, median, and mode from a set of two-digit data* identifies the classroom and computer lab as the primary places learning will occur. The teacher's answer to Question 13 would look like this:

Q 13 Where will the learning occur?	classroom and computer lab for input of data

Using the **BLM 4,** identify the location(s) where instruction and assessment will occur. Write them in the space next to Question 13.

Question 14: How do students show what they know during and after instruction?

Identify the basic types of measurements that are used while the content is being taught. These types of assessments produce evidence of student learning and include activities, processes, traditional tests, and products.

What this answer should include:	Examples:
• participation in activities	• taking notes; answering in class; participation in groups
• types of products	• book report; poster display; art work
• traditional tests	• multiple choice; true false; essay
• types of processes	• using six-step solution for science; applying the communicative property to solve a problem
• descriptions of work, skills	• student writes estimate number of M&Ms in a bag
• participation in groups	• cooperative group of 4; peer review of writing; group presentation with power point
• types of independent work	• individual report using technology; homework; personal daily agenda

Why answer this question?

The teacher should focus on which activities will be used to monitor progress and grade student learning. Because not all students demonstrate what they know in the same way, the teacher must consider using multiple types of assessments to collect evidence of student learning.

Case Study

The teacher assessing *calculating mean, median, and mode from a set of two-digit data* identifies a variety of assessments that will provide evidence of learning. The teacher's answer to Question 14 would look like this:

Q 14	How do students show what they know during and after instruction?	vocabulary test; worksheets with five problems for each concept; graphing information accurately; group presentation using rubric

 Using the **BLM 4,** identify the assessments that will be used . Write them in the space next to Question 14.

What have you created?

Take a look at your answers to these questions and you should see a very a detailed picture or framework of the way instruction is typically provided. **BLM 5** provides a completed set of questions based upon the case study. Notice how the instructional picture is painted by the answers to each question? The teacher has a complete view of the most important instructional information necessary for lesson plans.

Chapter 4

Essential Student Questions

Research and empirical evidence gathered over the past 23 years suggests that 99% of classroom learning challenges for students with disabilities can be identified as a mismatch between the content and instructional planning (Essential Curricular Questions) and how the student best learns (Moll, 1996). It becomes critical then that a teacher examines the mismatch and takes action to correct the problem. To identify the mismatch, the teacher not only examines the curriculum as done in the previous chapter, but also must analyze the needs of the student. In *Step 3: Analyze Student Needs*, the teacher identifies the strengths and areas of concern for the student that lead to a potential mismatch between instruction and student learning.

As in Step 2, here the teacher answers a series of questions, but now, the questions focus on the student. The Essential Student Questions (ESQs) work as a needs assessment survey by identifying the strengths and areas of need for the student. It is important for the teacher to know the strengths and areas of need for all students in the classroom so that planning for instruction and assessment matches the students' needs. However, when working with students with disabilities or learning challenges, it becomes CRITICAL to know this information.

The ESQs are not written for specific special education labels (e.g., learning disabled, visually impaired, emotionally disturbed) for two reasons. First, these questions are written to address ANY student who might be experiencing a problem (e.g., the student who is gifted and not being challenged or the student at-risk for failure), not just students with disabilities. Second, labels do not provide a picture of what a student can and cannot do. Two students with the same special education label may have extremely different characteristics, needs, and strengths. To differentiate instruction, the teacher must know what individual students can do and how they can do it.

The ESQs parallel the questions in the previous chapter. The reason to ask these questions separate from the content is to get a good look at what students can do and what they need to be successful without hooking it to specific content facts or skills. When the teacher has the essential information about the student, minor adjustments to the curriculum or learning environment - or differentiation - becomes easy.

Who should answer these questions related to the student? The answer to this question depends upon the teacher's situation. In some instances the general education teacher may be the only person involved in the process. In other situations, the general education and special education teacher might work together to answer the questions. Sometimes, when students with disabilities are first being included in the general education setting, the general education teacher does not know the student well enough to complete the questions. In this case, the primary responsibility falls on the special education teacher. Eventually the general education teacher learns enough about the student to use the questions for future planning. In a self contained teaching situation the special education teacher may be the only person involved in answering the questions. In any of these situations, the teacher(s) should gather information from a variety of sources including the student, parents whenever possible, and other specialists or persons with knowledge of the student, such as the physical therapist or instructional assistant, to get a complete picture of the strengths and needs of the student.

Let's Get Started!

Make a copy of **BLM 6, Essential Student Questions.** Apply each question to a student you know. If you cannot answer some of these questions try asking the student, parent, or other service providers who might have insight into the student.

For the purpose of consistency, each question is applied to the Case Study from Chapter 2 in which the teacher is preparing to teach *mean, median, and mode using two-digit number sets,* and is answered based on a case study named Nicholas. This is presented as **BLM 7**.

Essential Student Questions

Question 1: What does the student know about the content?

Identify what the student already knows about the content to be taught through reviewing old records, a pretest, or an interview. Pay attention to the concepts, processes, skills, or steps required of the content.

What this answer should include:	**Examples:**
• concepts (e.g., addition)	• knows addition up to 10
• processes (e.g., writing)	• can develop first draft
• skills (e.g., renaming fractions)	• knows simple fractions (e.g., 1/2, 1/3) but cannot rename any fractions
• steps (e.g., scientific process)	• knows the first two steps

Why answer this question?

Effective instruction not only addresses where the student is but takes the student to a new level of understanding of the content. If the teacher knows where the student is then instruction can begin at that point. Often teachers assume, based on the fact there is a disability, that the student cannot do anything or can do very little. Teachers use this as a reason to gear instruction toward the students who "can do" and overlook planning for the student with the disability. In most cases, students with disabilities <u>know</u> something about the content and <u>can do</u> the work. It is the responsibility of the teacher(s) to identify where the student is developmentally, and begin that student's instruction at that point.

Case Study: Nicholas

no exposure to mean, median, mode, but knows how to average	Q 1	What does the student know about the content?

 Using **BLM 6**, next to Question number 1(Q1), write down what the student knows about the content area to be taught.

Question 2: What are the interests (hopes and dreams) of the student?

Identify what the student currently likes to do in and outside of school. Find out what the student dreams of becoming when he grows up. The answer to this question should focus on the student's perspective, not the teacher or parents' (unless the student is incapable of truly speaking for himself). Getting the answer to this question will require a little detective work on the teacher's part!

What this answer should include:	**Examples:**
• interests	• cars; sports; reading comic books
• hopes and dreams	• be a stock car driver or farmer
• life long goals	• get a job; live alone

Why answer this question?

This question is important for students with disabilities for a variety of reasons. Students with disabilities may have shorter attention spans than their non-disabled peers. If the learning is connected to something they are interested in, their attention will be focused for a longer period of time.

Students who have disabilities might not always get the subtle connections between information and its use in the real world. It is important to help them make the connections between what is happening in the classroom and their real life.

Some students with disabilities may not ever master every aspect of a particular content area, but will need the basics of that content area for daily life (e.g., may not learn abstract formula of algebra, but can understand how to solve a real life problem like how many different types of pizzas are needed for x number of people). By understanding what the student likes to do in daily life or wants to do in the future, the teacher can gear the instruction toward those ends instead of just disconnected learning of the content.

Case study: Nicholas

likes sports, particularly football, wrestling and baseball; keeps scores; knows batting and football data	Q 2	What are the interests of the student?

 Using **BLM 6**, next to Q2, write down the interests of the student.

Question 3: What background knowledge does the student have for this content?

Identify what experiences the student has had in the past that are important for the teaching that is about to occur. Specifically, the teacher wants to know if the student has previous experiences that will relate to the topic and the examples that will be used in the discussions, behaviors that will be expected during the learning, and specific skills that will be necessary to complete tasks.

<u>What this answer should include:</u>	<u>Examples:</u>
• skills (e.g., measurement)	• can use a ruler; can mix chemicals safely
• behaviors (e.g., cooperative learning)	• can work as the scribe but not as discussant
• experiences (e.g., pulley systems)	• never seen an elevator system, but uses a hoist on the farm

Why answer this question?

There are several reasons that this question is critical for students with disabilities. Students with disabilities often spend an enormous amount of energy learning skills (e.g., decoding words, using a ruler, writing a sentence). While they are learning that skill, they often miss the content around which the skill was wrapped. If a skill that the student has not mastered is used during instruction, he may expend more energy trying to use the skill than actually getting the content. For example, a teacher may assume that the student understood the content of a reading passage in On the Way Home, by Laura Ingalls Wilder because he read a passage out loud. What the teacher may not realize was that the student used so much energy translating the words - just reading them out loud - that he did not get the full meaning of any of the text. So if the teacher knows the background skills of the student she can address the fact that those skills may interfere with the learning of important content.

Students with disabilities may have difficulty with behavioral expectations that other students have mastered. Two areas tend to be problematic in particular - transitioning from one type of activity to another (e.g., changing from independent to group work) and understanding the expected behaviors during instruction (e.g., staying in seat while teacher is talking). If the instruction calls for behaviors that the student has not mastered, the teacher can address these issues before problems arise.

Students with disabilities come from all walks of life and may have a wide range of experiences. However, some of these students may come to school with a limited set of experiences outside of their own home (e.g., a student with severe physical limitations whose parents do not have appropriate transportation will not have the same opportunities as another). So, expecting students to have had certain experiences may set them up for failure (e.g., expecting the student to know about zoo animals and their habitats when a student has never been to the zoo).

Case Study: Nicholas

can use a calculator to input a series of up to 10 numbers; add up to 1,000	Q 3	What background knowledge does the student have for his instruction?

 Using **BLM 6**, next to Q3, write down the background knowledge the student has for this content area.

Question 4: To what degree does the student understand the language of instruction?

Determine if the student understands the directional terminology, content specific terms, and project related terms. To find this information out, the teacher may need to review old work, give the student a pre-test, observe him in action, or interview him to determine his level of understanding.

What this answer should include:	**Examples:**
• directional terminology	• knows how to develop an argument; has difficulty with *explain* and *show*; trouble with words like *underline*, *circle*
• content specific terms	• understands <u>mix</u>, but not <u>combine</u>; knows meaning of <u>put together</u> but not <u>add</u>
• project/activity terms	• knows what a *model* is; can make a picture; does not understand what a five point paragraph includes

Why answer this question?

The teacher must attend to the behavior of the student when he is asked to act upon some instructional language. Unfortunately, this is a question that usually does not get answered until the student has met some failure. There are several important reasons to answer this question.

Students with disabilities often have trouble understanding basic pragmatics (meaning) and semantics (use) of instructional language. If a student does not understand the language common to most instructional settings, it will be extremely difficult, if not impossible, for the student to be successful in any activity.

Students with disabilities may have difficulty remembering a large number of content specific terms that may mean the same thing. For example, in math, when the teacher says to find the sum, does the student understand that <u>*find the sum*</u> is the same as <u>*add all the numbers*</u>, <u>*put the numbers together*</u>, and <u>*count them all*</u>? If a teacher is aware of the fact that a student may understand a content concept using one definition or set of terminology only, the teacher can make sure that the student hears the directions or has the information explained using that language.

Students with disabilities may not comprehend the subtle differences in the meaning of commonly used instructional words across content areas (e.g., the word *show* means two very different things in math and art). Teachers must be aware that the student may need an explicit explanation of what each word means within each context or classroom.

Students with disabilities may have difficulty remembering the steps or requirements for projects or activities in particular content areas (e.g., understanding that a research paper involves multiple stages not just a first draft). The teacher may need to provide step-by-step guides, or models of completed work to help the student complete each step of the task.

Case Study: Nicholas

difficulty with directional words like list, order, show your work explain; does not provide in-depth answers when asked to show or explain	Q 4	To what degree does the student understand the language of instruction?

Using **BLM 6**, next to Q4, identify the possible problems with understanding the language of instruction for the content area.

Question 5: What reading and writing skills does the student have that will impact using written materials?

Identify the reading capacity of the student including grade level, skills of reading for meaning and decoding words, approaches to reading, and comprehension of how to use different types of text for different purposes. Determine the writing skills of the student including level, skills, approaches, and genre use.

What this answer should include:	Examples:
• level	• reads at sixth grade level fluently; writes simple sentences
• skills	• does not read for meaning; difficulty with decoding; trouble reading basic sight words but understands other vocabulary; reads pictures but not words; subject-verb agreement; inaccurate verb tense; uses adjectives and adverbs
• approaches	• reads only for word, not meaning; skims only; does not use writing process; does not edit for grammar or spelling
• understands genre	• thinks comic books and biographies have same type of content; understands difference between a newspaper article and research report; can write a transactive piece but not a creative one

Why answer this question?

For students with high incidence disabilities (e.g., learning disabilities, mild mental retardation, ADD, ADHD, Behavior Disorders), reading is <u>the</u> single most interfering factor for learning **content** <u>because of the way we normally teach</u>, not because of the disability itself. Beginning around the third grade, most teachers use reading as the primary means for learning content and these students typically have not mastered the skills needed for reading at level by that age. By using reading as the primary means for learning new content, the teacher excludes those students who have poor reading skills from opportunities to learn the content.

It is important to note here that a disability in reading does not equate with an inability to learn content. The only time a student's inability to read impacts his learning content is when the teacher uses the reading as the only way to get the content. In most cases, the student with a disability in reading <u>can learn content</u> when it is presented in another manner (e.g., pictures, modeling, auditorily).

When the teacher knows the reading skills of the student, instruction can be adjusted to include methods for learning the content other than reading. Or the teacher can adjust the reading level of the work to meet the needs of the student.

While reading is the skill that most often interferes with learning new content for many students with disabilities, deficits in writing create one of the biggest interfering factors for showing what the student **knows** <u>because of the way students are normally asked to show what they know</u>. In most general classrooms, teachers have used written work as the primary mode for demonstrating knowledge. Students with disabilities may have difficulty using writing as the best vehicle to demonstrate what they know. By using written work as the primary assessment tool, the teacher excludes those students with poor writing skills from showing what they know.

Just as with reading, a disability in writing does not equate with an inability to learn content or to demonstrate knowledge in content. The only time a student's inability to write impacts his learning content or demonstrating knowledge is when the teacher uses the writing as the only way for him to express what he knows. In most cases, the student with a disability in writing <u>can demonstrate what he knows</u> when he can present it in another manner (e.g., verbally, drawing, acting, building).

When the teacher knows the writing skills of the student, instruction can be adjusted to include methods for assessing the content other than writing, or the writing level of the work can be adjusted to meet the needs of the student.

Case Study: Nicholas

reads two grade levels below his peers; word attack; skimming and reading for meaning are poor; understands pictures with simple directions better than text; no writing issues here	Q 5	What reading and writing skills does the student have?

 Using **BLM 6**, next to Q5, provide information pertaining to the student's ability to read and use written text.

Question 6: How does the student learn?

Identify the methods or styles of presentation that best reach the student. Every student has a style preference for learning new information. The simplest way to think about these styles is to approach them through the five senses: hearing, seeing, touching, tasting, and smell. There are other methods that are research-based and provide a better picture of the student's learning styles such as Howard Gardner's Eight Intelligences (Linguistic, Bodily-Kinesthetic, Logical- Mathematical, Visual-Spatial, Musical, Interpersonal, Intrapersonal, Naturalist).

What this answer should include:	Examples:
• five senses	• prefers to see pictures; likes symbols; needs to manipulate items; needs to hear it
• methods	• likes to read text over listening to lecture; learns better when with others; understands visual organizers
• intelligences	• logical-mathematical; bodily-kinesthetic; musical; verbal-linguistic; naturalist; interpersonal; visual-spatial

Why answer this question?

Students with disabilities are just like other students in that they have preferences for how new information is learned. Knowing how students learn guides the teacher in planning activities for learning new information. Just as with a student without disabilities, the teacher must recognize the learning style of the student with a disability and use that style in the classroom. However, this question is particularly important for students with disabilities because they often do not learn in the two traditional manners used in school: reading and listening. Students with disabilities often require that instruction include concrete, hands on, active learning experiences. This need for a variety of formats means that the teacher must look beyond using lecture format for teaching new information.

Case Study: Nicholas

learns best by seeing and doing quickly if he can physically manipulate information or see it modeled visually; auditory is he least effective learning mode	Q 6	How does the student learn?

 Using **BLM 6**, next to Q6, identify the learning style(s) of the student.

Question 7: What strategies does the student use to approach new learning?

Identify the specific ways the student acquires new learning including the techniques and approaches used before, during, and after learning. Techniques include specific steps or formats that allow the student to gain information (e.g., skimming, outlining, 5 step method, diagrams). Approaches are the methods for preparing for and connecting the learning (e.g., multiple drafts v. one final copy, prewriting on a topic, conducting a book walk before reading the story).

What this answer should include:	Examples:
• techniques	• does not outline when reading; uses a tape recorder for taking notes; moves right to left, not left to right
• approaches	• makes no predictions about the reading; random reading for details; does not use previous skills learned in other activities for new activity; looks for key words in text before reading

Why answer this question?

Students with disabilities often do not know how to approach a problem or how to use one specific method of learning for a particular learning situation. Ever had a student who successfully completed work one day and then on the very next day completely bombed the same type of work? It is likely the student did not have a method or strategy for approaching the problem! Attacking problems with random methods for solving them is characteristic of students with behavior disorders, learning disabilities, mild mental retardation, attention deficit disorder, and attention deficit hyperactivity disorder. While not true of every single student diagnosed with these labels, the student with disabilities often has difficulty developing strategies to approach problems and must be taught, in step-by-step fashion, how to approach different types of problems.

This being said, it is important for the teacher to know how the student approaches problems by asking the student to identify the logic or process used or observing as he approaches specific problems. For example, by watching the student in class, the math teacher can identify that he does not know how to skip count by five's, creating a situation where it takes the student more time than others to complete each problem. Knowing the methods a student uses allows her to adjust the instruction or teach the student a specific approach to learning.

Case Study: Nicholas

no specific strategies for learning; randomly approaches tasks; does not ask questions at the beginning for clarification; is not sure what is important in note taking; difficulty with directions with more than 3 steps	Q 7	What strategies does the student use to approach new learning?

 Using **BLM 6**, next to Q7, identify any learning strategies or lack there of this student displays.

Question 8: What activities will engage the student in learning?

Identify the types of activities the student would most like to do in real life when using this content and then connect the activity to the student's interests. This question is both dependent upon the age of the student and the immediacy of when the knowledge will be used. Young students have very different interests than older students. Using information immediately to attain something is typically more interesting than information that is not used for a long time.

This question is different from Question 6 which asks how the student prefers to learn or acquire new information. This question asks how the student prefers to act on the new information. For example, the content is on social and political reasons for W.W.II. The student's learning style might be auditory, so providing content through an auditory channel is important. The teacher might choose to lecture on the topic. However, the student is not engaged or excited about listening to the teacher. A better activity, one that would grab the student's attention, might be to allow the student to interview veterans or show a video that addresses the topic. The learning style (hearing it) combined with the student interacting with the content (via interviews) makes a better combination.

What this answer should include:	**Examples:**
• activities that grab attention	• likes interviewing people; likes to shop; create a web site; build a model of a cell; petition for a change to a rule in the school
• age/grade level interests	• likes music; loves to argue; playing a video

Why answer this question?

Students with disabilities are like students without disabilities in that they need to be excited and interested in what they are learning. They need to understand how the content connects to themselves personally. They need to act upon the content to understand how the content will help them in their future. However, there are subtle differences in some students.

Some students with disabilities may take longer to learn concepts and skills than their peers without disabilities and need very concrete experiences even after the content has been mastered. Because of this difference, the focus of activities for the student may be primarily on real world use (e.g., counting money to make a purchase in the lunch room instead of doing a worksheet on making change).

Some students with disabilities do not internalize the importance of *learning for learning's sake* and need a high level of external motivation to learn. One way this need for external motivation can be addressed is by using activities that attract or relate to the student.

Case Study: Nicholas

enjoys competitive events, pays attention to activities that relate to earning points, scores; likes games; loves talking sports scores	Q 8	What activities will engage the student in learning?

 Using **BLM 6**, next to Q8, identify the types of activities this student would enjoy being part of for instruction.

Question 9: What adaptive behavior skills does the student have that would impact learning?

Identify any adaptive behavior skills that the student uses well or has problems with, including transitions, interactions, behaviors, and work related skills. Transitions refer to changes from one event or area to another (e.g., moving from room to hallway, ending instruction in one content area and beginning another, altering between lecture and independent work). Interactions refer to the types of socially appropriate behaviors expected when the student works with another person (e.g., cooperative groups, answering a teacher's question). Behaviors refer to the broad spectrum of teacher-pleasing actions that are expected in the classroom (e.g., follows rules, sits in seat, shares with others). Work related skills include those actions students take to get assignments done or to participate in activities (e.g., put name on paper, work independently, bring materials to class, turn in homework).

<u>What this answer should include:</u>	<u>Examples:</u>
• transition	• difficulty moving from one activity to another without specific warning; takes 5 - 10 minutes to regroup after changing content areas; very flexible

---

• interactions	• works well in groups of 2-3; prefers working with an adult; takes a leadership role
• behaviors	• does not like to share materials; difficulty attending when lots of background noise present; gets frustrated easily; calls out
• work related behaviors	• cannot handle large group activities for longer than 15 minutes; long time to get organized; comes unprepared to class; forgets assignments

Why answer this question?

Many students with disabilities have some form of adaptive behavior problems that are either learned or natural to their disability. The student may have slight or extreme problems adapting to the normally fluid nature of the classroom or school setting. Each area is important to discuss.

Transitions

Most students deal with transitions relatively well. They learn to stop work when asked, put down their pencils, and listen to the teacher give new instructions or line up for some other event without it being traumatic. However, some students with disabilities cannot make such a quick transition. They may find it difficult to stop using the materials or to shift their focus from one subject to another. Students who have difficulty with transitions can often learn to deal with them if there is some cue or signal that prepares them for the change. If the teacher(s) can identify when transitions will occur during the instruction or between instructional events, they can develop a cue or signal that will help the student prepare and successfully move to the next event.

For example, Roger has trouble moving from one activity to another. Usually once he gets involved in an activity he does not want to leave it. If he is given a visual cue that indicates when a change will occur, such as a picture of a clock or a schedule, he transitions activities quicker. Knowing Roger needs a specific cue, the teacher can prepare a schedule on paper and use a clothes pin to mark what activity the group is moving to next when Roger has five minutes left. This helps Roger transition from one activity to another without major difficulty.

Interactions

Students are expected to interact with others in a variety of ways during instruction and throughout the day. Students are expected to adjust their interpersonal behaviors based on the situation. When asked to work independently the student is expected to do his own work and not interfere with others, but when asked to work in a large group the student is expected to pay attention and interact with others. Some students with disabilities have difficulty understanding the difference in expectations for these situations. They may have trouble keeping to themselves during independent work and may not understand why they are getting in trouble for the same behavior that was acceptable just five minutes before in a large group setting. Understanding that the student might have trouble with interactions allows the teacher to plan up front to help the student adapt to the new situation (e.g., reminder, a model, a picture of expected interaction).

Behaviors

The issue of behaviors is very complex. However, in most instances, there is a purpose to a behavior that the student uses. Students will sometimes show problems in adaptive behavior that are actually induced by requirements in the instructional environment. Teachers misinterpret some outward behaviors of students as emotional problems when in fact the problems are related to academic skills. Knowing that a student displays a behavior when certain academic events occur can help the teacher prepare for the behavior or will allow the teacher to adjust the academic situation in such a way that it will not create such a large problem.

For example, Rishad has difficulty working with other students and has displayed defiant behaviors to teachers during reading. He reads materials two grade levels below his peers. Rishad only displays the behaviors when reading at grade level is required. The behavior is meant to mask the fact that the student cannot do the required work. Knowing this, the teachers are able to adjust the reading to compensate for the behavior, and add a social skills training program to have him work on his anger/aggression.

Work related behaviors

Students with disabilities often have difficulty picking up on the skills that eventually generalize to the working world (e.g., remembering to bring specific items to the class—being prepared, raising their hands to answer a question—protocol for a meeting). The basic school skills that are required for every day functioning are important to students with disabilities. Without such skills, it will be more difficult for these students to obtain and retain employment. Because it may take more time to learn the skills, or they may need more support in demonstrating the skills, the teacher needs to be sure to identify the skills so they can be taught within the context of the content.

Case study: Nicholas

needs signals for transitioning from one activity to another; has good work related skills except forgets homework; trouble taking turns in some situations; acts as a leader; likes independent work; respectful of others	Q 9	What adaptive skills does the student have that impact learning?

Using **BLM 6**, next to Q9, identify the adaptive behavior skills the student has that will impact learning.

Question 10: What classroom management systems does the student use or have difficulty with in the classroom?

Identify how well the student uses or responds to the techniques used in a classroom to keep instruction flowing smoothly, keep students safe, and facilitate learning.

What this answer should include:	Examples:
• how to gain attention	• understands lights out means quiet; does not respond to teacher's "look at me"; claps rhythm when teacher does
• procedures	• puts homework in box; gets out of seat inappropriately; takes notes using a comparison chart
• routines	• does journal entry each day; forgets to write in agenda; forgets that calendar time is the first activity of the day; signs in for class each day

Why answer this question?

Classroom management systems are essential to the smooth flow of the instructional day. There are three potential issues that impact the success of the student with a disability. Students with disabilities may not pick up on the procedures and routines a teacher uses to keep the classroom organized or teach a new concept. The teacher may need to explicitly teach the routine or procedure more than once, or provide visual or verbal cues that a certain procedure is expected. For example, at the elementary level, on the first day of school, the teacher shows the students how to sit on the carpet appropriately (e.g., pretzel legs, hands in lap) and expects the students to respond when she says "pretzel please". The student with a disability might not understand that every time the teacher says "pretzel please" he should be sitting on the carpet appropriately. It may require reteaching the concept multiple times over several weeks or showing a real photograph of the student sitting pretzel style when the teacher says "pretzel please" to get the student to understand what is appropriate.

An example from the middle school level classroom shows Kendall having difficulty completing the journal activity at the beginning of the class. She does not understand the teacher wants her to respond to the question, without rewriting it from the board. Thus, everyday she copies the question from the board and never completes the activity. Her teacher may need to retrain her on how to read the question and then only write the answer, or provide her with a piece of paper with the question already on it so that she does not feel the need to rewrite the question each day.

Sometimes teachers do not use systems consistently in the classroom, which affects students with disabilities who need organization and systematic processes. Some students with disabilities need very organized and consistent environments. If a teacher is not consistent in requirements for class, the student becomes disorganized, disoriented, frustrated, and unable to complete tasks. The teacher may need to implement specific routines or procedures for the student so he can be successful.

For example Jeff, a student with traumatic brain injury, needs to have a specific schedule of events from the beginning of class to the end of class each day. He will flounder in a classroom if the teacher does not use any particular pattern for instruction each day. The teacher may need to arrange instruction in such a way that the same system is used (e.g., journal, discuss, read, write, discuss, close) or provide a daily sheet of paper with the schedule of events in the class that day.

Students with disabilities may need very specific routines to learn. Some students with disabilities learn using a very specific system. Without that system the student gets lost in the instructional activities. For example, Quentin has learning disabilities in reading and writing. He has learned to take notes using the concept comparison routine. The teacher may need to consistently use the routine in the classroom to ensure Quentin is getting the correct notes, or provide him with a study sheet using the routine if she is going to give notes in a different format.

Case Study: Nicholas

needs specific directions on how to get ready for every class; use a visual cue to get his attention; follows other typical class directions like raising hand, taking turns	Q 10 What classroom management systems does the student use or have trouble with that impact learning?

 Using **BLM 6**, next to Q10, identify the classroom management systems the student uses or has difficulty with that might impact learning.

Question 11: What physical and sensory issues does the student have that impact learning?

Identify any physical skills (fine or gross motor) or sensory issues (sight, vision, hearing, smell, touch, taste) that will help or interfere with learning.

What this answer should include:	**Examples:**
• fine motor	• holds a pencil; difficulty cutting with scissors; trouble writing legibly; can type quickly
• gross motor	• trouble sitting still; athletic; trouble walking without support; coordination is awkward; catches a ball
• sight	• trouble seeing up close; trouble discriminating different shapes; requires glasses for any size print; rapid eye movement
• hearing	• requires the use of auditory trainer, does not hear when there is a lot of background noise; acute hearing - high and low pitches are painful
• touch	• does not like certain textures; needs to feel textures of objects to calm down; does not like human touch but will accept touch from a stuffed animal
• taste	• aversion to sour tastes; puts everything in mouth
• smell	• highly aware of minute smells; certain smells create behavior problems; sensitive to molds or other odors
• physical and sensory	• difficulty standing and writing on board; difficulty maneuvering in classroom; likes certain smells and soft fabric to calm down

Why ask this question?

Students with disabilities may have physical or sensory issues that interfere with their learning. Knowing the issues ahead of time can circumvent potential learning barriers. Physical and sensory barriers prevent students from interacting with the materials and the people.

For example, Danny, a student with autism, has difficulty with certain tactile and sound sensations. He does not like to touch anything that is hot or rough in nature. Thus, when the teacher introduced sand as a method for writing letters, Danny threw the sand down and ran away. The teacher misinterpreted his behavior as not wanting to write his letters. If the teacher had known this behavior was based on the roughness of the sand she could have replaced his sand with shaving cream or pudding - thus differentiating his materials so he could participate.

Then there is Katrina who is visually impaired. She has limited vision and needs physical guidance or the use of her cane for mobility. If the teacher does not attend to this and rearranges the classroom for different activities without creating clear pathways for movement, Katrina's ability to move about the room in a timely fashion will be impacted. Katrina would also need large print books and braille for reading books and a braille machine for writing. Knowing these things ahead of time allows the teachers to create a suitable environment for her.

Charley is a student with ADHD. He has difficulty concentrating when he has to sit for long periods of time. However, he can concentrate for longer periods of time if he is allowed to stand up while working on a project or paper. The teacher allows him to tape his paper to the wall so he can stand up and read or write. This simple change in the physical requirements allows him to complete work on time and concentrate on the learning.

Consider Darryl, a student with severe physical disabilities. Darryl cannot sit at an ordinary desk. He must be in his wheelchair or in a position stand for support. He cannot grasp or hold hard objects. He does not have use of his left hand. Because of these physical needs, Darryl cannot participate in most typical class activities that involve being at a desk, using pen or pencil, or manipulating objects that are hard. Knowing this information allows the teacher to adjust or differentiate for him by placing a table in the room where he can interact with other students, wrap soft fabric around a marker to match his grasping ability when he might need to write, and use soft versions of materials (e.g., soft dice, sand bags, marshmallows) when he needs to manipulate objects.

Case Study: Nicholas

wears glasses consistently; no major issues in this area	Q 11	What physical or sensory issues does the student have that impact learning?

 Using **BLM 6**, next to Q11, write down any physical or sensory issues the student may have that will impact learning.

Question 12: What material or services does the student need for learning?

Identify the materials or services the student needs to have available during learning. Materials would include concrete tools the student uses and must have for learning (e.g., manipulatives, text types, writing tools). Services would include support provided by people or technology that help the student learn.

<u>**What this answer should include:**</u>

• materials

Examples:

• must have large paper; text in braille; alpha smart; calculator for math; auditory

	versions of reading materials; sticky paper to hold writing paper on desk
• services	• adult support for writing letters on paper; voice to text; computer programmed with answers; small group work with language pathologist when learning new vocabulary

Why answer this question?

Students with disabilities often require specific materials to assist them in learning. The types of materials will depend upon their physical and sensory capacities as well as their mental abilities. For example, one student might require the use of a laminated multiplication chart when calculating math problems, while another may need to use a large pencil to write because of a physical weakness in the hands.

Students with disabilities may require very specific services either from an adult or peer or through technology to fully participate in instruction. For example, the student who is deaf-blind will need an adult interpreter to translate the learning to the student through physical support and guidance. The student with severe speech problems may need a computer that has text to voice in order to participate in discussions in class.

If materials and services are not provided for students with disabilities it is likely they will not be able to fully participate in the instruction. Knowing what materials and services are necessary allows the teacher to plan for and have available what the student needs to participate in the instruction.

Case Study: Nicholas

uses a calculator for math; will need support from adult when trying activities with more than 3 steps to redirect his attention; not skilled in internet use for research	Q 12	What materials or services will the student need to be successful?

 Using **BLM 6**, next to Q12, write down the materials and services the student might need to be successful.

Question 13: What setting will allow the student to acquire, maintain, and generalize the content?

Identify the best learning environment for the student. Consider the difference between learning in the traditional classroom, labs, school, or community.

What this answer should include:	Examples:
• learning environment and rationale	• learns better in the real world using coins to make change; learns science content in the science lab with activities better than in the regular classroom with just reading

Why answer this question?

Students with disabilities, particularly those with cognitive disabilities, often need learning environments that reflect how information is going to be used in real life. They may have difficulty learning content in an out-of-context environment or have difficulty generalizing the same skill in the real world. For example, there is a big difference between writing a pretend check on a worksheet in the classroom and writing and cashing the check at a bank. Practicing in a classroom is important, but the final test might need to be in the real world.

Knowing the environment where a student will best learn allows the teacher to either adjust the classroom to be as close to the real world as possible or work with others to ensure that the student has the opportunity to try out new skills in real environments.

Case Study: Nicholas

ok in classroom; can use library and science lab for research	Q 13	What setting will allow the student to acquire, maintain, and generalize content knowledge?

 Using **BLM 6**, next to Q13, identify the setting or location that will be the best environment for the student to learn.

Question 14: How does the student best show what he knows and can do?

Identify the ways students can demonstrate their learning. Include verbal, written, and visual methods that best represent what the student knows. Consider the fact that the teacher must asses student learning and identify how it can be demonstrated. Include participation in traditional methods of assessment.

What this answer should include:	Examples:
• verbal	• cannot express self well verbally; explains in great detail; better verbal than written explanations; uses computer to verbally respond

• written	• writing does not reflect what they know; great writer - shows higher knowledge level in writing that verbal responses in class
• visual	• draws accurately and can depict learning through pictures; can act out the learning; uses pictures and symbols to represent learning; great at building models to demonstrate learning
• physical	• needs manipulatives to demonstrate
• test taking	• performs poorly on paper and pencil tests; needs extended time for written essays
• independent v. group work	• works better alone so cooperative learning is not best demonstration of knowledge; works better with a peer

Why answer this question?

Traditional paper and pencil tests, while useful, are not the only way to measure what a student knows. In an effective classroom the teacher will collect assessment data from a wide range of activities (e.g., observations, peer feedback, portfolios, paper and pencil tests, demonstrations). Unfortunately, not every teacher values the collection of data from such a wide range of activities. Many teachers limit their assessment of student progress to paper and pencil tests at the "end" of learning.

Students with disabilities will vary greatly on their ability to demonstrate their knowledge using paper and pencil tests. Some will perform well on traditional tests; others will fail miserably. Some students will need to attempt a test or task more than once to reach mastery. Students with disabilities need the opportunity to demonstrate what they know in the best possible platform. Knowing how a student best demonstrates learning allows the teacher to collect assessment data at appropriate times under appropriate circumstances.

For example, a student may need to be interviewed while the other students are taking a written test. The teachers might keep anecdotal records of how the student responds verbally to questions during class instead of basing his grade only on the paper and pencil response. A student might need to take a test three times before he can pass it so the teacher lets him take it mid-way through the learning, then near the end, and then with the class.

Case study: Nicholas

can take short paper and pencil tests; he may need to explain his written answers after an essay to better show what he knows	**Q 14** How does the student best show what he knows and can do?

 Using **BLM 6**, next to Q14, identify the best types of assessment for this student.

What have you created?

Take a minute to look over the answers you have provided on the **BLM 6** concerning a student from your class, or use the example of Nicholas that is on **BLM 7**. Notice how the information gives you a broad, yet specific picture of where the student faces challenges in a typical learning environment.

Chapter 5

Decisions on Differentiating Instruction: Gap Analysis

You have completed the first three steps toward differentiating instruction by focusing on the foundation for instruction and answering the Essential Curricular Questions and Essential Student Questions. In *Step 4: Analyze the Gap*, you will use these two sets of questions to determine where, when, and what differentiation might be necessary. By the end of this step, you will have very specific ideas of what areas to differentiate and how to accomplish the differentiation.

Exhibit 5.1 Step 4 of Process for Differentiated Instruction

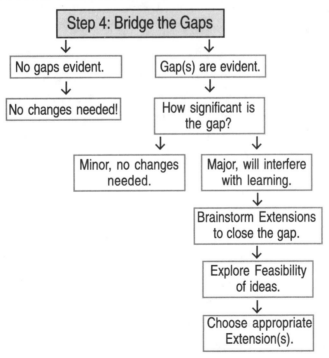

To complete **BLM 10, Gap Analysis,** you will compare the completed ECQs and ESQ Black Line Masters, analyze the answers to determine if there is a bridge or a gap between the planned instruction (ECQ) and student needs (ESQ), and decide what to differentiate using the Extensions and Feasibility tools provided in this chapter. **Exhibit 5.1,** on the previous page, shows the specific considerations within Step 4 that lead to the decision of what to differentiate.

To determine if there is a <u>bridge</u> or a <u>gap</u> between the planned instruction (ECQ) and student needs (ESQ), this chapter offers a specific set of questions to use when a gap is found. Through these you can determine if the gap is serious enough to warrant differentiation. It then supplies a set of Extensions for Learning, around which you can base your differentiation to bridge any serious gaps. In the course of this chapter, you will find the process for the Gap Analysis has been applied to each question with ideas on how to close any gaps found. The process has also been summarized in **BLM 11, Gap Analysis Case Study: Nicholas and mean, median, and mode**, as a model to help you analyze your own case study developed in Chapters 3 and 4.

Analyzing the Questions for Bridges and Gaps

Bridges are instances in which there is a match between what the instructional situation (ESQs) calls for and what the student needs(ESQs). For example, an instructional plan will require a student to use graph paper (materials) to plot points (process) and it turns out that the student already knows how to use graph paper to plot points. In this case there is an obvious connection, or bridge, between instructional expectations and student's abilities. The teacher will not need to differentiate the materials or process for the student. When a bridge is identified, the teacher knows that aspect of the instructional situation should work for the student.

Gaps are instances in which the instructional situation requires something the student may not be ready for or may not be able to do without some level of change to the learning situation. For example, an instructional plan calls for the students to work cooperatively (adaptive behavior) to complete a project and the student does not work well in groups. In this case, there is a disconnect, or gap, between what is expected and what the student can do. The teacher will need to attend to the fact that the student usually does not perform well under those circumstances and determine what differentiation might be necessary.

A bridge or gap?

The first decision is <u>determining where there is a *bridge* or *gap*</u>. The next decision is <u>what to do with the information</u>. If there is a *bridge*, teachers can assume that no differentiation is needed for that aspect of the instruction. When there is a *gap*, teachers must then determine if the gap is significant enough to create a barrier to learning. **Exhibit 5.2, Comparing ECQ, ESQ, and Gap Analysis,** on the following page, provides a glimpse into the process.

Exhibit 5.2 Comparing ECQ, ESQ, and Gap Analysis

Essential Curricular Questions	Initial Instruction Plan	Student Information: Nicholas	Essential Student Questions	Is there a gap?	Yes/No Maybe	Ideas for Differentiation	Try First
Q1 What is the content to be taught?	Introduce mean, median, mode using double-digit number sets	No exposure to mean, median, or mode, but knows how to average	**Q1** What does the student know about the content?	**Q1:1** Content	No		
Q2 How will the student use the content in real life?	Statistics; stock market; sports scores (e.g., batting averages); voting outcomes; weather patterns; shopping	Likes sports, particularly football, wrestling, and baseball; keeps scores; knows batting and football data	**Q2** What are the interests of the student?	**Q2:2** Real life / Interests	No	Be sure to use sports ideas in teaching	
Q3 What background knowledge is needed for this content?	Addition of double-digit numbers; rank ordering number sets; numbers up to 1,000; use of calculator	Uses a calculator to input a series of up to 10 numbers; adds up to 1,000	**Q3** What background knowledge does the student have for this content?	**Q3:3** Background	No		
Q4 What is the language of instruction for this content?	Order, rank, add, subtract, sum, count, graph, categorize, average, show work, divide	Has difficulty with directional words such as list, order and "show your work", does not provide in-depth answers when asked to "show" or "explain"	**Q4** To what degree does the student understand the language of instruction?	**Q4:4** Language of Instruction	YES – Directional words	Model and explain specific words; perhaps provide a picture of each word's meaning/process	both

The Significance of a Gap

Overall, out of the 14 question pairs, no single pair of questions is more important than another. The significance of a gap will be dependent upon the unique characteristics of the student's disability and the instructional plan. For example, for one student using specific learning strategies may be more important than use of materials, while for another student attention to adaptive behaviors may be more important than content. The teacher will need to make professional decisions on the seriousness of the gap. In some situations there may be multiple gaps that are considered very important while in others there may only be one gap considered significant enough to address.

To determine if a gap is significant enough to create a barrier to learning, the teacher must consider what will happen if the gap is not addressed. When working with students with disabilities, the teacher must pay attention to the information provided on the Individualized Education Program (IEP). If the IEP outlines specific areas for differentiation, the teacher *must* consider that area a priority and address that within the instructional plan. Even if the area of concern is not expressly written on the IEP, the teacher must still determine the significance of the gap. When determining the importance of the gap, some typical questions to consider are:

- Will this gap prevent the student from participating in any aspect of learning?
- If not addressed will the student develop behaviors that interfere with learning?
- Is this gap the most significant problem preventing the student from learning?
- Does the gap represent a short term or long term difference between what the student needs and the instruction planned?

Deciding what to Differentiate

Once the significance of the gap has been determined, the teacher must decide what changes or differentiation will bridge the gap. Here the teacher brainstorms ideas that will close the gap. Empirical evidence collected by Moll (1986-02) indicates there are at least 15 areas of differentiation to consider. These areas are named Extensions for Learning for two reasons. First, many of the terms you will read in this section are often associated with modifications and adaptations in the special education field, but Moll's collection of evidence comes from the general education, special education, and gifted and talented fields, suggesting that these methods for differentiation are used for a wide range of students, not just those with disabilities. The term Extension fits the larger challenge of differentiating instruction for <u>any student who needs such support</u>, while the terms adaptations and modifications are typically used just for students with disabilities.

The second reason the term Extensions is used relates to the negative connotations often associated with the terms modification and adaptation. Often teachers refer to adaptations or modifications as "doing the work for the child" or "dumbing down the work". *Extensions* suggests the action that will help the student <u>reach</u> the work and increase the likelihood of success, regardless of disability or ability. Think in terms of an extension ladder that helps us to reach the second story windows on our house. The extension ladder is the tool that helps us reach the level we need to wash windows. The ladder does not wash the windows for us, but gives us the opportunity to reach those windows. We still have to do the work. Extensions in differentiated instruction offer the same thing - the tool that helps the student get to the work. The student still has to perform the work. Extensions in no way should dumb down or do the work for the student.

The Extensions are described below with corresponding examples. **BLM 8, Extensions for Learning,** provides a similar version of the information. It can be used during the Gap Analysis process described later in this chapter. Some examples have been modified from the <u>Program of Studies Implementation Manual, Kentucky Department of Education</u> (1998).

Extensions for Learning

1. <u>Application and Demonstration of Knowledge</u>

Consider the ways the student can demonstrate in measurable terms what he has learned or mastered. Some examples:

- student who has trouble writing can draw accurate pictures and flow charts to show what he has learned instead of writing a paragraph;
- student who has difficulty with presenting in a large group can video tape presentation and show to class;
- student who has difficulty taking a written exam can take an oral exam or audio tape responses.

2. <u>Complexity of Task</u>

Consider altering the level of difficulty or the degree of decision making involved. Some examples:

- student measures a line to the nearest half inch instead of quarter inch means decreased complexity—still requires accurate measurement, but not the same degree;
- student has difficulty reading long passages to get information so he uses highlighted texts to focus on the information, not the length of the passage;
- student works on addition of double-digit numbers while other students are working on triple digit which is decreased complexity - still requires regrouping, but not the same number of times per problem;

- student writes a research paper on the political causes of the civil war while other students are only studying the logistics of different battles; digging into the political causes equals increased complexity requiring deeper understanding of war;
- student writes three sentences while other students are writing 5 point paragraphs which is decreased complexity - still requires writing meaningful sentences, but not as organized or pointed.

3. Environment

Consider a variety of settings or locations for the learning. Some examples:

- student with mild mental disabilities has difficulty transferring information from one environment to another so the teacher arranges for the student to use the math skill of counting money in the lunch room, the bookstore, and the grocery;
- student is easily distracted by visual or auditory stimuli so the teacher arranges for his seat to be away from distractions during independent work;
- student learns best when "near the action" so seating is arranged to be within 10 feet of the instructional focus at all times;
- student has problems with florescent lights so classroom is outfitted with softer lighting in areas of importance.

4. Independence Level

Consider varying the amount of direct and indirect assistance the student needs to participate. Some examples:

- student has difficulty completing tasks independently so the teacher ensures a peer or the teacher check on the student every 5 minutes; this requires that the student work independently but with more frequent support than other students;
- student works better alone so the teacher provides directions and lets the student be independent while the rest of class is working as a large group, allowing the student to participate, but with less support;
- student with significant mental disabilities requires physical guidance from an aide to complete a written activity; the student is still writing, but given a higher level of support;
- student has difficulty keeping track of assignments, so teacher writes them on the board and checks the student's agenda at the end of each class; the student still has responsibility for collecting information, but is supported to a greater degree.

5. Language of Learning

Consider changing the words used to explain, demonstrate, or demand action during instruction. Some examples:

- student has difficulty with higher level learning words like "compare" or "judge" so the teacher uses "find similarities or differences" or "give your opinion and use some facts";
- student has trouble understanding that certain words mean different things in different settings (e.g., *show your work* in art is different that *show your work* in math) so the teacher models what the words *show your work* mean or creates a visual model of the differences;
- student has difficulty with the meaning of different types of words associated with genres for writing (e.g., persuasive and transactive) so the teacher models types, puts examples on the walls, provides laminated mini-charts for the student, color codes each type, and uses alternate words (e.g., convince or list steps).

6. Motivation

Consider adding extrinsic and intrinsic motivators that match the student's interests. Some examples:

- student loves cars, so teacher uses miniature cars for manipulatives in math;
- student wants to get out of school so teacher focuses writing skills on getting a job;
- student likes to have independent time so teacher hooks completion of work with earned time to work, read, or play on his own;
- student has specific interests in history so the teacher lets him choose a topic of interest to research;
- student needs constant reinforcement but teacher does not want to disturb class so she gives him sticky notes with positive comments on them instead of verbal praise;
- student takes great pride in others viewing work so samples are placed on bulletin board.

7. Order of Learning

Consider altering the instructional sequence and progression of learning. Some examples:

- student does not have prerequisite knowledge for content so the teacher focuses on the pre-learning to bring the student up to speed;
- student has not memorized multiplication facts but can work the problems on paper or calculator, so teacher lets the student use a calculator so that he can move to higher level math skills instead of just skill and drill for memorization; student jumps the "requirement" for rote memorization because the student can do the higher level process/problem without it;
- student requires longer time to learn about one state and the class has already moved on

to another, allow the student to jump in with the class without penalty for missed material;

- student already knows the information to be presented so she moves to the next level independently.

8. Pace

Consider reducing or increasing the speed or acceleration of the learning. Some examples:

- student masters information after 10 trials so the teacher eliminates unnecessary practice problems;
- student usually requires more time to learn the information so the teacher provides same information over three weeks instead of two;
- student needs information repeated more often so centers for learning are used in addition to lessons in class, and student uses both each day.

9. Participation

Consider changing the amount and type of participation that would be appropriate for the student. Some examples:

- student with severe mental disabilities might need to participate in the activity to develop friendships instead of develop knowledge of content; the student is exposed to the content, but participation is focused on developing the life-long skill of interacting with people;
- student with problems processing questions is only expected to answer questions out loud in class when the teacher gives him the question prior to class; encourages the student to participate and gives him time to think through the answer;
- student has difficulty remembering to raise hand to speak out, so the teacher has him be the "caller" for the class, where he gets to call on only the people who raise their hand when the teacher asks a question.

10. Procedures and Routines

Consider changing or adding specific procedures or routines to the classroom to support learning. Some examples:

- teacher requires students to raise hand to answer question, but student does not have use of hand so teacher allows him to hit a buzzer with his knee;
- teacher turns light off to get attention, but student has significant anxiety in darkness so teacher uses bell instead;
- teacher expects students to sit on the floor in circle with legs crossed but due to physical problems student has trouble sitting that way on the ground, so teacher allows student to sit on telephone book which gives enough room for the student to cross legs; the routine of

sitting on the floor is changed to allow sitting on a small object;

- teacher verbally gives homework each day, but student has trouble writing information down when heard, but can write it down when seen so the teacher begins writing homework on the board each day; the routine of verbal directions is augmented with written directions.

11. Purpose and Appropriateness

Consider changing the intent, goal or reason for the learning. Some examples:

- 18 year old who has difficulty with math might need to work on math activities similar to those required in an after school job instead of abstract formulas - the purpose being to learn math as a daily life skill, not an abstract concept;

- student with language problems may need to work more on using vocabulary appropriately in conversations than on spelling the words for a test - the purpose being to use language appropriately, not just to spell words;

- student with severe mental disabilities may need to practice making healthy food choices in natural environments more so than drawing a food pyramid - the appropriateness being the student learns how to use information about nutrition, not just what a food pyramid looks like;

- student who has difficulty interacting appropriately with other students may need to focus primarily on group behaviors instead of content - the purpose being to use the instructional lesson as a method for learning appropriate behaviors.

12. Resources and Materials

Consider using people, materials, and furnishings that will facilitate learning. Some examples:

- student has poor fine motor skills and cannot hold a pencil, so he uses a fat marker for writing;

- student knows the process for multiplication and division but cannot memorize the facts so he uses a calculator;

- student has physical disabilities that prevent sitting at typical school desk so teacher ensures there is a table and form board chair available;

- student does not have use of arms or legs, but mentally is capable of the work so he uses a computer with adaptive switch for the head;

- student has minimal hearing but can read and speak American Sign Language, so the teacher ensures there is an interpreter available; or

- teacher uses overhead projector to write notes, but student has figure ground problems with black letters against white background so teacher uses color overlay on overhead so background is color other than white.

13. Size

Consider adjusting the quantity or proportions of the instructional activities. Some examples:

• student has difficulty writing numbers quickly so the teacher reduces the number of problems on the sheet; student still must do the math, but a smaller quantity;

• student has difficulty comparing multiple aspects of two concepts so the teacher allows him to compare one aspect of each concept at a time, or only focus on one aspect and compare it in depth; student must do the work of comparison, but with fewer components;

• student can handle long term projects better than short term so the teacher gives him one research project for the semester instead of three smaller ones; student still conducts the research but the proportion is different.

14. Strategies for Learning and Presentation Styles

Consider changing the way information is organized, manipulated, and presented within the instruction. Some examples:

• student with mild mental disabilities needs visual symbols for abstract concepts; this anchors the idea in concrete terms;

• student with reading problems needs books on tape to play while a book is being read silently by the class, thereby allowing the student to gain information auditorily;

• student with attention deficit needs to move to stay focused so teacher incorporates "dancing definitions" into the language arts class and allows student to act out the knowledge and allows for movement;

• student is disorganized so teacher models and requires the use of organizational routine of a binder with tabs for daily notes which allows student to use specific method to organize and use information.

15. Time

Consider reducing or increasing the duration, length, or intervals of instruction and assessment. Some examples:

• student has trouble staying focused for longer than 10 minutes so the teacher breaks lecture into mini lectures and activities alternating every 10 minutes;

• student cannot type fast nor write fast, but can create excellent written papers so the teacher allows additional time without penalty; student produces quality work and is not measured by how fast the work completed;

• student can learn information in smaller chunks so the teacher breaks up the 8 week science unit into 4 mini-units with tests in between.

Determine the Feasibility of the Idea

When multiple ideas are brainstormed for a particular gap, the teacher determines which one is most likely to help the student. Determining the feasibility of an idea is critical to effective differentiation. If the teacher chooses ideas that are not most appropriate, the students will experience failure and the teacher frustration. **BLM 9, Feasibility Worksheet,** provides a compressed version of the information to follow. It can be used during the Gap Analysis process. To determine the feasibility of an idea the teacher should consider the following:

- **rapid results** - Will the change create visible results in student performance quickly? The best scenario is to chose an extension that will create results relatively quickly.

- **disturbance level** - Will the change create significant disruption to the routines and procedures of the classroom? The best choice is to find an appropriate extension that will create the least amount of disruption to the classroom. Remember however, that unless the change causes considerable disruption (e.g., makes it impossible for other students to learn), the extension will likely be considered appropriate under federal law (IDEA).

- **access** - Is the resource, service, or material readily available to the teacher? The teacher wants to choose resources, services, or materials that are relatively easy to acquire so that a time lapse between need and service does not exist. Remember, IDEA requires a school to provide appropriate supports, services, and materials, so just because something is not available does not mean the teacher should not ask for and get it.

- **ease of implementation** - Can the change be implemented without an extraordinary amount of work or training for the adults involved? The best route is to find Extensions that are easy to implement for a teacher. Choices that require extensive training are not usually as easy to implement nor considered popular choices for general education teachers. Remember, however, that under IDEA there will be instances when a particular type of differentiation will be required for a student and teachers will be required to get training to implement it (e.g., the use of an auditory trainer).

- **age appropriateness** - Does the idea fit the age of the student or will it use materials, methods, or situations that are not appropriate? Even though some students with disabilities might be developmentally at a much lower level than their peers, the differentiation must be appropriate for the student's age (e.g., an 18 year old student working on writing his name should not be using 1st grade paper, but should be using a job application form).

- **usable by others** - Is this an Extension that might be beneficial to other students in the room? When an Extension can be used by other students in the room, the teacher is more likely to use it and continue using it (e.g., COPS sentence writing strategy is good for any student who needs to remember to capitalize, organize, punctuate, and check their spelling).

- **length of time** - How long will this particular extension be needed? It is important to recognize that some Extensions will be required throughout the student's life in school (e.g., use of braille machine). Other Extensions may only be needed temporarily and can be faded as the student becomes more competent (e.g., highlighted texts to teach the student how to find important information).

- **person implementing** - Who will be the primary implementer of this Extension? In some instances, the person *is* the Extension, meaning that a student needs direct support from an adult or peer (e.g.,student requires a sign language interpreter). Some Extensions can easily be provided by the general education teacher (e.g., outline of the notes) while other Extensions may require the expertise of a special education teacher (e.g., text rewritten to the grade level of the student) or other specialist. Other Extensions can be implemented by the student (e.g., uses calculator) or a peer (e.g., checks agenda for homework assignments).

Decide on the Differentiation

Once the questions have been analyzed and ideas brainstormed and checked for feasibility, the teacher can choose the forms of differentiation that will support the student. At this point, the teacher considers how many gaps have been identified and determines if one or many levels of differentiation are necessary. In some instances there may be gaps in several areas, but one type of differentiation will address or bridge all the gaps. For example, if a student can tell what he knows better than write it down, the teacher can make adjustments to the instructional plan in the strategies (Q7), activities (Q 8), and the assessment (Q14) by adding methods that use student discussion and audio taping.

Once the analysis and decision making process is complete, the teacher can move to the instructional design phase in which differentiations are embedded within the instruction. This process is explained in Chapter 6 and 7. For now, let's get some practice analyzing and choosing differentiated instruction.

Let's get started!

Place your completed **BLM 4** and **6** side by side, with **4** on the left and **6** on the right so that the answers you filled in are next to each other. See **Exhibit 5.3, Side by Side ECQ and ESQ**. With the questions side by side, begin reviewing each pair of questions. As you read each pair, use the information that follows to help you make decisions on what differentiation you might need and how to provide it. Make a copy of **BLM 10,** on which there are pairs of questions written as Q #:# (e.g., Q1:1) meaning you are comparing a question on curriculum to the corresponding question about the student. Use **BLM 10** to make notes on each pair of questions for your own case study.

Exhibit 5.3 Side by Side ECQ and ESQ

Essential Curricular Questions	Initial Instruction Plan	Student Information: Nicholas	Essential Student Questions
Q1 What is the content to be taught?	Introduce mean, median, mode using double-digit number sets	No exposure to mean, median, or mode, but knows how to average	**Q1** What does the student know about the content?
Q2 How will the student use the content in real life?	Statistics; stock market; sports scores (e.g., batting averages); voting outcomes; weather patterns; shopping	Likes sports, particularly football, wrestling, and baseball; keeps scores; knows batting and football data	**Q2** What are the interests of the student?
Q3 What background knowledge is needed for this content?	Addition of double-digit numbers; rank ordering number sets; numbers up to 1,000; use of calculator	Uses a calculator to input a series of up to 10 numbers; adds up to 1,000	**Q3** What background knowledge does the student have for this content?
Q4 What is the language of instruction for this content?	Order, rank, add, subtract, sum, count, graph, categorize, average, show work, divide	Has difficulty with directional words such as list, order and "show your work"; does not provide in-depth answers when asked to "show" or "explain"	**Q4** To what degree does the student understand the language of instruction?

Q1:1 Is there is a gap between the content to be taught and what the student knows?

Sometimes it turns out that a student knows little or nothing about a particular content area. Often this is not a problem, because the teacher is treating it like new content for all students in the class. This gap in knowledge only becomes a problem when the instruction places a student in the middle of concepts or activities without any review or preview. If the instructional plan expects the student to jump into the middle of a concept, there may be a need to differentiate how the student will reach the content. Several Extensions might be helpful here: changing the level of complexity, altering the order of learning, or increasing the level of support during learning.

Some ideas for gap closure:

- pre-teach the concept to the student before it is introduced to the class as a whole;
- ensure the student gets the most basic information about the content at the beginning of the instruction instead of jumping in to the middle of the content;
- conduct a review of what has been learned with the whole class before introducing the new concept;
- assign a peer buddy to bring the student up to speed with the content covered thus far;
- only measure the student's progress on learning the basics of the content for the first few instructional sessions.

Case Study: Nicholas

introduce calculating mean, median, mode using double-digit number sets	no exposure to mean, median, mode, but knows how to average

In comparing the answers for Question 1:1 there is no real gap because the planned instruction is at the introductory level, so other students will not know the concept and Nicholas does have knowledge of one key element: averaging.

 Use **BLM 10,** Q1:1 to note if there is a gap and draft ideas to address the gap.

Q 2:2 Do the student's interests match the real life application of the content?

If there is a match the teacher simply needs to ensure to help the student make the connection. If there is not a match between the interests of the student and the content, there may be a need for differentiating the situation to create interest. The extension most commonly used in this case is motivation. Some ideas to fill the gap:

- offer external incentives for participation, completion of work;
- use a token economy system in which the student earns points for appropriate work or behavior;
- contract with the student for time doing something of interest after work is completed; or
- allow student to earn special events or prizes for self and peers for appropriate work or behavior.

Case Study: Nicholas

statistics; stock market; sports scores (aka averages); voting outcomes; weather patterns; shopping	likes sports particularly football, wrestling and baseball; keeps scores, knows batting and football data

In this question, there is no real gap because the planned instruction relates to statistics, which relates directly to sports scores, which Nicholas finds very motivating. The teacher wants to ensure that at several points during the instructional work on mean, median, and mode the concept is applied to sports.

 Use **BLM 10**, Q2:2 to note if there is a gap and draft ideas to address the gap.

Q3:3 Does the student have the background information necessary or expected for the planned instruction?

If the student does have the background knowledge, the teacher wants to be sure to help the student connect that background knowledge to the new learning. If there is a gap between what the student should and does know, the teacher will need to consider differentiating the situation to either build background or eliminate the importance of the background knowledge. Extensions commonly used where a gap exists in background include time, pace, order of learning, resources, and environment. Some examples that close the gap:

- conduct a review of previously learned knowledge - it serves as a jump start for the student, bringing him up to par with classmates;
- allow the student time to develop the background knowledge by having study sessions at different times in or out of the classroom;
- provide the student with materials that will quickly develop the necessary background;
- allow the student to jump in and later reteach whatever is necessary as it occurs;
- take the student to the environments where he can learn about the topic quickly;
- have peer explain or demonstrate knowledge needed.

Case Study: Nicholas

addition of double-digit numbers; rank ordering number sets; numbers up to 1,000; use of calculator	uses a calculator to input a series of up to 10 numbers; adds up to 1,000

There is no significant gap because the planned instruction requires knowing math concepts and use of a calculator in which Nicholas seems to have some degree of skill. In this case the teacher may want to make note that Nicholas can input up to 10 numbers. If any activities require input of more than 10 numbers Nicholas may need some support.

 Use **BLM 10,** Q3:3 to note if there is a gap and draft ideas to address the gap.

Q4:4 Is there a gap between the language of instruction and what the student understands?

If there is not a gap, the teacher can use the language and feel confident that the student will be successful. If there is a gap, the teacher must consider ways to differentiate the language so that the student will be successful. Extensions that are commonly used in this situation include level of complexity, language, and procedures and routines. Some examples for filling this gap:

- use visual symbols or pictures next to written word, or with verbal words that tell the student what to do;

- explain the directions two times, using the more complex language first, then using simpler words or vice versa;

- have a student act out/demonstrate the language as you use it;

- laminate a pictorial version of common instructions that demonstrates the student actually performing the task and put written words next to the pictures.

Case Study: Nicholas

order, rank, add, subtract, sum, count, graph, categorize, explain, show work, divide	has difficulty with directional words such as list, order, or show your work; does not provide in-depth answers when asked to show work

There is a gap between the language of instruction and the language that Nicholas understands. He may have difficulty with the language implying direction such as *rank order*, *show*, and *explain*. Here the teacher may need to differentiate by teaching him the concepts behind the language, using different words for those concepts, or providing models of what answers look like using each word. It may be necessary to explain, demonstrate, or use a model every time Nicholas is expected to act on those words.

 Use **BLM 10,** Q4:4 to note if there is a gap and draft ideas to address the gap.

Q5:5 Is there a gap between the reading or writing skills required and the student's abilities?

Reading Skills. If there is no gap, the teacher can use the reading materials with relative confidence that they will not interfere with the student getting the content. If there is a gap, the teacher must consider ways to differentiate the reading requirements. Extensions used for this type of gap include: purpose and appropriateness of learning, complexity, materials, size, pace, and amount of time.

A special note must be made here: differentiating reading materials so that the student can access the content is very different than teaching a student to read. Too often teachers confuse the two. Many teachers do not feel it is their responsibility to teach a student to read, so they hesitate working on issues related to reading materials. While most professional teachers would argue every teacher should work on student's ability to read, the issue does not have to interfere with a student gaining *content* knowledge if differentiation is used. Teachers tend to assume a student cannot learn the content if he cannot read the material. If the goal is to *learn the content*, and reading is the *primary method* used to get to the content, the teacher must differentiate the method for the student who cannot read so he can access the information. Some examples of ways to close the gap:

- use a parallel novel that is written at a lower or higher level; (The Story of Anne Frank, by Brenda Ralph Lewis, Dorling Kindersley Readers Level 3 or Anne Frank, Beyond the Diary, a Photographic Remembrance by Ruud van der Rol and Rian Verhoeven - instead of Anne Frank: the Diary of a Young Girl by Anne Frank);
- rewrite the materials using simpler language;
- provide audio or video tapes that correspond to the reading;
- provide the student with the reading material in advance of class and review important points prior to class;
- offer a study guide with the most important points from the reading;
- break the reading into manageable chunks;
- use texts with visual/pictorial explanations;
- highlight important points in the text for students to use as focal point.

Writing Skills. If there is no gap, the teacher can use the writing requirements with relative confidence that they will not interfere with the student demonstrating what he knows via writing. If there is a gap, the teacher must consider ways to differentiate the writing requirements. Extensions used for this type of gap often include: complexity, independence or support, participation, size, amount of time, resources and materials, and application and demonstration of knowledge.

Differentiating writing requirements so that the student can demonstrate what he knows is very different than teaching a student to write. Teachers tend to assume a student did not learn the content if he cannot write about the material. If the goal is to *show that he learned the content*, and writing is the *primary method* used to demonstrate this learning, the teacher must differentiate the method for the student who cannot write so he can be assessed on what he learned, not on how well he writes. Some examples of ways to close the gap:

- allow the student to make a list instead of writing complete sentences to answer a question;
- a peer or the teacher provides a copy of notes taken in class that are more complete than the student is capable of taking during lecture;
- allow the student to audio tape instead of writing notes or answers to questions;
- interview the student using questions from a test instead of having him write essay questions;
- provide an outline shell for note taking with some information already filled in so the student only has to write some of the information down during note taking;
- offer additional time to complete written tasks that will be graded;
- use the computer for word processing, grammar and spell check;
- let the student illustrate concepts learned in a science lesson instead of writing a report.

Case Study: Nicholas

read directions, numeric symbols for meaning (worth); decipher word problems, 7th grade level terms; write numbers 1-1,000; write short answers using vocabulary	reads two grade levels below peers; word attack, skimming and reading for meaning are poor; understands pictures with simple directions better than text; no writing issues here

There is a significant gap between the reading level required and Nicholas' skills, but no gap in writing skills. He is reading two grade levels below his peers which indicates that he will probably struggle with the seventh grade level terms. In addition, Nicholas has difficulty reading for meaning, so he may experience trouble deciphering the word problems used for the content. The teacher could differentiate the reading skills for him by rewriting the word problems on a fifth grade level, teaching him the specific words needed for the word problems, or using the strengths listed and provide pictures with the directions or word problems to better explain them.

 Use **BLM 10**, Q5:5 to note if there is a gap and draft ideas to address the gap.

Q 6:6 Is there a gap between the way information is typically presented and the way the student learns?

If there is a bridge between the two, the teacher can reasonably assume the methods of presenting the content will support this student's learning. If there is a gap, then the teacher must differentiate the teaching method(s) to support the student's learning.

It is important to note here that every student, disabled and non disabled, learns differently. It would be impossible for a teacher to incorporate techniques into every single lesson that would match each student's learning style. However, it is critical that during the instructional process students have some opportunity to learn the information in a manner that best suits their style. A student may not need to have information presented in his learning style every day, or all the time. A good rule to follow is that the material is presented the first time in his learning style and that at least half of all practice/review sessions use that learning style also. However, for a student with a disability, the more the information is presented in his learning style, the greater chance he will learn and retain the information.

Extensions that address a gap in teaching methods and learning styles include procedures and routines, materials and resources, pace, environment, complexity, application and demonstration of knowledge. Some examples of closing the gap:

- if the student is not good with pure lecture, add student discussion to class time;
- if reading is the primary mode for teaching but the student learns better by doing, add role playing or manipulatives;
- for the student who learns better with visual cues, use a web, map or other graphic organizer;
- for the student who works better in quiet, reduce the amount of lecture and discussion and add quiet zone work;
- for the student who cannot take notes and listen intently at the same time, provide a note taking guide partially filled in so he can concentrate on what is said and still be required to take notes;
- for the student who needs hands-on learning, use manipulatives or models;
- for the student who needs more time to get notes down on paper, audio tape the lecture and let him listen to it later, and update his notes;
- for the student who needs real life application, take him to the location where the skill will be used instead of just talking about it in class.

Case Study: Nicholas

overhead calculator to demonstrate; demonstrate each concept using multiple problems on board	learns best by seeing and doing; he learns quickly if he can manipulate information or see it modeled visually; auditory is his least effective learning mode

There is no significant gap because the planned instruction methods include visual demonstrations. However, because Nicholas does have trouble learning auditorily, the teacher will want to make sure to demonstrate visually while providing the mini-lectures or go back over the main concepts using visuals after the lecture. In addition, it might be important to consider using number tiles or other manipulatives to help him move numbers around when learning the rank ordering for determining mode.

Use **BLM 10**, Q6:6 to note if there is a gap and draft ideas to address the gap.

Q 7:7 Is there a gap between the learning strategies expected and those used effectively by the student?

If there is not a gap, the teacher can safely use the learning strategies. If there is a difference between the strategies expected and those the student uses, the teacher must consider differentiating the strategies to support the student. The Extension typically used to differentiate instruction under these circumstances is instructional procedures and routines. Some examples of differentiating the procedures or routines to bridge this gap include:

- for the student with a random approach to tasks, teach a specific step-by-step process;
- for the student who has difficulty determining what are important notes from a lecture, provide a graphic organizer routine;
- for the student who counts manipulatives by ones, teach them to use skip counting to improve speed;
- for the student who does not have an approach to solving a problem, model a metacognition skill like self talk as you teach the process;
- for the student who does not know how to skim for important words, use a highlighter in the text and fade until the student can use the highlighter on his own.

Case Study: Nicholas

ordering highest to lowest; checking for accuracy; note taking; discovery	has no specific strategies for learning; randomly approaches tasks; does not ask clarification questions; not sure what is important in note taking; difficulty following directions of more than 3 steps

There is a significant gap between the strategies expected in the instruction and those Nicholas uses for learning. Nicholas does not approach tasks with an organized format; this will interfere with his ability to follow steps to compute mean, median, and mode. He does not know what is important in note taking, so he may take notes on unimportant information during lecture. There are several ways the teacher might differentiate to support his learning including modeling self talk during the step-by-step process for calculating each math process, having him use self talk during the different phases of learning, writing down a particular step-by-step format for approaching the tasks, physically manipulating the steps, and/or providing notes from lectures either before or after the mini-lectures.

Use **BLM 10,** Q7:7 to note if there is a gap and draft ideas to address the gap.

Q 8:8 Is there a gap between the planned activities and the types of activities that motivate or engage the student?

If there is no gap the teacher can use the activities planned. If there is a gap, the teacher might consider ways to differentiate the activities. As with Question 6:6, it is not possible for a teacher to connect every activity in a classroom to each student's needs. However, it is important to remember that the more the student is connected to the learning, the greater the learning. For students with disabilities it becomes essential that the activities are highly connected to their lives. Extensions commonly used to address this problem are application and demonstration of knowledge, motivation, and environment. Some examples include:

- for the student who likes to speak or act, use role play instead of discussion for political viewpoints;
- for the student who loves competition, use games and puzzles;
- instead of just practicing writing persuasive letters, the student writes a letter and sends it to the person he is trying to persuade;
- use daily living reading materials like the newspaper instead of commercial school texts to read for detail;
- let the student draw what he knows before he writes it;
- have the student research a true-to-life problem within the school instead of arbitrary problems from a book.

Case Study: Nicholas

7th graders are interested in fairness, social issues, and consumerism so activities like graphing income levels from different jobs, collecting personal data for comparison; comparing items at different shops or restaurants by using mean, median, or mode might get them more interested in the topic.	enjoys competitive events, likes earning points; likes games; loves tallying sports scores

There is a gap between the teacher's ideas for the lessons and Nicholas' interests, but it is easy to bridge. Knowing that Nicholas likes sports, the teacher can use sports scores in some of the activities or assignments to reinforce, or introduce the concepts. (e.g., determining which baseball players will be drafted based on the mean, median, mode of players in the American league; determining the mean, median, and mode from points scored by a pro basketball player over five years).

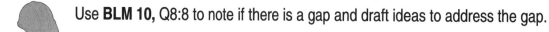 Use **BLM 10,** Q8:8 to note if there is a gap and draft ideas to address the gap.

Q 9:9 Is there a gap between the adaptive behaviors expected and the student's ability?

If a student has the adaptive behaviors expected for a particular teaching situation, then no further action is needed. However, even the slightest gap in this area can create real problems for the student, the classroom, and/or the teacher. Many teachers will tell you that they can handle a student who learns at a different pace much easier than the student with adaptive behavior problems. Therefore, it is important for teachers to discuss any instances in which there might be a difference and consider differentiating the instructional situation to prevent or contain the behaviors so the student can remain in the classroom.

Poor adaptive behaviors have so many different causes and purposes. It is difficult to always know precisely how to differentiate without conducting some analysis of the behavior. (To learn more about analyzing and addressing adaptive behaviors, check out the excellent resources listed in the Appendix.) For example, if the student does not work well independently, is it because he has trouble concentrating, difficulty reading the instructions, or does he lack self confidence? Each possible reason would give rise to a unique method of differentiation.

The good news is that when a teacher differentiates instruction in the other areas covered through these question pairs, the student's adaptive behaviors often improve because the cause of the poor behavior is often related to instructional issues. For example, in a non differentiated setting, a student may show behaviors such as lack of attention or aggression toward others when the reading materials are above his level. The student uses the poor behavior to avoid the reading work he already knows he cannot do. However, in a differentiated classroom the teacher employs reading materials that the student can use and the student is less frustrated or embarrassed, and more successful. The student does not need to use bad behaviors to avoid doing the work.

Any one of the Extensions could possibly address the problems in adaptive behavior depending upon the reason behind the behavior. Some examples include:

- for the student who has difficulty changing from one activity to another because he does not handle quick changes easily, the teacher might consider using the extension of procedures and routines by adding in a specific signal to the instructional environment that warns the student when the time to transition to another activity is coming;

- a student shows aggressive behaviors whenever it is time to begin math class; teacher determines that the student cannot do simple math without manipulatives and manipulatives are not typically used in class; teacher decides to differentiate the size of tasks, level of support, and materials used by having the student complete fewer problems in the beginning, attends to the student more frequently during problem work, and uses manipulatives in the instruction and independent work;

- student slips into "stealth mode" (e.g., slinks down in seat, never raises hand, plays with other things) when teacher begins reading story from a literature book; teacher determines the student does not find the stories relative to his life; teacher differentiates by using stories that connect to the student's background, culture or area of interest;

- student does not pay attention, answer questions or complete work; teacher determines that the student is not interested in the work; teacher differentiates by creating a contract for completing work and participating in class through which the student earns time or points toward activities of interest.

Case Study: Nicholas

independent and small cooperative learning groups; movement around the room and to the library; change from teacher demonstration to student work approximately every 10 minutes	needs signals for transitioning from one activity to another; has good work skills but forgets homework; trouble taking turns sometimes; acts as leader; likes independent work; respectful of others

There are both bridges and gaps between the teacher's expectations and Nicholas' adaptive behaviors. Nicholas likes to work independently and can be a leader in a group. The instruction calls for some independent and some cooperative work where the teacher could let him be a leader from time to time. However, Nicholas has difficulty transitioning from one activity to another and the teacher transitions every 10 minutes. The teacher may need to differentiate by using a specific signal to let him know a transition is coming.

 Use **BLM 10,** Q9:9 to note if there is a gap and draft ideas to address the gap.

Q10:10 Is there a gap between the classroom management systems used by the teacher and those the student needs?

If the management systems the teacher uses match what the student needs and can use, then no differentiation is necessary. When there is a gap between the management systems and student needs and abilities, the teacher must consider other methods of getting the student to follow the system, participate in the activity, or demonstrate the behavior expected. The most common Extensions used when this gap appears include time, size, motivation, procedures and routines, and participation. Some examples include:

- teacher has random system for when students turn in homework so sometimes the student misses the event of turning it in, even when he has it; teacher implements a "first foot in the door" routine where all students turn in their homework the first moment they walk in to class;

- student has trouble knowing what to write down for notes when a teacher lectures so the teacher uses an organizational web on chart paper during lecture to pinpoint most important information;

- teacher has student use a laminated checklist every day before class starts to make sure he has everything for science class;

- student has difficulty remembering how to edit his own written work so the teacher models and has student use the C.O.P.S routine (COPS teaches student to check their capitalization, organization, punctuation, and spelling before they turn work in);

- student has difficulty remembering to bring materials to class so teacher has special packet made up in which the student leaves an extra set of the items he usually forgets in the room at the end of the day so he has less to remember.

Case Study: Nicholas

at beginning of class pick up math packet with calculator; bring book, paper, pencil to class; check in at the door using chart; raise hand to answer questions; turn lights off for attention	needs specific directions on how to get ready for class; needs a visual cue to get his attention; follows typical classroom directions like raising hands, taking turns

In this case most of the information matches, so there is not a great gap in the procedures and routines area. However, there is one area that Nicholas has trouble with that might pose a big problem: getting ready for class. If Nicholas has trouble remembering what to bring to class it could create real problems with the teacher and with the smoothness of getting started each day. Here the teacher will want to consider providing some cue or system for helping him remember what to bring. The teacher could use a variety of techniques like laminating a card that has each item listed; putting a list on his locker or his desk that he has to check off before class starts; giving him a verbal reminder; using a peer buddy to double check his readiness; or keeping a baggy of items he needs for class in the room with his name on it.

 Use **BLM 10**, Q10:10 to note if there is a gap and draft ideas to address the gap.

Q 11:11 Is there a gap between the physical or sensory skills required and those the student can use effectively?

If the student does not have any problems with physical or sensory skills, then the teacher does not need to attend to this issue. However, when a student has a physical or sensory sensitivity or challenge that interferes with learning, the teacher must consider ways to differentiate for that problem. Extensions for bridging the gap in this area include materials, pace, time, level of participation, support and independence, and activities. Some examples:

- student has fine motor skill trouble and cannot use a regular scissors; the teacher gives the student loop scissors (which require a lot less fine motor work);

- student has five minutes to get from one room to another and the student walks slowly on crutches so the teacher allows the student to leave class three minutes earlier than others to get to new locations;

- teacher uses a lot of group work where the noise level is relatively loud and the student has sensitivity to certain loud sounds including small group conversations in the classroom, so the teacher provides a set of headphones or ear plugs to reduce the noise;

- teacher uses text and pictures often and the student has reduced vision so the teacher ensures text and objects are enlarged for the student;

- teacher expects students to discuss ideas in class and the student cannot use voice to answer questions so the teacher ensures the student has drawing pad and pencil or a voice synthesized computer available during discussion.

Case Study: Nicholas

punching numbers in a calculator; viewing information from paper, board, books; listening to directions; writing using a pencil; talking with peers; standing to write on board	wears glasses consistently; no other issues in this area

In this case, as long as Nicholas remembers to wear his glasses, there should be no problems in the physical or sensory skills required for the planned instruction.

 Use **BLM 10,** Q11:11 to note if there is a gap and draft ideas to address the gap.

Q 12:12 Is there a gap between the materials or services used and ones the student needs to be successful?

If the materials or services planned for instruction can be adequately used by the student, the teacher can proceed with the instruction as planned. When there is a gap between the plan and the student's capabilities the teacher must determine what can be altered to adapt the situation to the learner. Some examples include:

- student cannot hold a pencil, but can hold larger writing utensils so the teacher ensures student has fat pencil or marker for writing (material);

- student has difficulty sitting upright without supports so the teacher ensures a bean bag or adult is there to help the student sit when in circle time on the floor (service);
- student has difficulty reading material, but can understand it when read aloud so the teacher ensures the student has taped texts or text on computer so the student can hear the information (material);
- student needs extra learning sessions for new concepts so the teacher ensures the student has access to the resource teacher for additional time (service);
- student cannot memorize multiplication facts but can find an answer on a multiplication chart (material).

Case Study: Nicholas

calculator; paper and pencil	use a calculator for math; will need support from an adult or peer with activities requiring more than 3 steps

The materials for the instruction are ones that Nicholas will be able to use. It appears there may be some resource or service support needed. He may need someone to keep him focused when the activities require four or more steps so the teacher might consider hooking him up with a peer or adult to keep him focused.

 Use **BLM 10,** Q12:12 to note if there is a gap and draft ideas to address the gap.

Q 13:13 Is there a gap between the location where instruction is provided and the needs of the student?

If the location or setting of the instruction matches the needs of the student, the teacher can be assured that no major problems will occur. When there is a gap between the normal location for learning and what a student needs to learn, the teacher must consider how the location or setting can be modified or altered to address the student's needs. Common Extensions used here are environment and routines and procedures.

- student has trouble generalizing information from one environment to another so when learning money skills he is taken out to stores, banks, or on the job (environment);
- student has difficulty sitting in confined spaces so he is allowed to remain at desk while other students are sitting in small circle on the floor (routine);
- student needs to manipulate information to gain understanding so he is allowed to go outside to collect rocks with different textures before instruction begins on the classifications

of rocks (environment and routine);

- student has difficulty learning new information in large group so he moves to a small area of the room or to another room for small group/individual instruction when new information is presented (environment).

Case Study: Nicholas

classroom and computer lab for input of data	ok in classroom; can use library and science lab for research

It appears there is no real concern over the environments where instruction will occur and where Nicholas can learn.

 Use **BLM 10,** Q13:13 to note if there is a gap and draft ideas to address the gap.

Q 14:14 Is there a gap between the methods of assessment and how the student can demonstrate what he knows?

If the student can show what he knows in a reasonable manner using the techniques the teacher has planned, then there is no need for differentiation. When the methods to assess do not match the ways the student best demonstrates knowledge, then the teacher must consider differentiating the methods so that a fair assessment can be made of the student's learning.

It is important to note that there are multiple ways a teacher can assess a student (e.g., observation, anecdotal records, video tape, audio tape, written work, projects, dramatizations). For a more comprehensive list of ways to assess students and resources on those types of assessments see the Appendix. It is also important to note that the teacher cannot physically collect data on every student, in every area, every day. Too often though, teachers do not collect any information other than paper and pencil tests or worksheets. For students with disabilities, this type of assessment is often the <u>least</u> reliable method for determining what they know.

When a gap in assessment exists, the teacher must consider other ways to collect data on the student's learning. To close this gap, she focuses on the way the student applies and demonstrates his knowledge. Some examples:

- teacher uses end of unit tests, but student has difficulty taking long tests so the teacher differentiates by using smaller, more frequent tests during the unit;
- teacher uses traditional spelling test and the student can spell the words when writing sentences but cannot spell them in isolation, so the teacher differentiates by letting the student write sentences using the words;

- teacher uses paper and pencil tests but the student cannot read quickly enough to finish the test on time so the teacher differentiates by putting the questions on audio tape so the student can listen to them and write answers;
- student always bombs big tests but participates in class, answers questions, does independent work with great accuracy so the teacher weights the student's grade to put more emphasis on class performance than tests;
- teacher is assessing student understanding of the history of transportation in the United States, student cannot write a research report, but uses drawings and photographs to depict the people, places, and things that have changed as transportation changed.

Case Study: Nicholas

vocabulary test; worksheets with 5 problems for each concept; graphing information; group presentation with rubric	can take short paper and pencil tests; may need to verbally explain his answers later after an essay

It appears that there are no major gaps between the assessment and Nicholas' abilities. The teacher may want to attend to the fact that Nicholas does not explain things in writing very well. So if the vocabulary test requires explanation of the terms, the teacher might need to give him an opportunity to verbally tell what else he knows.

 Use **BLM 10,** Q14:14 to note if there is a gap and draft ideas to address the gap.

What have you created?

Using this analysis and decision-making process, you have created an outline of ideas to use for differentiating instruction. Use **BLM 11, Gap Analysis Sheet Case Study** to view a summary of the gaps and ideas for bridging those gaps for the Case Study: Nicholas.

Now you have a visual and detailed picture of three things: (1) what does not need to be changed, (2) what differentiation is needed to support the student's learning, and (3) additional ideas for specific situations if the student begins to show signs of failure due to the barrier.

Notice that in several instances the teacher identified a series of ideas in order from most natural to most intrusive (e.g., question 10:10). Whenever possible, the teacher wants to avoid using differentiations that are extremely intrusive or highly noticeable when less intrusive methods will work. For example, the list on the locker is less intrusive because only the student sees the intervention and the student has the responsibility for completing the task of coming to class prepared. A specially marked bag with the student's name on it, kept by the teacher, given out in front of other students is more intrusive because others see it and the student carries little responsibility for coming to class prepared. There will be instances, however, where the best differentiation may indeed seem somewhat intrusive because the student absolutely needs that differentiation to be successful.

If you used **BLM 10** for your case study and have not already done so, remember to go back to analyze your ideas for feasibility and then rank order them, beginning with what you want to try first.

The Case Study: Nicholas — What does the teacher know?

Based on the **Gap Analysis of the Case Study: Nicholas, BLM 11,** it is clear that there is no need to change anything related to the content, real life connections, background, teaching style, physical or sensory skills, and location of instruction. The Gap Analysis indicates there are some areas that might need attention if problems begin and persist including the use of interesting activities, materials, and assessment.

There are definitely areas that the teacher needs to differentiate for Nicholas including the language of instruction, reading, learning strategies, class management, and adaptive behavior. In each of these areas, the teacher identified at least two different ideas of how to address the gap and rank ordered the ideas for feasibility. This rank ordering provides specific choices for differentiation in each area.

It may seem a little overwhelming at first to think of changing five different areas of a planned instructional situation, but in reality, there are only a few basic changes to be made. In essence, it looks like the teacher will need to consider changes to the techniques used to introduce and demonstrate the concept of *calculating mean, median, and mode using double-digit number sets* in three major ways.

First, the teacher will want to ensure the **<u>use of visual models</u>** for the

1. language of instruction - For example, when the concept of <u>rank order highest to lowest</u> for finding the mode is introduced, the teacher may need to model what *rank order* means using several different examples and let the students practice;

2. learning strategies - For example, the teacher will need to demonstrate on the board or overhead examples of a specific method/process for calculating each type of math concept.

Using visual models for teaching concepts is an effective strategy for any student, not just the student with a disability, so adding this to the instructional situation is natural, easy to do, and will increase the performance of many other students in the room.

Second, the teacher will want to **adjust or create materials used** including:

1. reading materials such as written word problems, directions on papers or books, and assessment questions;

2. materials that require more than 3 steps by highlighting or coding into increments of 3; and

3. development of physical cues (e.g., laminated cards, posters) that support the student.

It is important to spend a minute reflecting on the topic of reading materials. To determine if changing the reading level changes what is measured, the teacher must determine what is to be measured. For example, the word problem states:

Rank order the following numeric items: 84,56,24,43,56,93.

There are three possible ways the teacher might use this as assessment. Is the teacher trying to determine if the student can read the words? Is the teacher trying to determine if the student knows what the words *rank order* mean? Is the teacher trying to determine if the student knows *how to rank numbers highest to lowest* for use in a particular math problem?

If the teacher is trying to determine if the student can simply read the words, then all the student has to do is read them aloud, because simply reading the words does not mean the student has to act on the words (do what is asked). If that is what the teacher wants, then there should be no adjustment to the reading level of the words used. Remember the Differentiated Instruction Pyramid from Chapter 2? This purpose would fall at the bottom of the pyramid by measuring specific skills unrelated to the content to be measured.

If the teacher wants to know if the student knows what *rank order* means, then the reading level should not be changed because it is vocabulary specific – it is the actual words themselves that the student must act on. In this case, to help the student identify that the words are important, the teacher might change the reading cues to help him understand the importance like this:

Rank order the following numeric items: 84,56,24,43,56,93.

If the teacher is measuring this aspect of the content (vocabulary/language), it would fall in the middle of the Differentiation Instruction Pyramid focusing on important, but specific aspects of the content.

If the teacher wants to know if the student *can use the process of rank ordering* as part of a larger math problem, then the reading level or words can be changed because it is the process, not the specific vocabulary, that the teacher wants to measure.

Rank order, *from highest to lowest*, the following numeric items: 84,56,24, 43,56,93 and determine the range of the items.

If the teacher is measuring how the student uses the process required for this content she has moved to the top of the Differentiated Instruction Pyramid focusing on life long use and application of the content instead of more isolated events.

Third, the teacher will want to consider **attention to the behavior of the student** that supports the student's learning including:

1. reinforcement of independent, on task work;

2. use of specific routines for transitions in the classroom; and

3. organizational routines to prepare for and participate in instruction.

Paying attention to the behaviors of the student, particularly on-task, independent work, and organization is important for any student, not just a student with a disability. The difference in this case is that Nicholas may need someone to attend to him and guide him in these areas more often than another student in the room.

What do you think?

Is there anything about the changes that need to be made for Nicholas—using visual models, changing materials, and attending to the behaviors of the student—that cannot be done with relative ease? Will these changes possibly benefit other students in the room without taking away from the *content*? Using those changes to the instructional situation, can you still aim for the top of the Differentiated Instruction Pyramid?

What next?

Knowing the specific match between initial instructional plans and student needs enhances the teacher's ability to make simple adjustments to the learning environment that will create an accessible learning situation. It is time to begin developing specific plans that are content rich and differentiated for the students in the learning situation. There are still some questions left unanswered:

• Who develops and implements these differentiations?

• How often will they be implemented during the instructional situation?

• What will it look like when it is all put together in an instructional plan?

Chapters 6 and 7 help answer these questions by walking you through the instructional planning process and the decision making process for determining what type of teaching model you might need to serve the students in your room.

Chapter 6

Designing Differentiated Lesson Plans

Part 1: The Big Picture of the Lesson

Up to this point you have been collecting and analyzing the information needed to design appropriate instruction. In Chapter 6 you will use this information to make specific decisions related to how instructional lesson plans can be differentiated to meet unique student needs. By the end of the chapter you will have a completed *Step 5: Design the Instruction and Assessment* of the differentiation process which outlines the information necessary for an effective lesson based upon the curriculum and the students in the classroom. In Chapter 7 you will develop specific plans for implementation, including the acts and actions of teachers and students by completing *Step 6: Outline Instructional Actions and Responsibilities*.

Ideally, the process for developing and implementing a differentiated lesson plan is shared by the teacher and other professionals who work with the student. When all the service providers are involved in the planning process it is more likely that the differentiation will be successful. However, there are many instances when the teacher must make decisions on her own. If you are a teacher working on your own, take heart. If you followed the steps for completing the ECQ, ESQ, and Gap Analysis before trying to plan a differentiated lesson, rest assured that your differentiations will be appropriate and effective.

Before you can develop a complete lesson, it is important to discuss the components of an effective instructional lesson. This chapter will not attempt to teach how to write a lesson plan so much as it will focus on what each component of an effective lesson plan should include and how to combine information from the Gap Analysis into each component of the plan. For an excellent resource on writing lesson plans try Price and Nelson's *Daily Planning for Today's Classroom, 2nd*

Ed. (2003) or Bigge and Stump's *Curriculum, Assessment, and Instruction for Students with Disabilities* (1999). Pre-service teachers will find the *Bellarmine University Lesson Plan Format* provided in the Appendix particularly helpful with the details of each component of an effective lesson plan.

Let's Get Started!!

First, take the **ECQ and ESQ sheet (BLM 4 & 6)** and clip or staple them to the Gap Analysis Sheet, leaving the **Gap Analysis Sheet, BLM 10,** on top. Now, make a copy of the **Differentiated Lesson Plan Guide Part 1: The Big Picture, BLM 12.** As you read each section of this chapter, look at the Case Study example provided in that section and then use **BLM 12** to write your own lesson to match the content and student you have been working on in the previous chapters. For a completed copy of the Lesson Plan Guide Part 1 based on the Case Study: Nicholas and mean, median, and mode, see the **BLM 13.**

The Differentiated Lesson Plan Guide does not have to be used for this process. In fact, some teachers might find the boxes limit their ability to write all the information needed for a complete lesson. However, the benefit of using the Guide is that it puts in writing what will be done and it provides documentation of the expectations of teachers working collaboratively so that there are no surprises when it comes time for actually teaching.

What are the components of an effective lesson?

There are literally thousands of different resources explaining how to write a typical lesson plan and what to incorporate into the plan. Reviewing these resources, one will find that there are essentially 10 components to an effective lesson. The planning components of an effective lesson include two major phases: creating the Big Picture, and the Instructional Actions and Responsibilities. The big picture section outlines ultimate outcome for students through up-front planning or thinking to prepare for the lesson. The Instructional Actions section outlines the specifics, including the steps or stages of how the lesson will help students reach the outcome.

For the purposes of differentiation, however, there are few resources on how to write the lesson. This chapter provides a format for writing an effective lesson that includes differentiated instruction and assessment. To create a differentiated lesson plan, the teacher must include two additional phases: identifying student priorities, and teacher roles and responsibilities. The student priorities section is where teachers document very unusual issues related to specific students that cannot be included in the other sections of the big picture either because of the amount of detail or the degree of change needed. The teacher responsibilities section outlines who will be responsible for implementing the lesson. The sub components of each section of a differentiated lesson plan are listed on the following page.

Part 1

The Big Picture	Student Priorities
• Learning Principle • Context • Objectives • Assessment • Skills • Strategies • Vocabulary • Resources • Content Connections • Materials	• Any changes to items in the Big Picture section of the planning that are significantly different and need special attention.

Part 2

Instructional Actions	Teacher Responsibilities
• Advanced organizer/introduction • Direct/explicit teaching • Practice • Generalization/application • Closure	• Assignments for each person during the instructional process.

Take a minute to look at the **BLM 12, Differentiated Lesson Plan Guide Part 1: the Big Picture,** which provides the outline of the Differentiated Lesson Plan. Notice that there is a space for writing information on each item listed in the Big Picture section. There is also a small square located to the right hand side of each space. This small square will be used to indicate if there is a need for differentiation that is not included within the details of that section. When a small square is checked, it means there will be something related to that item described in the Student Priorities section of the lesson. In Chapter 7 you will have an opportunity to work through Part 2: Instructional Details and Teacher Responsibilities.

Let's work through each section of Part 1 and examine what the teacher must consider when creating a differentiated lesson.

Deciding What to Teach: The Big Picture

The first thing the teacher should do is create the big picture of the instruction by focusing the planning toward the top of the Differentiated Instruction Pyramid. The ultimate goal of any lesson is to create a learning environment that supports the four essential components of the pyramid: societal goals, real life application, genuine experiences, and authentic assessment. By aiming for the top of the pyramid, the teacher develops appropriate outcomes for all students. The teacher creates the big picture through the Learning Principle, Objectives, Context, and Assessment portions of the lesson planning process.

Learning Principle

The teacher identifies the critical Learning Principle to be achieved by the students. Here the teacher simply identifies the principle, without forming it into an objective. The Learning Principle includes the "bigger ideas" of the local school curriculum, as well as state and national standards. The Learning Principle is global enough to include a range of behaviors the students will display across specific content areas. The Learning Principle helps the teacher relate the content to the context of the student's life. Some examples:

- Students solve real life problems using mathematics;
- Students use a variety of written materials to gather information;
- Students write for a variety of purposes and audiences.

To further clarify, think about the teacher who has the specific instructional goal of teaching how to calculate mean, median, and mode using two-digit numbers. The Learning Principle of this activity would be: Students use mathematic equations to solve real life problems. Some teachers might argue using measures of central tendency (mean, median and mode) or two-digit numbers are the important learning principles, but in reality, the bigger picture is that we learn different methods of mathematics to solve life problems. We can solve real life mathematics problems using simpler methods; the methods may not be as efficient, but in reality the idea of using mean, median, and mode is a sub structure of the Learning Principle solve real life problems using mathematics.

Learning Principle and Differentiation

The Learning Principle is important for differentiation in three ways. First, to reach the top of the Differentiation Pyramid, the teacher must be aware of why the content is important in society, how it connects to the students, and where the students will use the information. The Learning Principle points the instruction toward this end. Knowing the ultimate purpose of the learning helps the teacher design instruction that provides genuine experiences and authentic assessment. When a teacher focuses on life-like experiences, a wider variety of learning experiences can be incorporated in to the classroom. The teacher can broaden the scope of activities and assessments which in turn will meet the unique needs of more students than using only one type of activity or assessment.

Second, for students with disabilities, acquiring the skill of the Learning Principle may be more important than the specific content for that individual lesson. The student with a disability might have difficulty with the particulars of one lesson, but can focus on the overall concepts of the content. This is where the teacher sets the stage for some levels of differentiation within the instruction. The teacher can analyze the gaps between instruction and student needs to determine if any steps need to be taken to adjust for student success.

For example, a teacher is planning to teach students how to write complex sentences using the transactive format. The Learning Principle is identified as *writing for a variety of purposes and audiences - transactive*. Through the gap analysis process, the teacher knows that there is one student in the room who will have difficulty writing complex sentences, but can write simple sentences. In a non-differentiated classroom, the teacher would either subject the student to the requirements of complex sentences and subsequent failure, or insist the student could not do the work and send him to a special classroom.

In a differentiated classroom, the teacher would recognize where the student is developmentally, and prepare the lesson in such a way that the student could use simple sentences to meet the goal of writing the transactive piece. The teacher would challenge the student to use complex sentences through teaching strategies (e.g., putting two simple sentences together) but also realize that the student's best performance might be writing the transactive piece using only simple sentences. Here, the student would be working toward the goal of writing for a particular purpose and audience, but not to the same level of complexity as the other students. In this instance, the teacher would be modifying the complexity of the lesson for the student. By understanding the options for the student participating and working toward the Learning Principle, the teacher sets the stage of both challenge and success for the student.

The third way Learning Principles are important for differentiation relates to instances when a student with a disability might need to be in a learning environment other than the general classroom. Some students might not be able to participate in the general classroom during a particular lesson or series of lessons. However, it is important that the student continues to have access to the general education curriculum. In this case, the special education teacher, or other specialist working with the student, needs to be aware of the Learning Principle for the lesson(s) so that the student can work toward that goal under different circumstances.

For example, a student with behavior problems might not be able to participate in the general classroom until the behaviors are under control. The student is working in a self contained classroom learning to control his behaviors. During this time, he should also be working toward mastery of the Learning Principle. If the student does not have the opportunity to work toward the

Learning Principle, he will transition back into the general classroom further behind, which will create frustration, and likely increase the inappropriate behaviors again.

Another example would be the student with more significant cognitive disabilities who needs to be learning through Community Based Instruction (CBI). The CBI teacher wants to make sure the student has the skills necessary for participating in the community as an adult. The Learning Principle focuses on what the student should know and be able to do in real life. The CBI teacher uses the Learning Principle as the guide for developing those skills. Using the principle mentioned above - *writing for a variety of purposes and audiences* - the CBI teacher might focus on teaching the student how to request a refund in writing, how to apply for a job, or how to invite someone to a party. Here, the Learning Principle allows the teacher to focus on skills that will help the student be successful in life and meet the standards of the curriculum. The instruction is differentiated to meet the unique needs of the student, but the integrity of the content standard remains intact.

When differentiation is needed that relates directly to the Learning Principle, the teacher writes the principle in the section and then puts a check mark ✓ in the square, indicating that information will be written in the fourth section of the lesson plan: Student Priorities.

In the Case Study: Nicholas and Mean, Median and Mode, the gap analysis indicated that Nicholas will need no differentiation related to the overall content. Therefore, the teacher would not check off the square in the Learning Principle section. If, however, the teacher had other students in the class requiring some differentiation, there might be a check in the box.

Case Study: Nicholas and Mean, Median, Mode

Learning Principle: *Students solve real life problems using mathematics*

 Using **BLM 12,** write in the Learning Principle for the content you want to teach. If there is an indication that your own case study (or other student in your class) might need differentiation related to the Learning Principle, put a check mark in the square.

Context

It is important for the teacher to keep in mind where the current instruction "fits" with the overall progress toward the Learning Principle and the top of the Differentiation Pyramid. Here, the teacher notes prior learning, or what has come before this lesson, and where it will lead in the future. For example, in the lesson on writing complex sentences, the teacher notes the following:

Students have been writing transactive pieces for simple tasks - e.g., short books on brushing teeth (purpose) for younger students (audience). The instruction moves to writing about more complex tasks and the audience changes to adults.

Context and Differentiation

By putting the upcoming lesson plan in context, the teacher has a perspective on what background knowledge the students should have prior to the lesson. If the teacher discovers through the gap analysis that a student does not have this knowledge, then adjustments can be made to close that gap.

However, it is also important to keep the context of the learning in the forefront of planning in case a student is not ready for that level of instruction and needs to continue to work on the skills or information that was presented previously. This information gives the teacher an idea of what to use in the instructional lesson. In a non-differentiated classroom the teacher would move on and not revisit the skills from past lessons.

In a differentiated classroom the teacher would consider what might bring the student up to par on previously covered material. In some cases, all the student needs is an intensive remediation session to acquire the skill. In others, the student may need to continue to work on the unmastered skill for a longer time. Each of these instances provides the teacher with a point for considering differentiation. In the first instance, the teacher might decide, by considering the Context and the needs of the student, to provide an intensive remediation session for the whole class before moving forward. Or she may ask a special education teacher to provide a session during study period for the individual student. In the second instance, where the student needs to continue working on the unmastered skills considered prior knowledge, the teacher might decide that the student can continue to work toward the skills or knowledge from previous lessons within the context of the planned lesson or does not have to master the skills to move to the next lesson.

The beauty of considering the Context is that in almost any classroom there will be non-disabled students as well as those with disabilities who will not have mastered the previous lessons and can benefit from differentiation through remediation or continued work on the previous skills. For example, the teacher recognizes there are four students, including one with a disability, who have not mastered writing simple sentences. As the teacher plans the lesson, an intensive activity involving just those four students can be planned while other students are working on their complex sentences.

Knowing that there is more than one student in need of work on mastering previous materials allows the teacher to incorporate activities to address this group in the normal lesson plan. By incorporating such activities in the lesson plan, the differentiation for the student with the disability becomes a natural part of the instruction instead of a secondary consideration.

In the Case Study: Nicholas, there does not appear to be any problem with previously learned material. His background and the expected knowledge and skill level appear to be even with each other.

Case Study: Nicholas and Mean, Median, and Mode

Context: *Students have been working on averaging, rank ordering, and analyzing data for information using graphs, but the numbers have been single digit.*

Using **BLM 12,** write in the Context of what you are planning to teach. If there is an indication that your own case study (or another student in your class) might need differentiation related to the Context, put a check mark in the square.

Objectives

Once the Learning Principle and Context are written, the teacher can focus on specific objectives for the instruction. For the purposes of differentiation, consider objectives to be goal statements suggesting progress toward the Learning Principle. Objectives are what the teacher wants to measure when all the teaching and practice is completed. Objectives define what will be assessed. The teacher can write objectives that allow students to complete the same work, but in a variety of formats without compromising the Learning Principle.

There is considerable debate on what constitutes an effective instructional objective. (For some teacher-friendly texts on how to write effective objectives see Mager (1997) and Gronlund (1995).) To develop lessons that have differentiation naturally embedded, the objectives have to be more than just the basic learning statements of a typical curriculum text book. Each objective should meet four basic standards:

- Student focused - outline what the students will do as the end result of instruction and activity;
- Measurable in nature - include actions that can be observed and counted;
- Include circumstances of the actions - what materials, models, location, or support are definitely part of the work;
- Indicate criteria for performance - the degree, level, or number of demonstrations required for success or mastery.

Here is one example of an objective from a lesson plan on democracy.

After reading passages and engaging in class discussion on democracy, students will defend the need for a balance between freedom and responsibility in a democratic society by writing and orally presenting a three minute argument with at least four major points.

Does it meet the standards for a good objective?
- student as the focus - yes, indicates the student will do the work
- observable actions - write and present an argument
- circumstances of the action - after reading and discussion
- criteria for performance - three minutes, includes four points.

There are at least three types of objectives the teacher might consider developing for a particular lesson: content related, behavior, and process. Content related objectives refer to specific information or knowledge within a content area (e.g., math, science, reading). Behavior objectives reflect important actions expected of the students during or after instruction. Process objectives refer to specific methods or procedures that are important (e.g., develop a character web, write a haiku). Each type of objective has its own purpose and level of importance. In some lessons, the teacher will only focus on one type of objective, while in other lessons there might be all three types of objectives.

Many teachers struggle with deciding how many objectives to write. There is no secret formula for that issue. In general, the teacher should consider what is most important and what will actually be measured. Using importance and assessment as the guide, most lesson plans consist of no more than 3 - 4 objectives.

Objectives and Differentiation

Objectives provide yet another place to pause and consider differentiation of instruction. The teacher uses information from the gap analysis to prepare for and incorporate changes into the lesson plan. Objectives might be adjusted if there is a potential problem with teaching methods, activities, materials, adaptive behaviors, or physical or sensory skills for the student with a disability. How the teacher approaches differentiation will depend on which type of objective the lesson will use. The teacher will need to consider the type of objective (content, behavior, or process), the circumstances of the objective, and the criteria for performance.

Content related objectives. The teacher uses information from the gap analysis to predict if the student will be able to master the objectives under the given circumstances. If the teacher sees that a student will be able to accomplish some, but not all of the content related objectives planned for the lesson, the teacher can rank order the objectives in order of easiest to hardest or lowest to highest. Then the teacher can identify which objective from the group is most important for the student to master.

For example, when teaching mean, median, and mode, the teacher identifies *mode* as the easiest, *median* as the next hardest, and *mean* as the hardest concept to learn. The teacher can write three different objectives, one for each concept. Then, if there is a student in the room who might not master all three concepts, she can check the box indicating that there is information on this in the Student Priorities section of the lesson plan.

Behavior related objectives. There are two different situations that might arise related to differentiation for students with disabilities. First, there may be situations where the teacher would not normally put a behavior objective into the lesson, but there is at least one student who needs to work specifically on certain behavior(s). The teacher must decide if the behavior objective is important enough to incorporate into the full lesson and assess all or most students on this objective. Often the teacher knows that most of the students have mastered the behavioral objective, but considers it very important for all students, so it is included with the lesson plan. For the student with a disability, if the behavior is the most important focus of their learning, then the objective should be documented in the lesson plan either in this section or in the Student Priorities section of the plan.

The other situation that might arise that calls for differentiation is when a specific behavior objective is listed for the lesson and it is clear through the gap analysis that the student with a disability will have difficulty performing the behavior. For example, the objective calls for students to work cooperatively in groups of four and the student with a disability has difficulty working in groups of more than two students. In a situation such as this one, the teacher must decide the degree to which the student will need to meet this goal, or if he is required to meet it at all. The teacher can decide to adjust the actual objective by removing the number of students required in a cooperative group or indicate that there will be differentiation for the student by placing a check in the box and clarifying the issue in the Student Priorities section of the lesson plan.

Process related behaviors. Using the gap analysis the teacher discovers that the student with a disability might have trouble with an objective related to a particular processes. For example, the objective requires students to use a five step scientific process and a student in the class has trouble following more than two steps at a time. Usually students with disabilities have difficulty with the number of steps in a process or degree of difficulty of the process. The teacher determines whether to change the type of process required or break the process into manageable chunks for the student. If the teacher determines that more than one process can be used to get to the same end, the objective can be written to incorporate both processes. If the student needs a variation of the process, the teacher can indicate this by checking the box and describe the difference in the process in the Student Priorities section of the lesson plan.

Circumstances of the objective. Each objective outlines what circumstances (e.g., materials, location, type of support) will be in place for mastery to be demonstrated. If during the gap analysis the teacher discovers that there is a potential problem with the teaching style, reading level, materials, physical or sensory skills, or location of the circumstance, then differentiation might be in order. For example, if the objective calls for students to use a ninth grade text book and the student with a disability can only read sixth grade materials, the teacher will want to consider how the objective will be differentiated. The teacher could adjust the wording on the objective to indicate the use of various text book levels or indicate there is a differentiation issue for a student by placing a check in the box and then clarifying the issue in the Student Consideration section of the lesson plan.

Criteria of the objective. The criteria of the objective defines what level or type of performance is expected of the student. The teacher can adjust objectives if there is a gap between the student's skills and level or type of performance expected.

For example, in a non-differentiated classroom, the teacher who wrote the objective above on democracy would require and grade each student on his verbal presentation. The teacher would not make any changes for a student with a communication problem who had trouble verbally presenting information. The student would be rated on his verbal presentation and would likely meet some level of failure.

In a differentiated classroom, the teacher knows up front that the student may need to present in a different form (e.g., visually representing the argument). The teacher then has two options. One option is for the teacher to leave the objective written as it is and adjust the requirements during the assessment phase of planning and implementation. The other option is to incorporate more choices for demonstrating knowledge into the objective. A differentiated objective, taking into account other methods of demonstration than just verbal presentations, might look like this:

> *After reading passages and class discussion on democracy, students will defend the need for a balance between freedom and responsibility in a democratic society by writing and presenting a verbal or visual argument which includes at least four major points, and takes no more than five minutes to present.*

Unless the teacher was planning on measuring *only* the student's ability to <u>verbally</u> present information, changing the objective to include the option of visually presenting an argument does not change the overall expectation for the student.

There are advantages to both techniques of dealing with the criteria of objectives. If the teacher waits until the assessment planning phase to make the differentiation, the objective outlines a single set of criteria for the class. Then the teacher documents what minor changes will be made for the student requiring differentiated assessment. The advantage here is that there is really only one major and one unique assessment. The advantage of adjusting the objective to allow for various methods of demonstration is that it will likely reach more students than just the one with the disability. In this instance more students might perform better if they have more than one option for demonstrating their knowledge. Either way, the teacher ends up creating different sets of criteria for assessment, but in the second situation the teacher opens the door for a wider variety of learners to be successful.

In the Case Study: Nicholas and mean, median, and mode, the teacher chose to write three different objectives for several reasons. First, each of the three concepts - mean, median, and mode - requires a different level of skill and different types of calculations. In addition, the teacher knows there are a few students who might have trouble with the process for calculating the mean so she has rank ordered the objectives from easiest to hardest and will allow the students to master the easiest first.

Notice in the objectives that the teacher did not list the level of reading for the word problems. This could be because Nicholas needs word problems to be written on a lower level than the other students. By omitting the reading level of the word problems the teacher designs the objective to allow for the differentiation(s) needed for Nicholas. The teacher has designed the objective to measure the math skill, not a reading skill.

The other item of importance is that the teacher incorporated the use of written or verbal responses for each objective. This is important for Nicholas because he sometimes has difficulty

> **Case Study: Nicholas and mean, median, and mode.**
>
> Objectives:
>
> Using word problems and note book formulas, students will:
>
> • *identify the mode for a series of two-digit numbers by circling or verbally identifying the number(s) with 90% accuracy.*
>
> • *identify or calculate the median for a series of two-digit numbers by circling, writing, or verbally identifying the number with 90% accuracy.*
>
> • *calculate the mean for a series of two-digit numbers by writing or verbally describing the process and the correct answer with 90% accuracy.*

 Using **BLM 12,** write the objectives for your lesson plan. If there is an indication that your own case study (or other student in your class) might need differentiation that is not incorporated into the objectives, put a check mark in the square.

Assessment

The final section of the big picture part of the lesson plan is Assessment. Assessment is more than just paper and pencil tests. Assessment refers to the total picture of student performance across settings and levels of application. The purpose of this section is not to teach how to assess, but to discuss differentiation issues that must be considered when planning assessment for a particular lesson.

The assessment section of the lesson plan is more than just stating that there will be a test at the end of the unit. The teacher outlines how objectives will be measured on the Lesson Plan Guide and provides, via attachments, the actual assessment pieces that will be used at the end of the learning. The objectives provide the basic structure of what should be measured, but the assessments outline how it should be measured. For example, using the objective on democracy again, the teacher would want to indicate how the students will meet the objective. The teacher would use the assessment section on the Lesson Plan Guide to indicate what will be used to assess the presentations and then attach a model of the assessment to the Lesson Plan Guide. The information on the Lesson Plan Guide might look like this:

> *Rubric for presentation will be used to rate written information, presentation styles, and four major points. Rubrics will be provided to students prior to beginning of instruction. See attached.*

Assessment and Differentiation

In a non-differentiated classroom there will be one test for all students to take at the end of learning. In a differentiated classroom you will find a variety of assessment techniques in use at various times during instruction, practice, and independent demonstration. In a differentiated classroom there will be a wide variety of assessment tools used including typical tests, demonstrations, presentations, projects, portfolios, observations, and self-rating scales.

Best practices suggest that assessments are developed before the instruction ever begins. Some teachers will argue that they cannot build a test until after the instruction is complete, but research suggests that assessment is more effective if the test is built first, so the teacher knows what is most important to teach. Then after instruction is complete, the teacher can adjust the test based on what did and did not get covered.

It is important to develop the assessment before teaching in a differentiated classroom so that the teacher can prepare for any modifications or adaptations that will need to be made for a particular student. Too often, teachers do not realize the need for a modification until after the student has failed the assessment. By planning ahead of time, the teacher can make the adjustments or work with another individual, such as the special education teacher, to make appropriate changes. By planning and modifying ahead of time, the teacher increases the likelihood of success for the student.

Typically, when there is a need to differentiate assessments the teacher can choose from two options: modify the assessment or develop/use a completely different assessment. Teachers want to ensure when they make changes to the assessment that they are attending to the <u>purpose</u> of the assessment, not the mode of the assessment. For example, if a teacher refuses to let a student answer test questions orally instead of in writing, the teacher is actually assessing the student's ability to <u>write</u> not necessarily his level of knowledge.

When it comes to modifying the assessment, the teacher has many different options or Extensions to use: change the time, size, pace, type of demonstration, or materials. Here is one example in which the teacher can consider several options depending upon the needs of the students.

> *The teacher plans a paper and pencil test with 50 questions and knows there is a student with a disability who has trouble quickly processing written information. The student can read the information and can process it, but needs more time to respond than the typical student. Knowing this ahead of time from the gap analysis, the teacher can assume the student will have difficulty taking the test in the allotted 50 minutes. Given this knowledge, the teacher can plan ahead of time for the student to (a) have additional time to take the test (time), (b) reduce the number of questions the student has to answer during the normal test time (size), or (c) take*

the test over two different periods such as during class and then during study period (pace).

Another student has trouble writing answers on paper, but can type. The teacher can allow the student to use the computer to answer questions instead of hand writing (materials) or allow the student to answer questions on a tape recorder (materials, demonstration).

Creating a completely different assessment can be simple or complicated depending upon the need of the student and the objective. In most cases the teacher can modify the assessment for the student using techniques like the ones in the example above. However, once in a while a student will require a very different method of assessment. For example, a student with significant cognitive problems might have difficulty passing a paper and pencil test on how to write checks and keep a check book, but can demonstrate these skills by actually going to the bank to cash the check and keeping a balanced check book over time.

The teacher can incorporate differentiations in the Assessment section of the Lesson Plan Guide or place a check in the box and indicate what types of changes are necessary in the Student Priorities section. Notice in the Case Study: Nicholas and mean, median, and mode, that the teacher decided to keep the assessment related to the objectives and included verbal and written responses.

Case Study: Nicholas and mean, median, and mode.

Assessment: students will complete daily assignments in workbooks; anecdotal records will indicate student verbal responses during class; mini-tests will be given on each concept, then one large test with four word problems for each concept; students can add audio tape answers to their written work during last ten minutes of each class.

Using **BLM 12,** write down the type of assessments you will use for the lesson to be taught and provide an example. If there is an indication that your own case study (or other student in your class) might need differentiation that is not incorporated into the assessment section, put a check mark in the square.

Skills

Skills are the basic acts or actions the student will need to complete the lesson. They include physical, cognitive, and adaptive behavior capacities that will be expected or needed for successful completion of the activity. For example, skills might include listening for information, writing, spelling, cutting with a scissors, using a calculator, following four step directions, or reading a paragraph.

Skills and Differentiation

It is important to identify the types of skills needed for the lesson so that the teacher can prepare or modify the level of skill for a specific student. Too often, teachers miss the fact that certain skills or lack of skills interfere with student learning. The teacher will want to include obvious and hidden skills. For example, an obvious skill in the objective on democracy would be *writing*, because it is listed in the objective. A hidden skill might be *listening for information*. This skill is hidden because it is implied in the objective, but not explicit.

There are several ways skills are differentiated. The first issue that usually comes up with skills and differentiation is when the lesson requires a skill and the student has not mastered it yet. Here, the teacher has to determine if the skill can be varied or perhaps omitted. For example, the lesson calls for the skill of creating an outline while listening to lecture, and a student has difficulty listening and writing at the same time. The teacher can choose to vary the skill (e.g., provide an outline with some information already filled in), allow the student to complete the outline later, or even remove that skill as a requirement for the student.

Another way skills might be part of the differentiation is when a particular skill listed on the Lesson Plan Guide is considered more important than others for a particular student. The teacher acknowledges that the student will be focusing on developing that particular skill and not on others. For example, the teacher lists these skills as important for a lesson: sharing materials, cutting with scissors, following directions. The teacher knows that one student will have difficulty sharing materials so that skill becomes the priority for that student during this lesson plan.

The other time that skills are sometimes used in differentiation is when a student might need to make the skills themselves the priority instead of mastering the overall lesson plan objectives. For example, a student with extremely inadequate social skills might need to focus solely on the skill of working in a small group and be measured on this skill instead of other objectives. In essence, what is considered a skill for most students becomes the primary focus for another student.

In the Case Study: Nicholas and mean, median, and mode, the teacher knows from the gap analysis that he will have trouble with reading skills if the information is provided on grade level and that Nicholas may have trouble with independent work. Therefore, the teacher has described the skills needed and checked the box indicating there will be some differentiation described in the Student Priorities section of the lesson plan.

Case Study: Nicholas and mean, median, and mode.

Skills:

• reading grade level • use calculator • listen and discuss • rank order
• number recognition • keep workbook • independent work

 Using **BLM 12,** write down the type of skills required for the lesson. If there is an indication that your own case study (or other student in your class) might need differentiation that is not incorporated into the skills section, put a check mark in the square.

Strategies

The teacher wants to identify any learning strategies that will be used for the lesson. Learning strategies are specific approaches or physical or mental processes used to teach or learn a concept. For example, strategies might include using a five step process for writing a paragraph, creating a comparison chart, or using C.O.P.S. for sentence writing.

Strategies and Differentiation

Through the gap analysis process the teacher knows a student needs a particular type of learning strategy to be successful. This strategy can become the primary strategy used for teaching the entire class or considered a secondary strategy the student will use instead of the other strategy. The teacher can either list the strategy in the provided space or indicate that a different strategy will be used for an individual student by placing a check in the small box provided.

In the Case Study: Nicholas and mean, median, and mode, the teacher discovered during the gap analysis that Nicholas randomly approached tasks and did not always ask questions for clarification. The teacher decided that he needed a specific method to approach each objective and included this information in both the Strategies section and in the Student Priorities section.

Case Study: Nicholas and mean, median, and mode.

Strategies:
teach step-by-step process using picture and words for each concept;
have students verbally repeat each step

Using **BLM 12,** write down the type of strategies required for the lesson. If there is an indication that your own case study (or other student in your class) might need differentiation that is not incorporated into the strategies section, put a check mark in the square.

Vocabulary

The teacher should consider what vocabulary is important for the learning including the background vocabulary, new vocabulary, and language of instruction. The teacher should identify the most important vocabulary, not random words from the overall teaching. The most important vocabulary can often be found in the objectives and assessments developed for the lesson.

Vocabulary and Differentiation

Students with disabilities may have difficulty with background vocabulary, new vocabulary, or the language of instruction. If the teacher determines during the gap analysis that the student might have trouble in any of these three areas it can be addressed in this section or in the Student Considerations section. For example, the teacher knows the student will have trouble with the words *show your work.* The teacher lists this term in the vocabulary section to indicate that the phrase needs to be explained and modeled for all students or the teacher omits the phrase from the vocabulary section but checks off the small box and puts the phrase in the Student Priorities section with an explanation.

In the Case Study: Nicholas and mean, median, and mode, the teacher discovered that Nicholas will have trouble with directional words used in instruction so those words are listed in the vocabulary section, indicating the teacher will need to address them during instruction.

Case Study: Nicholas and mean, median, and mode.
Vocabulary:
order, rank, categorize, average, divide

 Using **BLM 12,** write the vocabulary required for the lesson. If there is an indication that your own case study (or another student in your class) might need differentiation that is not incorporated into the vocabulary section, put a check mark in the square.

Resources

The teacher wants to identify the people and places that are important for the lesson to be successful. In some instances, there may be nothing listed in the resource section because the lesson can be completed without other people (e.g., specialist) or settings (e.g., computer lab). In other instances, there may be lessons that require several resources to complete the learning process. For example, a teacher might want to have a nurse or physician guest speak as part of a series of lessons on nutrition, or take the students on a field trip to the local courthouse to view a trial and interview a judge. In this section the teacher simply lists the types of resources needed for the instruction.

Resources and Differentiation

Students with disabilities might require specific services or support from individuals, specific settings for learning, or both to be successful. Individuals might provide direct support to the student in the general classroom or in a separate setting. For example, one type of resource might be a personal assistant for a student who has extremely poor social skills in large groups. Another might be a special education teacher who works with the student during study hall. The individual might provide support to the teacher (e.g., adapted materials).

Students with disabilities may need services available in locations other than the general classroom. For example, if a student needs to have access to a computer with voice to text and the only computer equipped with the software is in the computer lab, the teacher will want to list the lab and software as resources needed.

The easiest way to document needed resources is to list them in this section of the lesson plan. If the teacher finds the resources cannot be listed in this section of the plan because of the amount of detail necessary, the information can be recorded in the Student Priorities section.

In the Case Study: Nicholas and mean, median, and mode, there is no indication that the specific resource of a different setting is needed. It appears that Nicholas can participate in the general classroom with some differentiation. There is some indication that he might need additional support on following directions involving more than three steps, working with directional words, coming to class prepared, and some adaptive behaviors. None of these issues are so great that they obviously would require another person with Nicholas all the time, but there is indication that the general teacher might want to work with a special education teacher to develop materials or conduct mini lessons on these areas. The teacher decided to indicate this information in the resource section of the lesson plan.

Case Study: Nicholas and mean, median, and mode.

Resources:

no major resources needed;

work with special ed. teacher to develop materials & adaptive behavior ideas

---

Using **BLM 12,** identify the resources required for the lesson. If there is an indication that your own case study (or another student in your class) might need differentiation that is not incorporated into the resource section, put a check mark in the square.

Content Connections

The teacher should identify how this information connects to other content areas so that during the teaching activities these connections become obvious to the students. For example, we use transactive writing in science, history, economics, math, and social studies. The language arts teacher can plan assignments that cross these different areas. Using a variety of activities that demonstrate how skills cross content helps the students see the connections and ensures consistency in their performance across environments.

Content Connections and Differentiation

Students with disabilities may need more explicit or obvious experiences connecting skills or knowledge from one environment to another. It is important to consider this and incorporate experiences that will help the students make the connections. For example, a student with moderate cognitive problems might not understand that writing a sentence in language arts class has the same requirements (e.g., punctuation, capitalization) as writing a sentence in other content areas. The teacher would want to use activities that cross content areas other than language arts and reinforce the skill when teaching the other content areas.

In the Case Study: Nicholas and mean, median, and mode, there is no indication that Nicholas would need specific differentiation related to content connections.

Case Study: Nicholas and mean, median, and mode.
Content Connections:
use these math concepts in science, economics, social studies

---

 Using **BLM 12,** identify the content connections for the lesson. If there is an indication that your own case study (or another student in your class) might need differentiation that is not incorporated into this section, put a check mark in the square.

Materials

The teacher should list the specific materials that will be used in the lesson. This list helps the teacher make sure all materials are ready before instruction begins.

Materials and Differentiation

It is important for the teacher to include those special materials needed by a student with a disability (e.g., supported chair, computer voice to text) or any modifications to materials in use (e.g., adapted pencil, color coded notes). Such information can be listed in this section or in the Student Priorities section of the lesson plan.

In the Case Study: Nicholas and mean, median, and mode, there is some indication that Nicholas would benefit from laminated cards with pictures of the math processes on them, a laminated card listing what he should bring to class, and some type of modification to the multiple step directions such as color coding. The teacher decided to indicate this information in the materials section of the lesson plan.

Case Study: Nicholas and mean, median, and mode.
Materials:
calculators, workbooks, paper and pencil,
laminated models of each math process, color coded steps

 Using **BLM 12,** identify the materials required for the lesson. If there is an indication that your own case study (or another student in your class) might need differentiation that is not incorporated into the materials section, put a check mark in the square.

Student Priorities

For any section that has a check mark in the small square there should be some description of the issue in the Student Priorities section of the Differentiated Lesson Plan Guide Part 1: the Big Picture. This part of the lesson planning process allows the teacher to indicate in more detail any specific or very unique needs a student will have related to any one of the typical lesson plan components.

Ideally, the majority of modifications or adaptations to a lesson plan would be incorporated into the general lesson plan sections listed on Part 1 of the Differentiated Lesson Plan Guide.

However, there will be some instances when a student or group of students will need modifications or adaptations that are too unique to build in to the general plan, but must be addressed by the teacher. Some examples include:

- a teacher may have a group of students who must work with manipulatives while others are capable of working with abstract concepts. The teacher might want to list this in the Student Priorities section to guarantee that these materials are available;

- a student needs a sign language interpreter any time lecture is used for note taking. The teacher will want to note this in the Student Priorities section if lecture is planned;

- a student will need additional time to complete large projects or long tests. The teacher will want to indicate this when projects or tests are part of the lesson plan.

Sometimes teachers use student's full name or just initials. Some teachers put detailed information in this section, while others use it as a quick reminder. The important point is that this space is used to acknowledge that something different must be provided for the student other than what will be used for the other students in the class.

In the Case Study: Nicholas and mean, median, and mode, the teacher put a check mark in the sections on strategies and skills indicating that Nicholas will need some specific differentiations that could not be embedded in the normal lesson plan.

Case Study: Nicholas and mean, median, and mode

Nicholas needs laminated cards showing step-by-step approach to solving mean, median, mode. Reading level of word problems will need to be on 3rd grade level.

 Using **BLM 12,** write in any student specific information that is not included in the general lesson but must be considered for the student with the disability.

What have you created?

Using the Differentiated Lesson Plan Guide Part 1: the Big Picture, you should have created a detailed picture of what will be taught, how it will be assessed, and all the pieces that need to be in place before the teaching begins. This picture should include the differentiated aspects of the instruction and assessment in the Big Picture section, the Student Priorities section, or across both sections.

Notice, in the completed version of **BLM 13, Differentiated Lesson Plan Guide Part 1: the Big Picture for the Case Study**: Nicholas and mean, median, and mode, that the plans for

---

instruction focus on the content, but also address the major gaps identified in Chapter 5 and outlined in **BLM 10.**

These gaps have been addressed by improving the instructional objectives and assessment to incorporate Nicholas' learning style (and likely other students!), incorporating important skills (e.g., reading, adaptive behavior), and including learning strategies and materials that Nicholas can use to be successful.

Once the Big Picture and Student Priorities are complete, the teacher can begin to outline the activities that will move the instruction from beginning to end and indicate who will be responsible for completing each activity. These decisions are explained in *Step 6: Outline Instructional Actions and Responsibilities, as* found in Chapter 7.

Chapter 7

Designing Differentiated Lesson Plans
Part 2: Instructional Actions & Responsibilities

Step 6: Outline Instructional Actions and Responsibilities, begins once Part 1: Big Picture of the instructional lesson plan is completed. In this step, using Part 2 of the lesson plan, **BLM 14,** the teacher outlines the details of the activities and actions that are necessary to implement the differentiated lesson, and she indicates the actions that will lead the students through the learning as well as the responsibilities the teacher or teachers will take to deliver the differentiated instruction.

The Instructional Actions section of the lesson plan is very important for developing effective differentiation, and each step is significant to all students, particularly those with disabilities. By outlining the Instructional Actions, or steps to the lesson, the teacher ensures that there is a complete process in place to begin, practice, and demonstrate mastery of the learning. The completion of the process is important because it helps students see the entire picture of the learning instead of just separate pieces.

The Instructional Actions section is also important to differentiation because it is the basis for the Responsibilities section in which the teacher outlines who is accountable for the differentiation. Too often, in classrooms where differentiation is required, there is an uncertainty as to who is responsible for the differentiation. When teachers are unsure of their responsibilities the differentiation does not happen, or happens after the student has met unnecessary failure, and the student suffers. By planning ahead of time who is responsible for what actions, the likelihood increases that differentiation will occur.

This chapter approaches the Responsibilities section from two perspectives: (1) the teacher who is solely responsible for implementation of all instruction and support for an individual student, and (2) the group of teachers who share responsibility for the student.

Let's Get Started!!

Make a copy of the **BLM 14, Differentiated Lesson Plan Guide Part 2: Instructional Actions and Responsibilities.** As you read each section of the chapter, apply your own teaching situation and case study to the lesson plan. For a completed copy of the Lesson Plan Guide Part 2: Case Study: Nicholas and mean, median and mode, see **BLM 15.**

Instructional Actions

At this point in the planning process the teacher must outline the specific instructional actions that will be used to guide the students toward mastery of the objectives. The teacher wants to define the actions that will move the students smoothly through the learning. There is no overt reference to any differentiations, but the decisions made in Part 1 of the planning process are embedded in each activity.

This part of the planning process requires that the teacher outline five types of actions. Each type of action has a particular purpose and serves a very important role in ensuring all students have a greater chance at successful completion of the instructional objectives. If a teacher uses lessons from curriculum text books, it is important to note that the information that is written on the guide is not the same information teachers can find in these books. The information on the guide is a simpler version of what is provided in the text books and is meant to outline the essential activities. The curriculum text book lessons provide more details, such as specific questions or actual problems to be solved. The text book lessons can be great companions to the completed Lesson Plan Guide.

1. Advanced Organizer or Introduction

This action is considered the "hook". It is the piece that pulls the students into the learning process. During this action the teacher attempts to connect the students' previous learning to what they are about to learn and indicates how the information will be used in real life. The action can be intensive review of information for reteaching purposes or simply a preview of what is to come. The action may take place in a matter of minutes or take a day or two to complete, depending upon the type of lesson to be taught.

The Advanced Organizer is an activity that prepares the students for the learning. An Introduction is usually a little less informative and typically includes the teacher asking questions related to either a previous lesson or students' current knowledge about a particular topic. Both activities are meant to excite the students and help them see the connection between what they already know and the new knowledge, as well as real-life connections to the new learning. Some examples:

Advanced Organizer

- Create a visual web of the story *I Columbus, My Journal (Eds. Peter and Connie Roop 1990 Avon Books NY)*, before reading anything from the book.
- Use a KWL (Know, Want to know, Learned) chart to gather what the students "Know" about the topic.
- Put the word "freedom" on the board and have students journal, then discuss what the word means.
- Review vocabulary terms important to the story before beginning the reading.

Introduction

- Ask series of questions related to the reasons we use transactive writing in our real life.
- Ask students to discuss why we need to learn about money.
- Show pictures from colonial days and ask them why the pictures are stories from the past.

For students with disabilities this step is particularly important because they often need that overt connection from one learning event to another, real life application, and time to process what they are about to learn. Using the Advanced Organizer or Introduction will give the student this overt connection. This is where the teacher can incorporate information for students who may have gaps in background knowledge, vocabulary, and interest in the content. For example, if during the gap analysis and planning it is determined that a student does not have much background knowledge for the content to be taught, the teacher can use the Advanced Organizer to bring the student up to par for the learning that is about to occur.

2. Direct or Explicit Teaching

This action is considered the actual teaching of new information. The teacher identifies how the specific content, skill, or process will be presented to the students. Usually this action includes the teacher demonstrating or modeling the desired outcome, walking the students through the steps and preparing them for independent work. This action may take a few minutes, a day, or even a week or more depending upon the lesson plan. Some examples:

- Model rank ordering numbers highest to lowest on the overhead and use at least 5 different examples the students work through at the same time.
- Show a sample of a sentence without punctuation and model how to change the punctuation. Work through at least 5 examples as a large group before independent work.

• Demonstrate the meaning of new vocabulary words through actions and pictures using some students as actors.

It is during the direct teaching that the student will benefit most from differentiation when there are gaps in the content, language of instruction, or learning style. If a student does not have skills within the content, the direct teaching will build those skills. Using direct teaching, the teacher can explicitly demonstrate the language of instruction (e.g., when modeling the technique of rank ordering, emphasize that *rank order* and *low to high* mean the same thing). During direct teaching the technique used to model the new learning can be connected to the learning style of the student (e.g., teacher shows pictures of verbs being acted out while explaining what each means so the student needing visual cues for learning will have a better understanding). This is a critical component for students with any type of learning difficulty.

3. Practice

This action refers to what the teacher will do to guide the students in practicing or manipulating the new knowledge. The teacher should identify the actions students will use to learn the new information as a group or independently. Practice implies that the teacher will be systematically observing and guiding the student work, but not actively directing the new knowledge. Practice may be limited to a few problems or be as complex as the development of a data report taking several days to complete. The length of practice will depend upon the type of lesson being taught. Some examples:

• Form groups of 4, pull apples randomly from the bag and record data of color for each pull to develop ratio/percentages. Graph and discuss results.

• Provide 10 sentences to be corrected for capitalization and punctuation.

• Form debate teams and prepare arguments for and against slavery.

• Use science lab to combine chemicals and observe reactions. Compare to class demonstration.

Each of the examples above implies that direct teaching of some content has occurred prior to the practice activity. Practice provides the opportunity to further develop a student's understanding through trial and error. The teacher has the opportunity to guide or redirect a student who is having difficulty completing an activity on his own. This guided practice is particularly important for students with disabilities. Many students can complete activities when directly guided by the teacher in a group or one-on-one situation, but have difficulty completing similar problems on their own. The guided practice time provides an opportunity for the student to work as independently as possible and receive immediate feedback on his work.

Practice can also include using activities that engage the learner (e.g., use word problems related to World Wrestling Federation), which is critical for students with disabilities. It might also include a student going out into the real world to complete the task (e.g., goes to the grocery story and counts money to purchase items). It is also during practice time that the student can get more individualized attention which often aids with engagement and understanding (e.g., teacher sits with student to work through a few problems). Finally, it may be that during practice the teacher collects assessment data on progress toward individual goals in the content area (e.g., work samples that show high percentage correct to balance out poor performance on a timed test).

4. Application and Generalization

This action identifies what activities will be employed to enhance the learning and drive home the acquisition of skills beyond the single lesson. The teacher can either identify specific actions to be taken as part of the ongoing instruction or identify the upcoming lessons that will teach the students to apply and generalize the learning in the future. Some examples:

- Use data from M&M lesson to develop a report on the color of candy and consumer choices.
- Take field trip to the city's sewer treatment plant to discover how water is treated and prepared for drinking in their own community compared to a large city.
- Conduct fund-raising campaign to practice collecting money, accounting for the money, and using money for paying debts and purchasing items.

The Generalization and Application of learning is very important in that it provides the opportunity to put learning into context of the real world or future learning. Often students with disabilities lose the skills they learn when these skills are not reinforced across settings or within their own lives. Providing opportunities for the student to generalize information from one setting to another increases the chances that the student will remember and be able to use the information in the future.

5. Closure

This action refers to how the teacher will bring the instructional period to an end or at least to a transition point for new learning. Here, the teacher identifies how to wrap up, or finalize the instruction and lead into the next level of instruction. The Closure might be in the form of a simple transition from one content area activity to another or it might be a final piece that pulls together learning that has occurred over time. Either way, the teacher wants to use actions that highlight the most important aspects of the learning and prepare the students for the next phase of learning. Some examples:

- Have students clean up supplies, return to desk and then ask review questions to double check understanding; explain how this activity will be used next week; get them prepared for math;

- Complete the Learned column of the KWL to document what students have learned;
- Have students predict how they will use mean, median, and mode in their science classes.

The Closure actions can pull student's into the focus of the instruction for one last time. It provides an opportunity to recheck understanding or skills. The Closure action also provides an opportunity to address issues of the adaptive behaviors such as transition and preparation for class. The teacher can ensure that the student will be ready to transition from one activity to another if there is a specific action taken that highlights or emphasizes that a change is about to occur.

A Note on Assessment

Although assessment will be addressed more fully in Chapter 8, it is critical to recognize its importance at this stage in the process. Assessment is essential for both teacher decision-making and student performance. It must be on-going and considered at each and every point in the instructional process. No longer is it adequate to merely give a grade or mark at the end of a sequence; rather data from every aspect of instruction must be used.

Therefore, it is understood that assessment occurs during any and all actions of the instruction. During the Introduction, the teacher can collect data on what a student or group of students knows before instruction begins. While Direct Teaching, the teacher can observe, take anecdotal notes, or collect students' work completed during the modeling. The Practice and Generalization actions provide plenty of opportunities to collect data from work samples, demonstrations, projects, or paper and pencil tests. The Closure offers one last chance to check for understanding through activities such as asking questions, student explanations, or final journal entries.

In **Exhibit 7.1** on the following page, the teacher has outlined the basic actions to be taken when teaching the Case Study: Nicholas and mean, median, and mode lesson plan. Notice how the teacher connected sports immediately to the learning by using the topic in the Introduction. In addition, the teacher has organized the Explicit Teaching to teach the easiest concept first (mode), use visual models, and incorporate five model examples before having the students practice on their own. During the Practice time, the teacher pairs up students so they can check for understanding. In the Closure, the teacher expects the students to reflect on how the math concepts are relevant to other content and life areas. The teacher has embedded important teaching actions that will help Nicholas and others be successful in the learning.

 Use **BLM 14** to complete the Instructional Actions section of your lesson plan.

Exhibit 7.1 Lesson Plan Part I - Instructional Activities for Case Study

Instructional Actions	Teacher		Responsibilities
	Mrs. M. (Gen. Ed)	Mr. E. (Spec Ed)	
Advanced Organizer or Introduction Discuss sports scores and their meanings; tests %s; gallop polls; why we use certain types of numbers to report data.			
Explicit (Direct) Teaching On overhead, as each concept is introduced, MODEL 5 problems of each: mode, median, mean - in that order. Go to practice after introducing each concept.			
Practice Word problems - sheets with 5 more problems of each concept. Pair up for checking answers; Practice mode - after mastery move to median, then mean.			
Generalization and Application Will lead to M&M lesson using 3 concepts for colors in bags and how M&M company uses that data to sell M&M's.			
Closure Ask them to journal, then share how they will use the mean, median, mode in the future. Draw examples.			

Responsibilities

Now that the Instructional Actions have been defined, the last phase of differentiation can be completed. As mentioned in the introduction to this book, there are two different scenarios in the Responsibilities section that must be addressed. In some teaching situations an individual teacher bears the majority, if not all, of the responsibility for designing, implementing, and assessing differentiated instruction. Other situations allow for more than one teacher, or the teacher and other service providers, to work together to design, implement, and assess the differentiated instruction. In this section of the chapter these two different scenarios will be briefly discussed as part of the completion of the lesson planning process: Responsibilities.

Teachers Working Alone

In some respects, for the teacher implementing the differentiated instruction alone, Responsibilities is the easiest part of the process. Here the teacher simply identifies who is responsible for the implementation of the _Instructional Actions_. The teacher working alone has two choices for assigning responsibilities for those actions. One choice is for the teacher to assign all the responsibilities to herself. The second choice is for the teacher to assign limited responsibilities for instruction to the students within the room. This option is used more often when the students are older (e.g., middle school or high school) and the teacher has modeled and taught the students how to "be the teacher". Obviously, the teacher still bears full responsibility for the instruction, but involving the students in the instruction offers variety to the students and creates a sense of ownership in the learning for the students.

In the Responsibilities section of the Differentiated Lesson Plan Guide - Part 2 Instructional Actions, there are three columns. The teacher uses these to outline what actions she will take to make sure the instruction and differentiations are completed. The teacher is as specific as possible, creating a picture of what she will do during each of the Instructional Actions to support learning. In the first column the teacher always identifies the actions she will take. The second and third columns are meant for note taking. Often, in the second, the teacher indicates supporting information such as where she will get certain materials or ideas for implementation. Sometimes, in the third column, the teacher indicates how the instruction parallels other work the students are completing in other settings. Several examples follow.

Exhibit 7.2 on the following page, provides an example of how a special education teacher, working in a self-contained classroom, completed the Responsibilities portion of her lesson plan. Notice how she included ways she was going to acquire resources from others in the general education classroom to support her own actions and how her work is paralleling work in the general classroom.

Exhibit 7.2 Lesson Plan Part II - Instructional Activites for Case Study

Instructional Actions	Teacher		Responsibilities
	ME!		
Advanced Organizer or Introduction			
Ask students where they get air they breathe and how they think new air is produced. Air pollution. Remind them of the notes from last class.	Prior to class make sure chart paper and markers are ready, have pre-made pictures of the 7 components; create vocabulary sheet. Rewrite text pieces if necessary.	Get information from science teacher on the roundhouse diagram of the nitrogen cycle and modify it to meet the comprehension level of the students.	
Explicit (Direct) Teaching			
Use chart paper, draw or place pictures of each of the major layers of the nitrogen cycle and discuss each. Discuss each of the 3 components in detail.	Check students for materials needed for class as they come in.	Use text book materials from gen. ed. class, but use small portions and rewrite if necessary.	
Practice	Lesson will likely take 2 - 3 days so move at their pace. Introduce components as they were able to identify them in the beginning KWL.		
Students create their own nitrogen cycle and label the components.	Give them option of drawing, building, writing about the cycle.		
Generalization and Application	Make sure to use journals as they end each day to capture ideas and practice writing!		
Discuss ways to reduce carbon dioxide in the air; analyze their neighborhood for good/bad situations.			
Closure			
Start a research project on one activity to change how the school contributes to the problem.			

Exhibit 7.3 on the following page, provides an example of how a general education teacher, implementing the instruction alone, completed his lesson plan. Notice how she accessed information from other professionals to develop the plan and incorporated the use of a technique taught to her by the gifted and talented teacher.

The idea behind this section, for the teacher working alone, is to put the finishing details on paper. By placing the specific actions on paper, the teacher has a script to follow when implementing differentiated instruction. This script can serve as a reflective journal for the teacher after the instruction is complete. The teacher can revisit the Instructional Actions and Responsibilities sections to identify what was completed, as well as what did and did not work. Such reflection is particularly helpful for the teacher when she is first attempting to implement differentiated instruction because it provides a visual prompt for what was successful as well as what changes will improve her instruction in the future.

 If you are a teacher implementing the differentiated instruction alone, use **BLM 14** to complete the Responsibilities section of your lesson plan.

Teachers Working Collaboratively

In an ideal situation, the teachers and other professional(s) who will be providing services to students with disabilities are planning and completing the lesson plan together. At this point, the teachers must decide who will be responsible for implementing the different types of actions and differentiated aspects of the instruction.

On the Differentiated Lesson Plan Guide Part 2 there are three columns under the heading Responsibilities. Each column represents one person involved in the planning and implementation process. Typically there are only two people (e.g., the general education and special education; general education and speech pathologist) involved in implementing differentiated instruction. Sometimes there are other service providers also involved in some part of the planning and implementation. The Guide provides a third column for those instances when more than two teachers or specialists are working together at one time.

To determine who will be responsible for what actions in a differentiated lesson, the teacher considers the action to be taken, the differentiation needed (if any), and the person best suited to implement it. Here, the final decisions are made related to the adults involved in the instruction and documented in columns. The columns reflect a brief description of what each person will do related to the instructional actions and the need for differentiation.

To complete this part of the guide, identify the persons involved in the lesson at the top of each column. Underneath each name and across from each activity indicate what the person will do and be responsible for throughout the instruction. The information should be as descriptive as possible so that everyone involved has a picture of what will be done. If a teacher is going to focus on a student or group of students, save space by using the students' initials.

Exhibit 7.3 General Education Teacher Working Alone

Instructional Actions	Teacher	Responsibilities
Advanced Organizer or Introduction Introduce how we will use the game paper, rock, scissors to explore experimental and theoretical probability.	Check homework. Seat them in 4s. Demo the game if necessary. Model how to collect the information. Discuss and demonstrate vocabulary.	
Explicit (Direct) Teaching Introduce vocabulary, game, demonstrate how to collect data appropriately; model graphing results.	Several students will need to use the computer to graph information. G & J will likely need a partner to help input data.	
Practice Let them play game, collect data, graph, predict based on data; double check results.	W. will need pictures of paper, rock, scissors to point to because of limited physical movement. Get these fro spec. ed. teacher.	Sp. Ed. teacher said to have him point to paper, rock, scissors.
Generalization and Application Use theoretical probability of same game; tree diagram of possible outcomes; how will we use probability in our lives every day?	B. needs to do something completely different. See GT teacher.	GT teacher said to compress the info for B. by testing him out of it and provided a few other probability activities that are a higher level of calculation and comprehension to use with B. if he tests out of the simple level of implementation.
Closure Students explain their understanding of prob. Begin assignment on creating a research project on prob.		

If you are having difficulty picturing the different ways teachers might collaborate to teach an instructional lesson, see **Appendix A, Models of Collaborative Teaching,** which provides a description of three commonly used models and examples from elementary, middle and high schools.

In **BLM 15,** the general education teacher has worked with the special education teacher to outline the responsibilities for teaching the Case Study: Nicholas and mean, median, and mode lesson plan. Notice how the two teachers have shared the responsibilities for teaching the whole class, providing models, and checking for understanding. They determined that the special education teacher could provide the introduction and teach a specific process for note taking, which was one area of need for Nicholas. The general education teacher decided to be the one to model each method for the math concept, while the special education teacher wrote the instructions for each method on chart paper. The chart paper will provide a visual cue for Nicholas and other students later on when they may need a reminder. The special education teacher will hand out the practice word problems and make sure the students understand them. Both teachers will work with individual students during the practice session to check for accuracy and understanding. The special education teacher will pay particular attention to the students who might have more trouble (N, S, & B) while the general education teacher works with other students.

 Using **BLM 14,** complete the Responsibilities section of your lesson plan.

What have you created?

Using the Differentiated Lesson Plan Guide Part 2: Instructional Actions, you have created a detailed picture of the specific Instructional Actions necessary to complete the differentiated instruction and have outlined who will be responsible for ensuring that each action is completed as planned. This picture should include enough information so that any teacher could pick up the plan and know precisely what to do for each Instructional Action.

Notice in the completed version of the Part 2 for Nicholas and mean, median and mode, **BLM 15,** that the Instructional Actions are clear and easy to follow and that the responsibilities of both teachers are very specific for each action. The original plans from the curriculum are still in place. The teachers will be teaching about mean, median, and mode using double-digit numbers. The specific needs of the student are being met through a variety of differentiations including modeling of specific vocabulary or processes, specific approaches to the mathematics problem solving, use of a timer for transitions, use of sports examples, checking for readiness for class, and adjusted reading level of mathematics problems. None of these differentiations interferes with the teaching of the content and it is likely that all of the changes will improve not only Nicholas' success, but the performance of other students who have similar needs.

By now, if you have been completing each of your Work Areas from Chapters 3 - 7, you will have planned an effective differentiated instructional lesson plan for your content area and the students you serve. Your lesson plan should be complete with a sound content focus, appropriate differentiated instructional designs, and specific responsibilities for each person involved in the teaching of the lesson. Before you embark on the teaching experience, spend a few minutes reading Chapter 8, which outlines the final step in the process, *Step 7: Plan, Implement, Assess and Refine*.

Chapter 8

Pulling It All Together

Using the information in prior chapters the teacher has completed the primary steps toward differentiated instruction. Using the Process for Differentiating Instruction flow chart, **Exhibit 8.1** on the next page, there is one step left: *Step 7: Plan, Implement, Assess, and Refine*. This step takes the teacher to the point of teaching the lesson she has designed, determining how effective it was, and making decisions on how to improve her planning and implementation for the next lesson.

Chapter 8 outlines some details for the stages of Step 7. This chapter offers specific pointers for implementing differentiation that will help avoid common pitfalls and shows how to use the process for improving both student and teacher performance. In the section on Planning, there are important points of advice to consider *after* the lesson is designed, but *before* the teacher steps into the classroom to use differentiation, particularly for the first time. These pointers were collected through personal experience and interviews with hundreds of classroom teachers who have implemented differentiated instruction. The Implementation section offers ideas of what and how to collect information while implementing the differentiated lesson. In the Assessment section there are specific questions posed to help the teacher determine the effectiveness of the instructional lesson. The final section, Refinement, focuses the teacher on decisions for improving future instruction. Within the chapter there are references to tools that might be helpful when working through *Step 7*.

The purpose of this step in the process is to ensure that the teacher takes time to evaluate the entire picture of differentiation, including sound instructional practices, important content, and student success. This step will enable the teacher to make decisions on the next phase of instruction and will loop her back into the differentiation process at the appropriate step for improving differentiation.

Exhibit 8.1 Process for Differentiated Instruction

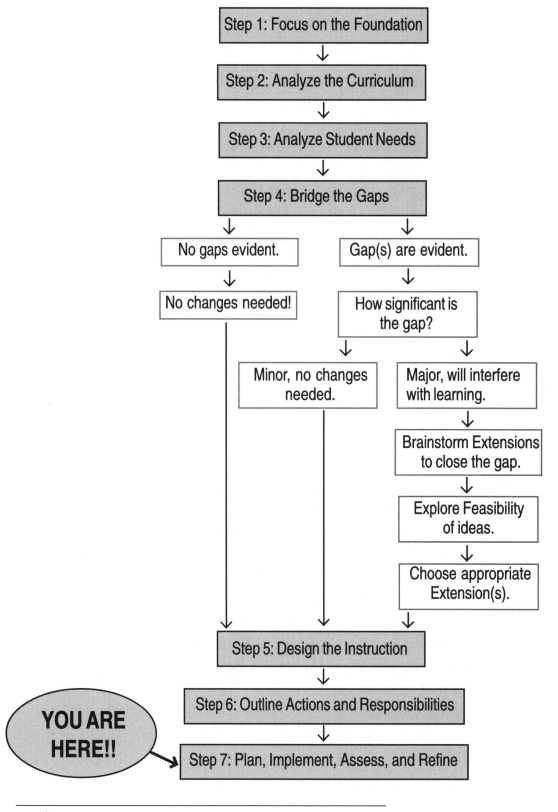

Plan for Instruction

There are several important points to consider before implementing the differentiated lesson plan. The first set of pointers are important for both the teacher who is working alone and the teachers who are working collaboratively. Additionally, there are a few important considerations that teachers who are collaborating must take into account. These are listed as *Team Issues* at the end of this section.

Pointers as the Teacher Prepares

Make sure everything is READY!

Materials and other types of modifications that are outlined on the lesson plan must be ready before instruction begins. A teacher must not wait until she is in the middle of instruction to gather materials or make the modifications that are listed on the lesson plan. For example, if the lesson plan calls for reading passages on the fifth grade level, then she must make sure to <u>have</u> those passages ready. There will be some times where she might need to make an unplanned modification during instruction, but having the planned modifications ready prior to instruction is critical for smooth implementation of the lesson plan.

Rehearse the lesson.

If a teacher is working on her own, she should take a few minutes, when the students are not in the room, to run a mental "dress rehearsal" to determine if what is planned makes sense and will work in the classroom, with the materials at hand. If teachers are working together, they should double check their understanding of how and when each teacher will implement her part(s) of the lesson and how each extension will be provided.

Develop a plan to collect data.

Because this is a new journey toward differentiation, the teacher will want to know if it is working or not. Particularly in the first few months of implementing differentiation she should ask: "How will I know if the instructional design worked?" Many times teachers rely only on the student outcomes (e.g., worksheets, journals) for this information. However, there is more to effective instruction than just students completing assignments. There are three primary areas from which data should be collected during the instruction: Student Progress, Teacher Responsibilities, and Instructional Effectiveness. It is important for the teacher to plan ahead of time how she will collect this information.

• <u>What to collect on Student Progress</u>.

During instruction the teacher will want to collect information on (a) students' progress toward the goals of instruction, (b) use of the extensions by students, including students for whom the extensions were not initially intended, and (3) the effectiveness of the differentiations tried during the lesson. If students are not making progress or if the differentiations are not effective, the teacher needs to know what changes to make for the next instructional plan. Common types of data teachers collect concerning Student Progress include: traditional work samples or projects, anecdotal records during the instruction focusing on the students' use of the differentiation, and private discussions with the students to gain their perspective on the usefulness of the differentiation.

Collecting such data is important because it can be used to generate new ideas as the teacher returns to the beginning of the differentiation process. The data should provide new insight as to the foundation of differentiation as it is outlined in the Differentiated Instruction Pyramid, the Essential Curriculum Questions, and the Essential Student Questions. The more the teacher knows about the students the better focused she can be on the content, instruction, and assessment to meet their unique needs.

In addition, this information will make the steps of the differentiation process easier. Student data collected during instruction will provide new information for the Essential Curriculum Questions and the Essential Student Questions. The more the teacher knows about the students, the better she can identify bridges and gaps in instruction. The better the gap analysis, the better the instructional design!

• <u>What to collect on Teacher Responsibilities</u>.

When working on her own, there are two things a teacher wants to know: Did I complete the instructional actions as planned? Did I implement the differentiation as planned? Examining how well the plan was executed allows the teacher to adjust future lessons. The teacher identifies her capabilities within differentiated instruction (e.g., teaching styles, comfort level with the change) and adjusts accordingly.

When teaching a lesson collaboratively, teachers will want to pay attention to how each teacher meets their assigned responsibilities. If one or both teachers fail to complete some aspect of their assigned roles in the instruction, it is likely that the lesson will not be as effective as planned. It is important to collect this information so the teachers can discuss the issue after the instruction to determine what happened and consider changes to their next plan based on that information.

• <u>What to collect on Instructional Effectiveness</u>.

Along with student progress and teacher responsibilities, the teacher will want to attend to the overall effectiveness of the instruction. Some common questions on instructional effectiveness include: Did the instruction produce the desired results? Was the instruction efficient? Would I use this lesson or differentiation again under similar situations?

The teacher needs to know if the students learned what was planned for them to learn. Sometimes a perfectly executed lesson plan creates results very different from what the teacher intended. If this is the case, the teacher must make adjustments to either the instruction or to the outcomes for the next instruction in the sequence.

It is also important to analyze the efficiency of a lesson. In an ideal world the teacher would have unlimited time, materials, and support to implement instruction. In the real world the teacher lives with limited time, resources, and supports. If a differentiated lesson requires a strategy that takes an inordinate amount of time, resources, or supports, the teacher may want to return to the gap analysis and feasibility stages of the process to identify a different strategy that might be more efficient.

In addition, the teacher should look at lessons for their usefulness in the future. If she has developed a differentiated lesson that worked well for all the students, she can keep that lesson or a particular strategy from that lesson and use it in the future. Teachers find this particularly helpful when they teach the same content every semester (or year) and often have students in each classes who need similar strategies. Some examples:

One strategy a math teacher found worth using again was putting math materials in gallon size zip bags with the students' names on them. This strategy was originally implemented to help a few students who had trouble keeping their materials organized, but it helped all the students in the room and made for easier storage. This teacher found that she often had students who had poor organizational skills in her classes so she still uses this organizational procedure for her students when necessary.

One strategy used as a form of differentiation in a series of lessons in reading a long passage was "popcorn reading". Basically popcorn reading allows all students to randomly read aloud different words that "speak to them" from a passage or poem. This "popping" of words from the text allows the students to experience the overall flavor of a piece before reading it verbatim. The words can be as basic as "the" or "and", or as complex as the highest vocabulary word in the piece. This strategy was used to allow the students who were not reading on the actual level of the passage to be part of the reading. The students could pick simple words already within their repertoire. In addition, the strategy allowed the students to hear words from the passage prior to reading them, and not feel intimidated by the passage. The teacher found that using this technique before reading the passage word-for-word increased the confidence and reading comprehen-

*sion of all the students in the room and decreased the reading anxiety level
of many students, including some who were not initially the aim of the
differentiation. She continues to use this strategy in her classes.*

- How to collect the data.

Collecting information on the students, teacher responsibilities, and instruction requires that the teacher be an active investigator, meaning she must collect data as the instruction transpires. Such data collection is called "On-the-Spot" collection. On-the-Spot collection refers to how a teacher, while teaching, garners data that will help her determine what worked in the lesson and what did not. On-the-Spot collection is important because it allows the teacher to collect information that, if undocumented when it occurs, might be overlooked by the teacher when analyzing the effectiveness of the lesson at a later time.

The teacher wants to use a simple system to collect data during the instruction. Data collection can take many forms. Some common formats include anecdotal records, student work samples or performances, journals, video tapes, and running records. The method for collecting data will depend upon the teacher and the type of data to be collected. For example, one teacher used a notebook that she carried with her throughout the room as she conducted the lesson. As events occurred that she thought were of importance she would jot them down. Another teacher used a clipboard and sheet of printer labels. She would write different information down on each label. Later, he transferred them to the inside of a folder according to the area of impact - student, teacher, or instruction. For example:

Doing the KWL took 15 minutes instead of 5! (Instruction)

*Brian chose to use the dark lined paper for his math calculations
and had 100% - usually gets 50%. (Differentiation/Stdt Progress)*

*Forgot to model the technique on the overhead - had to go back and
do this after many got frustrated. Should have done as planned -
would have saved time (Teacher responsibility)*

BLM 16, On-the-Spot Data Collection, offers a note taking guide for collecting data that the teacher might find useful the first time she is planning to collect specific data from the instruction. By planning ahead of time to collect information on the success of the lesson the teacher will know specifically what to watch for during and after instruction. She can identify simple ways to collect the information (e.g., using sticky notes at various points of the instruction to jot down ideas, concerns) and prevent lost opportunities. The more she knows about the instruction and its impact, the better able she is to adjust and improve future instruction.

Decide how to "introduce" differentiation.

It is important to consider how to introduce the use of differentiated instruction if such instruction is drastically different from what the teacher normally uses with the students. Two common concerns or questions often arise before teachers implement differentiated instruction:

- How do I/we explain differentiated instruction to students and parents?
- How do I/we explain to students and parents why two teachers are working together in the same room?

To inaugurate students and parents to the use of differentiated instruction the old adage, "the best defense is a good offense", works well. The teacher should plan to address the issue if necessary on the first day of school or implementation. The best way to explain differentiated instruction is to share with the students and parents her desire to improve <u>each</u> and <u>every</u> student's learning. The teacher must share her philosophy on providing students with the tools they need to learn, explaining that every student will need different tools at different times. Remember, the effective instruction with differentiations is not just designed for the student with special needs, but should be open for other students too!

- <u>Explaining to students</u>.

    The teacher should emphasize the importance of each student attending to his own needs and not comparing himself to other students in the room. Usually, once the teacher has told and shown the students that each of them will get to use whatever tools or techniques are necessary to be successful, the students pay little attention to the differentiations around them.

    The amount of emphasis on this issue changes depending upon the age/grade level of the students and how much prior exposure they have had to this type of instruction. For example, at the kindergarten level the teacher can simply explain that each student will use what they need, emphasizing individual differences as strengths (which is part of the curriculum!), and help each student identify the tools they need to get their work done. At the high school level, students are often a harder audience, particularly if they have been inculcated to competitive school environments. Often teachers use role playing and lessons on fairness to help students understand the ideas behind each student needing something different to be successful.

The teacher must also practice what she preaches. As she implements the differentiated instruction she must ensure that all students are progressing and using the tools they need to be successful. It is important that the teacher not get locked into using effective strategies only for students with disabilities or gifts. For example, if a listening center has been set up with the content textbook on tape for a particular student with reading disabilities, the teacher should remember that other students might also benefit from listening to the text while reading it and allow them to use the center as appropriate.

• <u>For parents</u>.

As with the students, the first thing the teacher needs to do when addressing parents is share her philosophy of teaching. When speaking with or writing to parents, she must focus on her desire to ensure that their child will be in a classroom where a wide variety of strategies are being used so that every student will be successful. It is sometimes necessary to explain that in a differentiated classroom competitiveness is downplayed and uniqueness is highlighted. In 23 years, working with the richest and poorest schools in the nation, I have never had a parent complain about the fact that their child was getting what he needed when differentiated instruction was used. In fact, in many schools, parents of students who did not have significant needs made special requests to have their child placed in classrooms where differentiated instruction was used, because they had come to realize the benefits to being in such a positive learning environment.

• <u>Special Issues where there are two teachers</u>.

When two teachers are working collaboratively in one learning environment they must set the stage for mutual respect and purpose from the very beginning. Students and parents must understand that both teachers are highly skilled individuals who are working toward improving the learning of each student in the room. It must be clear to the students and parents that <u>both</u> teachers are working as one to create the most effective learning environment possible and that they carry equal weight and responsibility in managing, teaching, grading, and decision making within the classroom.

When explaining the collaborative situation to the students it is important not only to explain the benefits of having two teachers in the room, but to impress upon the students that both teachers have equal authority. Such explanation avoids the students trying to "play" one teacher off another and deflects mixed messages of power within the classroom.

With the parents, the best way to explain this situation is to tell them that there are two highly skilled professionals ready to help each student learn. Sometimes the teachers feel it is necessary to offer an explanation of each teacher's role. The following excerpt from a letter sent home to parents is an excellent way to explain role differences.

We have exciting news! Your child will have two teachers in his/her classroom to help the children learn. One of us is an expert in all the content areas your child will need to learn this year. The other is an expert on learning strategies that help students learn difficult information. We will work together to ensure that your child has great learning strategies to use when learning new content! Plus, with two of us in the room we can answer twice as many questions in half the time!

• <u>Addressing disabilities</u>.

      Often teachers feel compelled to address the issue of students with disabilities being served in a general classroom. In many schools this aspect of differentiated instruction is no longer an issue because so many students with disabilities are integrated into general classrooms from the kindergarten level that the students without disabilities no longer see it as unique. There will be some instances, however, when the teacher will likely want to address the uniqueness of a student with a disability to the entire class. This is particularly true when the student has specific physical or medical needs that will be evident no matter what modifications are provided (e.g., continuous medical assistance) or when the students without disabilities in the class have not had previous exposure to students with such disabilities.

      For example, one of my students had a specific genetic hip disorder that prevented her from walking upright. She used both her feet and her hands for walking. She was new to the school and while there were other students with physical disabilities in the school, there had not been any other student like her there before. Another student had epilepsy which was not completely under the control of medicine. He had frequent episodes that required immediate medical attention. In both instances we felt it was important to discuss these differences with the class.

      There are different theories or beliefs on how to facilitate understanding, respect, and relationships between students without disabilities and those who have disabilities. Some theories advocate for letting the students learn about each other in facilitated activities (e.g., role playing, 20 questions). Others suggest telling the students without disabilities about the student with disabilities before he comes in to the classroom. The strategy I used in my classrooms depended upon the age of the student with the disability, his comfort level in discussing his gifts and uniqueness, and the age and maturity of the students without disabilities. The most successful strategy I used was a combination of both open discussion and discovery.

      It is important to note that the teacher must tread carefully when addressing issues of students with disabilities being in general education classrooms. The majority of students with disabilities who are in general education classrooms *will not* have disabilities so obvious or severe that the issue should be addressed with the entire class. For example, it is not necessary, nor legal, to point out that a student has a reading learning disability. In fact, two federal laws, the Family Educational Rights to Privacy Act (FERPA) and Individuals with Disabilities Education Act (IDEA), require that without parental permission, personally relevant information is not communicated to others. If a teacher feels that a student's disability is such that the entire class should know about it for purposeful reasons (e.g., potential medical attention), the teacher should first get permission in writing from the parent.

There should be *no instance* in a differentiated classroom when the students with disabilities are segregated physically (e.g., taught only in the corner of the room) or on paper (e.g., list of grades separated into non-disabled and disabled). In fact, in a true differentiated classroom an observer should be able to walk into the classroom and not be able to tell which students are disabled and which are not.

Decide on a Grading System.

The teacher should plan grading strategies ahead of time by deciding what to grade, how to grade it, and how to communicate those grades to students and parents. There has yet to be written a really good book on grading and differentiated instruction. However, there are several books on grading that can be applied to differentiated instruction which may be helpful, most notably that by K.O'Connor, as cited in the Bibliography. What follows are issues the teacher should consider when deciding on a grading system.

• What to grade.

Remember, there is a difference between grading and feedback. Nearly everything a student does deserves some form of feedback, but not everything should be graded. The teacher should look at the objectives and assessment outlined on her lesson plan as a guide in deciding what to grade. If it is not listed there and does not match the specific objectives of the plan, then it likely does not need to be graded. Save grading for the tests, projects, products, and presentations that represent significant milestones in the students' learning.

• How to grade.

There are two issues to consider in how to grade students: how to grade individual pieces of work and how to calculate overall grades for report cards. In a differentiated classroom, students will be working on the same content area, but may be going about it in very different ways. Some students will be working on very different goals than others. For example, one student may be working primarily on improving the grammar of his writing while another may be working on the content of his writing piece. Such differences often concern a teacher because she wants the grading to represent what the student is doing in relationship to his own work and not the work of others, but she knows that students will notice the differences. As mentioned above, communicating a teaching philosophy that promotes individual performance not group competition helps alleviate the problem of students comparing grades. Beyond the teaching philosophy, the teacher must communicate the grading process to the students.

For individual pieces of student work, scoring rubrics and rating scales are some of the best tools for grading. They provide details around which teachers can make decisions and offer very specific feedback to the students for improving their performance. Some teachers write a short phrase with grades when the grade does not represent assessment of the total product (e.g., "graded as first draft", "graded for content"). There are also grading stamps that help define how certain grades or feedback were developed or defined. For example, one grading stamp offers the teacher the following:

Graded only for:

❑ **spelling**

❑ **grammar**

❑ **content**

❑ **effort**

❑ **sentence structure**

(Note: This stamp was found at a teachers' convention, with no company identification. This or any stamp you design can be made by any company that produces ink stamps for envelopes.)

In relation to calculating overall grades for report cards, the teacher's decisions are sometimes mandated by local school policies (e.g., percentages, checklists). In some school districts, teachers are allowed to develop their own methods for calculating grades. (O'Connor's *Grading for Learning* provides multiple scenarios on how to develop grades for report cards and those ideas will not be featured here.)

• How to communicate grades.

The teacher must decide how she will relate grades to students and parents. Will it be symbols such as letters (A, B, C) or numbers (1, 2, 3), or written dialogue (reflection boxes)? The teacher should use a system that best reflects the age and needs of the students. No matter what the system, it should be carefully explained to parents and students. In a differentiated classroom the teacher typically finds that using a combination of symbols and written dialogue effectively communicates grades because the instruction and progress of each student becomes so individualized that a symbolic grade alone would not represent his whole progress.

Every teacher has a different method to address these three grading issues. Therefore, it is extremely important for teachers working collaboratively to discuss and decide on their preferred methods before beginning instruction.

Failure to decide on a grading system prior to implementation can create problems that are often difficult to resolve after the fact. It is possible that the grading plan a teacher outlines may change once she implements the instruction, but usually that change is an improvement over the original plan. To have no plan sets the teacher up for problems when she must address the differences in student performance using differentiated instruction.

Start Small.

One of the biggest mistakes teachers make when implementing differentiated instruction for the first time is to either try to change too much at one time or differentiate in too many different places before they have the basics down. Applying this process to every single content area of every class period at once would be a daunting task. Start small by beginning with one class period or one content area. The teacher should get the system of differentiation down and her comfort level up before adding new content or classes to her repertoire.

- Team Issues.

It would be impossible to over emphasize how important it is that teachers who are implementing instruction together in a collaborative situation discuss in detail very specific aspects of the collaborative work that is about to begin. Beyond the pointers provided above, veteran collaborative teachers offer the following pointers for teachers working together for the first time.

Prepare for the mistakes.

The first few times you implement this type of instruction it is very likely that there will be some mistakes. That is all part of the learning process. Consider how you will handle important missteps during the instruction. Discuss up front how you plan to handle the situation if something major comes up during instruction.

For example, Mrs. Carroll and Ms. Melton had agreed that if something big came up during instruction, either teacher could call for a huddle in which they would quickly whisper to each other what was wrong and generate a solution. They had to use that huddle plan in the following situation: on Monday one teacher taught the students that the x axis of a graph was the vertical line and the y axis was the horizontal line. On Tuesday, the other teacher when reviewing the learning from Monday said the opposite. Needless to say,the students noticed the teachers had taught x and y axis two different ways. The two teachers called a huddle and came up with a brilliant solution! They turned to the students and said, "Yes! Now you get to prove one of us wrong!" The students immediately dove into their books to research the problem. The teachers' huddle plan allowed them to develop a positive solution to a potentially embarrassing mistake.

Discuss Management Styles.

When two teachers start working together the dynamics are very important. Sometimes simple issues cloud the teachers' ability to work together, if they are not discussed up front. For example, one teacher does not want students getting up to sharpen pencils during instruction and the other allows it. A student gets up to sharpen his pencil and loses points for being out of his seat. Such a simple issue can cause problems if the teachers do not discuss it up front. Often the students get caught in the middle and suffer from the differences in management.

Research conducted by Moll (1996) identified six pivotal areas that can interfere with effective collaboration if not discussed prior to implementation:

- Routines and Procedures - the day-to-day methods each teacher uses to create smooth flow in the classroom;

- Room Arrangement - the organization, storage, and use of furniture, equipment, and materials;

- Student Supervision - the methods used to manage the students as they work including rules, reinforcement, and expectations;

- Instructional Planning, Implementation and Evaluation - the ways each teacher approaches each area (e.g., teaching style, grading, use of textbooks);

- Communication and Working with Instructional Assistants - how each teacher works with adult assistants, including their role in instruction and classroom discipline; and

- Communication and Interaction with Parents - the way each teacher prefers to work with parents of students in the room.

To help address these issues, a tool was developed for teachers who are just beginning to collaborate. The tool, **Appendix B, Defining Management Styles,** lists a series of questions under each of the six areas. Each teacher answers these questions independently and then shares her answers with her partner. During the discussion, the teachers are able to identify areas where they agree and potential problem areas. The idea is to use the tool to find those differences and come to some consensus on how to address those differences so that they do not interfere with student learning.

Find Time to Plan Together.

One of the most common complaints of teachers working collaboratively is the lack of time to plan together for their instructional lessons. It is important that the teachers candidly discuss their need for common time to plan with the appropriate administration. While it sometimes takes Houdini-like skill to coordinate schedules, administrators can usually find some common time for the teachers. However, sometimes it requires a little creativity. In the **Appendix C, Creative Ways to Make Time,** offers some real life examples of how other teams have created time for planning.

Communicate.

Perhaps the capstone for teachers working collaboratively is open, honest communication. Each teacher should consider it an essential part of the job to talk with her partner about all aspects of the differentiated instruction experience from student progress to personal comfort levels. Learning to communicate with another professional is not always an easy task. It is important for teachers who will be working together to discuss how they would like to communicate with each other, particularly during instruction and when there is a problem that must be addressed after the instruction.

• <u>During instruction.</u>

Discuss methods to signal to each other during instruction concerning problems that arise. For example, consider what you want to do when one or several students in the room are not getting the instruction and one teacher sees it but the other does not. Most teachers would not want to announce that aloud to the class. One team decided to use a "green/red flag" signal. At each desk the students had a green and red flag. The students kept the green flag up when they were understanding instruction but put the red flag up when they started having difficulty understanding something. Each teacher also had a green and red flag she could use. They agreed that either could put up the red flag if it appeared some students were having trouble and a change needed to be made. This signal allowed the teachers to communicate with each other in a non-confrontational manner and modeled the importance of asking questions.

• <u>When there is a problem.</u>

Discuss methods of sharing ideas or issues if some problem arises that cannot be immediately addressed or must be addressed after instruction. Different people prefer different methods of communication. Some prefer face-to-face discussion while others prefer written information with time to deliberate. For example, one high school teacher team liked to address problems immediately in what was called a "standing meeting". They would meet in the hallway, between classes and briefly discuss an issue and decide on a solution to try. In one middle school team, the special education teacher had to leave the room at the end of class and could not stop for a standing meeting. The teachers agreed to write any concern they had during instruction on a post-it and place it on the door frame. If the general education teacher had written it, the special education teacher would pick it up on her way out the door. If the special education teacher had written it, the general education teacher would pick it up between classes. They would meet for lunch and discuss the issue and make changes to instruction before the next day's lesson.

Take time to talk, as often as possible, particularly when you are first implementing instruction together. The tools presented in the next sections may help facilitate that conversation for beginning collaborative teams.

These pointers for planning are very important for the successful implementation of differentiated instruction. Making decisions related to assessment, grading, and management sets the stage for an effective learning environment by outlining the expectations and means of communicating student performance within a differentiated environment. Being mindful of the potential problems by preparing everything in advance, rehearsing the lesson, and mapping out how the differentiation will be addressed with students and parents prevents any unnecessary discontinuity in the lesson or instructional environment. For teachers working collaboratively the conversations and planning together solidify instruction and create a team focused on student outcomes.

Take time now to address each of these pointers in relationship to the implementation of your lesson plan. For example, use **BLM 16, On-the-Spot Data Collection,** to identify the areas for which you will try to collect data during instruction by checking the boxes under each question. If you are working in a team situation, refer to Appendix B, Defining Management Styles, to help work out differences. For the first few times you use this process write down your ideas for each pointer above.

Implementation

Once the teacher has completed the differentiated lesson plan and the planning for implementation she is ready to go! How she implements the instruction will depend upon the type of lesson plan she has developed. Thus, there is little to discuss in this chapter concerning the actual implementation of the lesson. However, there are a two basic pearls of wisdom teachers have passed along for those first attempting differentiation.

• <u>Stay Flexible and Nurture a Sense of Humor</u>.

Flexibility and humor were listed at the most important skills needed by teachers first beginning to implement differentiated instruction according to more than 400 teachers (Moll, 96). The classroom is filled with hundreds of variables that potentially can impact a lesson (e.g., fire drills, announcements, mass absences due to the flu). The teacher should understand that no matter how well an instructional plan is laid out, events beyond her control might interfere with its implementation. Veteran teachers of differentiation recommend learning to "go with the flow", live with the missteps, and focus on the next lesson.

• <u>Do Collect the Data</u>.

Data collection is the first item to be thrown out the window when instruction begins to get busy. Teachers tend to get so immersed in the instructional actions that they do not take time to write information down while the instruction is going on. Many teachers, with all the good intentions in the world, plan to write it down later. Usually it does not get written down or the information is incomplete because so much time has elapsed.

It will take some time to get used to teaching and collecting data at the same time. But it is well worth the effort. Without accurate data the teacher will be teaching without a compass, meaning she may not have a good idea of where the learning is headed. Students may end up learning nothing, or something very different than what the teacher had originally planned. Without the data, the teacher will have difficulty keeping instruction wrapped around the content, students, and authentic assessment of the Differentiated Instruction Pyramid.

You have been planning for this a long time.
Go to WORK!!!! Teach your lesson and do your best to collect the data you identified in the preparation phase.

Analysis of Data

Once the lesson is completed, it is important to take some time to analyze what happened. By looking at the information collected on the students, the teacher's responsibilities, and the effectiveness of the instruction, the teacher can determine what steps to take next. She can use the information to consider immediate steps to improve individual and group performance as well as future use of the lesson in similar situations.

Using the information collected from anecdotal records, student work, and answers to the questions outlined on **BLM 16, On-the-Spot Data,** the teacher can reflect on what happened and draw some conclusions. This information provides both a panoramic view of the instruction and outcomes and detailed information that can be used for content and student-specific decisions in future lesson plans.

When considering the overall effectiveness of the instruction and the outcomes, the teacher can narrow the questions she asks to the following:

❑ To what degree did all students make progress toward the intended goals, using the differentiations provided?

❑ To what degree did I/we complete the instructional actions as planned?

❑ To what degree did the instructional actions and differentiation facilitate the intended results?

❑ Overall, was this an efficient and effective way to deliver this instruction, given the content and students in this classroom?

❑ Based upon this information, what refinement should be made for the next instructional plan?

With each of these questions the teacher reviews all data collected and describes the results. By answering these questions in terms of *degree* it allows the teacher to speak to both the positive results and possible negative findings. For example:

To what degree did the instructional actions and differentiation facilitate the intended results?

The instructional actions worked well - using the steps outlined helped the students progress without frustration.... the differentiations were great - particularly using the text on tapes. Students showed a much higher level of comprehension this time!

To what degree did I/we complete the instructional actions as planned?

We both forgot to redo the reading level of the passages - this resulted in real problems for several students - their behavior went south! S. skipped a step where modeling was needed and it caused a lot of problems... we lost a lot of time reteaching! Need to stick to using the modeling technique!

BLM 17, Data Analysis Notetaking Sheet offers a note-taking sheet for analysis using these questions. This sheet is particularly helpful for teachers working in teams to discuss and write out results.

Notice that the data collected during instruction and the questions used to analyze the data reflect directly back to the first six steps of the Differentiation Process. Attending to the progress of the student, the teacher's implementation, and the success of the lesson provides the teacher with new and specific information to use when starting the process again. She will have new data for the Essential Curricular Questions and Essential Student Questions, new ideas for bridging gaps between the curriculum and the students' needs, and better insight as to specific instructional steps to take in the future. Once the teacher has answered these questions she has the knowledge to move to the final phase of this step in the process for differentiation: Refining Instruction.

 Using **BLM 17, Data Analysis Notetaking Sheet,** analyze the data you collected from your lesson.

Refine the Instruction

The most important question a teacher asks once the data have been analyzed is: What should I do next? The teacher will use her reflections on **BLM 16** to decide how to refine instruction for the future. It is important to note that the questions and answers generated on **BLM 16** are interconnected and a decision on what to do next must be based upon the total picture, or all answers. For example, if the data suggests that the students are not progressing toward the intended goals using the differentiations, there might be several different causes: the teacher may not have completed the instructional actions as planned, the instructional plan itself might not have been efficient, or the differentiations may not have been appropriate.

Based upon the results of the analysis, the teacher can now move toward improving instruction. She will have collected enough information to determine the following:

❏ Is it time to move on to new content or continue to teach the current content?
❏ Do the students need new types of differentiation or can they continue with the current differentiations?
❏ Did these instructional actions work well in this situation, should they be used in future lessons, or should changes be made?
❏ Was the right assessment information collected or are there other assessments that would have provided better information?

For each lesson, analysis of the answers to these questions will be different.

The answers to each of these questions lead the teacher directly back to the beginning of the differentiation process. With new information, the teacher begins considering the new focus of instruction including the essential elements of the curriculum, the needs of the student, and assessment techniques. Data analysis and instructional refinement, in essence, lead the teacher back to the Differentiation Guide Pyramid where the teacher must again decide how to keep her work focused at the top of the pyramid where instructional outcomes have significance for students.

The data analysis after each instructional lesson also provides the teacher with new data that can be used to plan new differentiated instruction to meet the unique needs of the students in her room. She will have data specific to individual students for whom Extensions were designed, data concerning other students' performance within the instructional lesson, and information concerning the students' level of content mastery. All of these will help her complete a new round of planning using the Essential Curriculum Questions, Essential Student Questions, and Gap Analysis.

While it may appear that *Step 7: Plan, Implement, Assess, and Refine* could be broken into four separate pieces, in reality the components are seamless once the teacher becomes accustom to using the entire differentiated instruction process. Teachers who have consistently used this process have become so attuned to this step that they can identify needed refinements as they are in the middle of the teaching. Such refinement creates effective instruction, increased student performance, and a more focused purpose for teaching.

 Using the information from the data analysis, identify areas in which you need to refine instruction, student outcomes, assessment, or the content.

What did you create?

Is your first differentiated lesson perfect? Rarely so. However, using this process increases the likelihood that the lesson plan you created is closer to "perfect" than any you have created before. Each time you implement the process and follow through with all the steps, you will see increased effectiveness in your lessons, which will produce improved student outcomes.

Chapter 9

Research-Based Results: Success with the DIGIT Process

As stated in the Introduction and Overview, Differentiated Instruction (DI) is a gift that gives the teacher the *knowledge* to design differentiated instruction, the *power* to implement the instruction using national and local curricular standards, and the *promise* of improved student performance. The major *premise* for using DI is that ALL children can learn, with the outcome of higher levels of achievement for all learners, regardless of any educational label used to "define" them.

This Chapter is dedicated to the research-based cases of teachers who are using this DIGIT process and the students who are in their classes. All of these cases are research-based in that the teachers were trained to use the DIGIT process and purposefully collected data to measure the changes in student performance. They are across elementary, middle, and high school levels from urban, suburban, and rural schools. They come from schools where "inclusive" education is NOT in "full implementation". Five of the research cases are from teams of teachers who use collaborative teaching models like those described in the Appendix A, while one research case is from a teacher who is not in a collaborative teaching situation. All of these teachers are striving to improve the performance of all students in their classrooms.

The fact that this research is coming from situations where inclusive education is not "perfected" is signifiant because many times teachers will refrain from trying DI until their entire school is in full support of the concept. The important point being that teachers can use this process and have success with student achievement within their classroom, even without full district support for inclusion.

The purpose of this Chapter is to share:

(1)   how teachers are using the DIGIT process at different school levels;

(2)   what types of Extensions/strategies teachers are using to bridge gaps;

(3)   the simplicity of the process;

(4)   the impressive academic results.

Each research case has five sections: Demographics, Background, Extensions, Implementation and Results, and Points to Ponder about the Process and the Outcomes. The Demographics piece outlines the basics of the school, the teaching situation, and highlights the instructional gaps and Extensions used to bridge those gaps. Next, the Background section explains why the teachers engaged this **DIGIT** process. Included in this section are the specific gaps the teachers found using the process. The Extensions section outlines what the teachers decided to use and why the Extension(s) was chosen. The Implementation and Results section explains how the teachers used the Extensions and what happened while using them. The final section, Points to Ponder, provides a summary of the key elements that make this process efficient and effective for meeting the needs of students. It increases academic performance without changing the curriculum or the general landscape of the classroom.

Case 1

Demographics

School Level: Elementary   **Grade**: 1st/2nd Split and 2nd grade

Location: Rural

Teaching Situation – Collaborative – Content/Skill Development Model

Content: Science

Instructional Gap(s) BLM 10: Language, Writing, Learning Styles

Extension Focus BLM 8: Teaching-Learning Style

Background

This collaborative team was planning to teach *classification of mammals' characteristics within a unit on animals*. Using the DIGIT process, the teachers completed the ECQ (BLM 4) and ESQ (BLM 6). Based on that information, they identified 3 basic areas where there would likely be gaps for some of the students in their class. The teachers identified the following gaps.

Gap Analysis Questions (BLM 10)	Area of Gap
Q4:4 Language of Instruction	Five (5) students struggle with the concept of *compare and contrast,* which is how the unit is normally taught – comparing one type of animal subset to another
Q5:5 Reading and /or Writing Skills	Writing full sentences is too complicated for three (3) students when taking notes, which is how it had been taught in the past; these students need visual model with limited writing during concept development
Q7:7 Learning Strategies	Two (2) students struggle taking notes for important content; they do not always know how to identify the most important information; they need organized visual model for important concepts

Extensions Identified for Differentiation

(BLM 8) – Strategies for Learning and Language of Learning

The teachers determined that they needed to approach the learning by providing a *specific strategy* (Learning Strategies gap) for the students to address note taking (Writing Skills gap) and the procedure of comparing and contrasting concepts (Language of Learning gap). The teachers chose the Concept Diagram strategy from the Kansas Learning Strategies. The Concept Diagram strategy provides students with a graphic organizer for organizing data when classifying information. The diagram allows for students to identify the concept, key words, characteristics that are *Always Present, Sometimes Present, and Never Present,* examples and nonexamples, and finally a definition based on that information. The team modified the strategy to fit their needs. They thought the original form seemed too "high schoolish" so they drew pictures on the page to add some interest and provide some visual cues about the topic.

They liked this graphic organizer strategy because they thought it would bridge the gap by:

❑ Q4:4 visually outlining the idea of *compare and contrast* in the Always, Sometimes, Never Present Categories and the Examples and Non Examples Columns;

❑ Q5:5 not requiring students to write complete sentences (use of key words), with the only complete sentence being the final definition; providing a visual model; and

❑ Q7:7 providing the students with a specific strategy or technique to compare what they know and learn about one type of animal (mammals) to others; the team thought this same strategy could be used with the other animal areas to be taught (e.g., fish and birds).

Implementation and Results

The team used this strategy across the study of mammals, birds, and fish. When the Extension was used for the first unit on mammals, the students initially gave multiple characteristics that did not apply to mammals, indicating that they thought most animals were mammals. When studying the next two units (fish and birds) the students gave fewer characteristics in the "Never Present" category each time and more correct characteristics in the "Always Present" category, indicating that they were understanding that not all animals were of one type (e.g., mammals) and could identify the specific characteristics of different animal types more accurately using the compare and contrast concept.

These teachers used ✓-, ✓, and ✓+ on tests to indicate student performance. The ✓- equated with a performance of below 80%, ✓ comparable to 80 – 90%, and ✓+ reflected a 90% or above. The students in the target class typically attained scores across all three check mark levels (from 50% - 100%). The students who were the focus of the Gap Analysis usually scored in the ✓- (50 – 79%) range on written tests. After using the strategy for 3 units, the class performance improved to the ✓ and ✓+ range (80-100%). All students in the class were scoring at least an 80% on the written test indicating that the Extension the teachers used was successful in helping the targeted students improve their performance.

In addition to using this Extension with the targeted class, these teachers chose to use it with an "excelled" class to see if it was a technique that might help this group with learning. The team discovered that the scores of the "excelled" class improved, with more students scoring the in ✓+ range than before. This change in score indicated to the teachers that the strategy was useful to these students also.

A comparison of the scores between the two classes indicated that the academic gap on written tests between the two classes had closed significantly by the end of the third cycle of using the strategy. Prior to using the strategy, the targeted class' average was typically between a ✓- and ✓ (around 78%) and the "excelled" class' average was typically at the high end of the ✓ range (around 88%). By the end of the third cycle, the targeted class' average was around 87% and the "excelled" class' average was around 93%. The average gap in academic score between the two groups prior to using the Extension to fill the gaps was 10 percentage points. Using the DIGIT process, the gap in test score averages between the two classes was reduced to 6 percentage points.

The teachers reported that the implementation of the Extension required a little more planning time in the beginning because it required them to focus on what they were going to cover in the class. However, in the long run, the teachers noted that using the strategy literally gave them more instructional time because they only taught what was important and the students who normally would have required more re-teaching after the initial teaching were successful using the Extension.

Points to Ponder about the Process and the Outcomes

Several points are important to note in the summary of this research case.

1. The teachers used the DIGIT process to identify specific gaps and choose a simple Extension or instructional strategy to bridge the gap. (No complex, high maintenance techniques were employed.)

2. The teachers did NOT change their content or their test methods or types. They contin-

ued to use the typical tests given for these units. (No "dumbing down" of the curriculum. No use of tests that had been modified.)

3. The teachers *changed their behaviors* (by organizing their lecture/discussion around a specific visual method), which in turn changed the students' performance. (They did not "fix" the students' problems; they gave them tools to use for learning.)

4. The students who were targeted in the gap analysis increased their performance levels to at least an 80% level from a 50 – 79% level in the past.

5. The overall performance of the entire class increased by using the strategy. (It was not a "special" strategy just for one student.)

6. The differentiated instruction helped close the performance gap of the targeted class. (It brought their scores in line with more a more "excelled" class.)

7. The "excelled" class benefited from the strategy also. (No child got left behind!)

8. The teachers felt that using the Extension actually increased their instructional time.

Case 2

Demographics

School Level: Elementary   **Grade**: 4th Grade

Location: Suburban

Teaching Situation – Collaborative – Role Exchange Model

Content: All/Writing

Instructional Gap(s) BLM 10: Teaching-Learning Style, Adaptive Behaviors

Extension Focus BLM 8: Adaptive Behavior

Background

    This collaborative team identified one particular student in the class who was posing significantly challenging behaviors including bullying, inappropriate verbal responses, incomplete and poor quality work, and failing to follow classroom rules. The behaviors were present across content areas and in social situations. The teachers were concerned about the behavior and its impact on the student's performance, and the level of disruption it was creating in class. They knew the student was capable of better work but could not determine what was happening to create the poor behaviors.

    Using the **DIGIT** process, the teachers completed the ECQ and ESQ to identify any gaps for differentiating instruction. The major gap they found in their analysis was in Q6:6 Teaching – Learning Style and Q9:9 Adaptive Behaviors.

Gap Analysis Questions (BLM 10)	Area of Gap
Q6:6 Teaching – Learning Style	Student appeared to struggle when left to work independently after large group instruction but did better when given a brief one-one review after large group; typically the teachers used a lot of independent work right after large group
Q9:9 Adaptive Behaviors	One (1) student struggled with appropriate behaviors across content and in social situations (bullying, fighting, few friends); seemed to have poor self esteem and a lot of self doubt when it came to work; teachers questioned whether the amount of independent work might have been triggering the problems in class

Extensions Identified for Differentiation

(BLM 8) – Motivation and Procedures and Routines

The teachers recognized that there were two gaps to address: the jump between large group and independent work; and the motivation level of the student. The first gap was relatively easy to address. The teachers decided to change their method of instruction by ensuring that immediately after large group instruction ended and independent work started, one of them would go directly to this student and his group for a review. (Procedure and Routine Extension). They thought this immediate assistance might prevent the student from becoming frustrated and displaying inappropriate behaviors.

The second issue, the self-esteem, did not seem as simple to resolve. The teachers decided to conduct a survey to determine how often they had positive interactions with the student. What they found was that their positive interactions were almost zero and their negative interactions were phenomenal in nature – as many as twenty during one 45-minute period. The teachers realized this high level of negative interaction might be the crucial gap. They decided to use the 3 for 1 Positive Interaction Strategy (Motivation Extension), as developed by Randy Sprick. This strategy suggests that for every 1 negative interaction a teacher has with a student there should be 3 positive interactions to counterbalance the negative interaction.

Implementation and Results

Because writing is such an important focus in the 4th grade (the first level of state assessments is conducted here and a writing portfolio is a major piece), the teachers decided to implement the change in teaching routine and increase the number of positive interactions with the student, particularly during writing and other content areas when writing was required. They made sure that one of them went directly to this student and the group of students around him to review the writing lesson as soon as large group work was over. They also used that time of review to give the student positive praise (e.g., you can do it, we know you are working hard). They did not provide any material rewards solely to this student, only verbal praise and attention. The teachers did provide material rewards to the class during writing scrimmages.

Just prior to using the DIGIT process, the teacher conducted an Open Response Scrimmage in writing. In this scrimmage, the targeted student produced two incomplete sentences during a thirty-minute period and scored a 0 on the scrimmage. In addition, during this time, he was so disruptive to other students he was removed from the classroom.

First
Scrimmage
0

Reading

7. A. Nice drums beats

B. Makes it sound a
hole lot better

Over the next three weeks the teachers implemented the two strategies and noticed a significant change in the behavior and performance of the student – and other students in the class. The teachers reported that his attitude in the classroom and other social settings improved dramatically, that the bullying had vanished, the student had become somewhat of a leader in the class and was developing friendships. In addition to the improved attitude and behavior, the student's academic work was improving dramatically. On the next writing scrimmage he scored a 4/4 and produced a paper filled with appropriate information, including at least 20 sentences and neat handwriting. See below.

READING ④ Second Scrimmage

5. The first step you would do is get a news paper cut it into squares then you will get some envelopes for whiteness. Now you get some vegtable peelings and dried grass for texture. And some dried herbs for scent. After you do that get a blender if you don't have a blender get a food prossor. Warm water, a spoon, a dish pan; a a piece of window screen smaller than the dishpan, paper towels, some sheets of news paper, and a rolling pin. Then put a handful of news pape the little squares. And bits of other materials into the blender or the food prossor if you fill it half full it is ok. Add some warm water but put in one spoonfull at a time, the blend all the materials together then it should be a mushy pulp. Don't make it too runny. Pour all of the pulp into the dish pan. Add warm water to make sure the dishpan is more than half full then you will need to stir it. Lower the screen into the pulp use both hands when you are lowering the screen into the pulp. Lift the screen out of the pulp. cover the pulp with another paper towel then use the pin rolling to roll exess water from the new piece of paper. Then the last thing you do is put the new piece of paper onto a old piece of paper.

The teachers reported other benefits to using this strategy. They found that other students who had been struggling in writing were also improving in writing. In addition, they found that the overall climate of the classroom become more positive with fewer inappropriate behaviors from other students and more supportive behaviors between students. The teachers attributed these changes to two things. First they found that they were giving more direct review and attention to the struggling students as soon as the large group activity was over so as not to draw complete attention to the targeted student. Second, they found that they were trying very hard to have a high level of positive interactions with all of their students and believe that this positive interaction created a more positive environment for the students.

The teachers reported that the use of the review strategy and 3/1 technique with the targeted student did not take away time from other students. They were able to help several students at a time in most reviews that happened after the large group activity so it was not a one-on-one teaching requirement every time. In fact, they reported that it actually *created more time with other students* because this student's negative behaviors were no longer requiring immediate attention.

Points to Ponder about the Process and the Outcomes

There are several important points to emphasize concerning this research case.

1. The teachers <u>used the DIGIT process</u> to identify specific gaps and choose two simple Extensions to bridge the gap. (No complex, high maintenance techniques were employed.)

2. The teachers <u>did NOT change their content</u> or their requirements for Open Response Scrimmages or appropriate behavior. (No "dumbing down" of the curriculum. No use of tests that had been modified. No "turning the other way" for inappropriate behaviors.)

3. The teachers *changed their behaviors* (by adding in review directly after large group instruction for individual and small groups AND increasing their positive interactions with students), which in turn <u>changed the students' performance</u>.

4. The student who was the target of this process <u>significantly improved both **academic** and **adaptive behaviors**</u>.

5. The overall <u>performance of the entire class increased</u> by using the strategy. (The Extensions did not detract from other students.)

6. The use of the Extensions actually <u>increased instructional time</u> by decreasing time spent on inappropriate behaviors.

7. The Extensions chosen <u>did not cost anything</u> and were easy to implement.

Case 3

Demographics

School Level: Middle School   **Grade**: 6th Grade
Location: Rural
Teaching Situation – Collaborative – Parallel Dedicated Support
Content: Humanities – Practical Living
Instructional Gap(s) BLM 10: Teaching – Learning Style; Learning Strategy
Extension Focus BLM 8: Teaching-Learning Style; Learning Strategy

Background

In this teaching situation, the general education teacher did the majority of the instruction alone. He worked directly with the special education teacher who came into the classroom on a consistent but not necessarily daily basis.

The teachers were frustrated because several of their students who were at-risk or had IEPs were not performing well on class tests. They decided to use the DIGIT process to identify a possible gaps that might be impacting the students' performance. They found there were gaps in Q5:5 Reading/Writing Skills and Q7:7 Learning Strategies.

Gap Analysis Questions (BLM 10)	Area of Gap
Q5:5 Reading/Writing Skills	Students were struggling with the reading – having difficulty in determining what was important to know
Q7:7 Learning Strategy	Students did not appear to have specific strategies for gleaning important information from reading, activities, and lecture.

Extensions Identified for Differentiation

(BLM 8) – Order of Learning and Strategies for Learning and Presentation Styles

The teachers recognized that the two gaps were highly related but felt like the gap in Q7:7 was the biggest barrier to success. The students were capable of reading the material at least at a level high enough to pick up the basic information (e.g., highlighted vocabulary, facts). The students could take notes from lecture, but upon examination of the notes, the teachers found them to be disorganized, with more trivial information included than important factors. Given that information, the teachers believed the trouble deciding what was important might be the most interfering factor in the students' performing at a higher level.

The teachers decided to use the NNE Strategy, as developed by this author. With this, the teacher identifies three layers of learning for the content. The first N represents what the teacher believes all students NEED to know – the basics of the content. This level is the information or skill level that is critical for use or application in daily life (e.g., how to figure basic sales tax). The second N represents what is NICE to know – the additional details that make the content, skill or process interesting and useful at a higher level (e.g., how tax laws are created and maintained). The E represents the EXCELLENT to know information – the depth in details or full breadth of content (e.g., understanding the complexity of how taxes are distributed for government use). This level includes information that is not necessary for daily use, but might be necessary for further application at higher level of study or use in a profession.

Implementation of the NNE Strategy required the teachers to create a study guide for each of four units to be taught in Practical Living. They made a decision that the information in the first layer (Need to Know) represented approximately 75% of the information from the unit. The second layer (Nice to Know) represented an additional 15% of the content, and the third layer (Excellent to Know) represented 90 – 100% of the content.

Using this technique required the teachers to change how they provided information to the students. They presented the information in a written, three-tiered study guide format (Presentation Style Extension). In addition, the technique required them to change the sequence in which information was provided. The teachers exposed the students to all of the information, on all three tiers from the very beginning (Order of Learning).

Implementation and Results

When the first study guide was introduced the teacher emphasized to the students that if they learned the information in the first layer they would likely pass the test with a 75% and further defined what score was likely if they learned what was in layer 2 and 3 of the study guide. The teacher gave the students choice by saying they could use or ignore the study guide. Additionally the teacher highly encouraged them to reach for the third layer of learning but made it clear that the first layer was acceptable. The teacher felt the need to emphasize that the first layer was acceptable because there were students who normally would not even strive to meet that goal and did not want to overwhelm them by suggesting that only the third layer was acceptable.

The teachers introduced each unit with the study guide, reviewing all of the information in the guide at each level. Throughout the unit of study, the teacher would reference the study guide each time an important piece of information was discussed, discovered, or practiced in an activity. The students saw the study guide every day. The teacher reminded the students to use the study guide as they prepared for each test.

The teachers reported that during their planning sessions they decided NOT to change the test content levels or format from previous tests. There were a few instances when they realized their tests needed a slight adjustment up – meaning they did not have enough level 3 questions on them.

The general education teacher collected three types of data related to the use of the study guide Extension. Test scores were recorded for each unit test. The teacher asked the students to self-report on whether or not they had used the study guide to prepare for their tests. The teacher disaggregated the range of scores of the targeted students. The results of the data are below:

	PreImplementation	Unit/Test 1	Unit/Test 2	Unit/Test 3	Unit/Test 4
Test Score Average for Class	84%	88%	88%	87%	94%
Students reporting they used the study guide	N/A	65%	69%	61%	71%
Targeted Students range of test scores	40 – 75%	70 – 90%	75 – 93%	80 – 93%	80 – 94%

The data clearly show that the average tests scores for the target students increased dramatically, closing the achievement gap for these students. The teacher reported that the students who were targeted for this strategy reported using the study guide Extension to prepare for each test.

In addition to the positive results for the targeted students, the class average increased dramatically after the implementation of the NNE Strategy. Who can argue with a class average of 94% on traditional tests?

The teachers reported that using the NNE Strategy initially took more planning time than they were use to, but in the end saved instructional time. They found that the process became easier, and thus quicker, after planning the first one because they developed their own pattern of identifying what went into the three levels. The general education teacher felt the study guide Extension helped to focus the lecture and activities, thus spending less time on unimportant information. The teacher also reported that the integrity of the content was actually improved because there was a distinct focus on all three levels, whereas in the past the instruction may not have made it to the 3rd level because students would struggle with the first two levels of information without a method for taking appropriate notes.

Points to Ponder about the Process and the Outcomes
There are several important points to emphasize concerning this research case.

1. The teachers <u>used the DIGIT process</u> to identify specific gaps and chose one Extension to bridge the gap. (No complex, high maintenance techniques were employed.)

2. The teachers <u>did NOT change their content</u> or their requirements for tests. (No "dumbing down" of the curriculum. No use of tests that had been modified.)

3. The teachers *changed their behaviors* (by focusing on what was important to teach *before* teaching it and making direct and distinct connections to important information on the study guide throughout the lecture and activities), which in turn <u>changed the students' performance</u>.

4. The students who were the target of this process <u>significantly improved **academic** perfor-mance</u>.

5. The overall <u>performance of the entire class improved</u> by using the strategy. (The Extensions did not detract from other students.)

6. The use of the Extensions actually <u>increased instructional time</u> by decreasing time spent on unimportant information.

7. The Extensions chosen <u>did not cost anything</u> and were relatively easy to implement.

Case 4

Demographics

<table>
<tr><td><u>School Level</u>: Middle School</td><td><u>Grade</u>: 11th Grade</td></tr>
<tr><td colspan="2"><u>Location</u>:   Urban</td></tr>
<tr><td colspan="2"><u>Teaching Situation</u> Non Collaborative – teacher on own</td></tr>
<tr><td colspan="2"><u>Content</u>:   Literature</td></tr>
<tr><td colspan="2"><u>Instructional Gap(s) BLM 10</u>: Teaching – Learning Style</td></tr>
<tr><td colspan="2"><u>Extension Focus BLM 8</u>: Participation and Assessment</td></tr>
</table>

Background

In this situation, the teacher was concerned over the standardized test scores and Open Response writing performance of many of his students. In particular, there were 3 students with learning disabilities and one student identified as gifted and talented who were not performing up to average. Using the DIGIT process, the teacher identified possible gaps in Q6:6 Teaching – Learning Style and Q14:14 Assessment.

Gap Analysis Questions (BLM 10)	Area of Gap
Q 6:6 Teaching - Learning Style	The teacher was using reading and lecture to cover the content, but many of the students learned through discussion or action.
Q14:14 Assessment	Standardized tests and open response writing were common methods, but several of the students could draw or discuss what they knew better than write information down.

Extensions Identified for Differentiation

(BLM 8) – Participation and Assessment

The teacher determined there was a need to change the level of active participation (Teaching – Learning Style) in the class and to provide an additional method for students to show what they had learned beyond the standardized test and open response writing activities (Assessment).

To address the active participation, the teacher chose a pair-share type of strategy, such as that identified by Spencer and Lori Kagan. Typically, this strategy gives students time to discuss questions with partners before sharing with a large group. However, the teacher modified the strategy by using pair share time for students to discuss new ideas and review previously learned concepts.

In addition, the teacher decided to add another method for students to demonstrate what they knew by allowing them to illustrate the most important points of any concept to be tested.

Implementation and Results

The teacher used the Pair Share strategy at least two times per week. While students were engaged in the activity, the teacher observed and collected data on how often the targeted students verbally interacted in their small group.

The teacher used the illustration strategy one time per week and then once with the unit test. For each unit illustration opportunity, the teacher provided a basic rubric of what the students should include. For example "Create a timeline for the events in the story and identify which events were pivotal in resolving the problem. With your illustrations, include a phrase or sentence that explains why the events were important."

Data was collected on the number of times students participated, standardized test scores, open response questions, and illustrations. Students' scores were grouped into three categories: students who verbally responded an average of 3 or more times during a pair share activity, those who responded an average of 2 times, and those who responded an average of 1 time. One student responded an average of zero times during the implementation. This chart represents the average test scores for the total number of students in the class who responded 3, 2, 1, 0 times.

Average # of Times Students Responded in Pair-Share Activity	Standardized Test Average		Open Response Average		Illustration	
	Pre-Implementation	Post - Implementation	Pre-Implementation	Post - Implementation	Pre-Implementation	Post - Implementation
3	80	83	80	87	NA	98
2	72	71	78	90	NA	95
1	73	74	80	88	NA	85
0	50	68	50	70	NA	80

The teacher also disaggregated the data for the four students targeted for these Extensions.

Student	Avg. # of Responses in Pair Share	Standardized Test Average		Open Response Average		Illustration	
		Pre-Implementation	Post - Implementation	Pre-Implementation	Post - Implementation	Pre-Implementation	Post - Implementation
1 (LD)	3	73	80	70	81	NA	92
2 (LD)	3	78	82	72	85	NA	100
3 (LD)	1	73	79	71	79	NA	98
4 (GT)	3	80	85	81	87	NA	100

The teacher reported that the overall average of the class improved across the tests after using the Extensions of Pair Share and illustrations. Students who responded more often in the Pair Share activities on average performed better than those who responded less often. The biggest gains overall appear to be in the written Open Response events.

All four of the students targeted for these Extensions improved test scores in both standardized and open response events. In addition, all four scored extremely high in the illustrations test event.

The teacher indicated that using these two Extensions did not decrease or increase the amount of time it took to cover material. The only major change for the teacher was to plan out how often to let the students share and to give explicit directions on what the students should discuss during each sharing session.

Points to Ponder about the Process and the Outcomes

There are several important points to emphasize concerning this research case.

1. The teacher worked alone to solve a problem. This was not a collaborative teaching situation but the process worked.

2. The teacher used the DIGIT process to identify specific gaps and chose two Extensions to bridge the gap.

3. No complex, high maintenance techniques were employed.

4. The teacher did NOT change the content or the requirements for tests. (No "dumbing down" of the curriculum. No use of tests that had been modified.)

5. The teacher *changed his behavior* (by allowing the students to participate more often in discussion and demonstrate through illustration their understanding of concepts), which in turn changed the students' performance.

6. The students who were the target of this process significantly improved **academic** performance.

7. The overall performance of the entire class improved by using the strategy. (The Extensions did not detract from other students.)

8. The use of the Extensions actually did not decreased instructional time.

9. The Extensions chosen did not cost anything and were relatively easy to implement.

Case 5

Demographics

School Level: High School	**Grade**: 10th Grade

Location: Suburban

Teaching Situation – Collaborative – Role Exchange

Content: Social Studies – Forms of Government

Instructional Gap(s) BLM 10: Teaching – Learning Style

Extension Focus BLM 8: Order of Learning; Presentation Style

Background

The teachers in this situation were frustrated with the scores students were making on tests and quizzes. In particular, there were 6 students who had specific learning disabilities who were not performing well on tests and quizzes. The teachers used the ECQ (BLM 4) and ESQ (BLM 6) to determine if there were any specific gaps between the instruction and the needs of the students. The teachers identified one potential gap that could be addressed.

Gap Analysis Questions (BLM 10)	Area of Gap
Q 6:6 Teaching - Learning Style	The class period was 90 minutes long and the teaching (e.g., lecture) was in large segments; the students needed information provided in smaller chunks.

Extensions Identified for Differentiation

(BLM 8) – Learning and Presentation Styles

The teachers determined that there was a need to change how the teaching occurred in the 90-minute block. They felt that the direct teaching or lecturing needed to be broken into smaller portions to make the information easier to understand. They chose the CPR Strategy[1] (Content, Process, Review) that is attributed to Bob Pike. In this teaching strategy the normal direct teaching time is broken into smaller segments and each segment has three layers: teach a small segment of Content, use an activity to allow the students to Process the content, then have a specific Review of student learning before moving on to the next segment of content. The time element is different in that the time frame for teaching content is between 10 – 20 minutes, unlike many classes where the teaching encompasses 30 – 40 minutes with an activity stuck on the end.

Using this technique required the teachers to change how they presented information to the students. They had to rework the presentation of information into smaller chunks, or mini-lessons, create mini-activities that were meaningful or break up larger activities into smaller units, and generate a method to review the learning of the student after each mini lesson. The additional challenge was to ensure that one mini-lesson segment was connected with the next so that by the end of the class block of time the students experienced the full scope of the intended content.

Implementation and Results

The teachers developed 3 mini-lessons for their 90-minute blocks with a short 2-minute transition period (mind stretch) between the mini-lessons. In each of the mini-lessons, they designed a handout for note taking for each of the 3 mini-lessons that included the three tiers of information noted in the NNE Strategy mentioned earlier. The students were given highlighters and were asked to highlight important information covered during the lecture. The teachers thought this method would expedite the lecture portion of the teaching, require students to read the content, and identify important information. The teachers also hoped this method would signal for them any student not picking up on what information was most important from the lecture.

After the lecture portion of the mini-lesson the teachers conducted a processing activity in which students would have to take important information that was highlighted and apply it to a particular situation. Following the processing activity, the students were engaged in a review of the content. For example, in one unit, the teachers lectured briefly on the different forms of government and provided basic definitions. After the lecture, to process the information, the students identified how each government form impacted them as high school students. Finally, as review the students played a matching game that required them to 3-way match the correct form of government to its definition and daily application to their own life.

Using the highlighting method within the mini-lectures, the teachers discovered that several of the targeted students were having difficulty deciding what to highlight during the mini-lecture. The teachers reported that they would not have picked up on the trouble with note taking had they continued to use the larger time blocks for the lecture. The use of the CPR strategy allowed them to stop and have the students process the information. During this time, it became evident the students were not understanding the important points. Had they continued to use the previous method of lecturing for a large block of time, the students would have been significantly behind in their compre-hension of the material (which may explain the very poor grades on tests).

They used this information to change how they cued the students into what information was most important. Initially, the teachers decided to make poster size examples of the note-taking handout for each mini-lesson. While one teacher was lecturing, the other would highlight on the poster that items were important and then explain why it was more important than other information around it using a metacognition method (talking out loud about their thinking process). The teachers kept the poster size examples up on the walls for several days and used them to review information with the class and to emphasize how to pick important information before each new lecture session. After 2 weeks of using poster size examples, finding that the students were picking up on how to choose important information, the teachers changed to using an overhead projector and a copy of the note-taking handout to highlight the important information. Using the overhead was a more natural method for note taking (meaning it is how many teachers give out information) so the teachers thought they needed to transition the students away from the poster size and into the overhead size in hopes the students would transfer the skill to other classes.

The teachers reported an increase in the ability of the targeted students to identify important information from a lecture. The students' accuracy in highlighting the correct information increased from an average of 50% to an average of 89%. In addition, the teachers found that the targeted students' test scores improved. Over a four-week period, their average test scores rose from 69% to an 83%, with some of the students receiving 100% on individual tests for the first time in this govern-ment class. Test scores for the rest of the class did not show much change.

In this case, the Extension strategy used to bridge the instruction gap certainly improved the performance of the targeted students. As their scores improved, the academic gap decreased between the targeted students and their classmates.

The teachers reported that using the CPR Strategy took more time in initial planning because they had to determine where to break up the lecture into meaningful units, develop or segment activities for each lecture piece, and determine how to review the smaller portions of information. However, the teachers note that this change in their teaching style has increased instructional time. They found the students maintained important information for a longer period of time using this method so they spent less time before the unit tests reviewing, thus opening up time for more instruction.

Points to Ponder about the Process and the Outcomes

There are several important points to emphasize concerning this research case.

1. The teachers used the DIGIT process to identify specific gaps and chose one Extension to bridge the gap. (No complex, high maintenance techniques were employed.)

2. The teachers did NOT change their content or their requirements for their tests. (No "dumbing down" of the curriculum. No use of tests that had been modified.)

3. The teachers changed their behaviors (by delivering instruction in a three tiered mini-lesson format that included processing and review), which in turn changed the students' performance.

4. The students who were the target of this process improved **academic** scores.

5. The use of the Extensions actually increased instructional time by decreasing time spent on reviewing prior to a unit test.

6. The Extensions chosen did not cost anything and were easy to implement.

Case 6

Demographics

School Level: High School   **Grade**: 9th Grade

Location: Urban

Teaching Situation – Collaborative – Content/Skill Development

Content: Math

Instructional Gap(s) BLM 10: Teaching – Learning Style, Assessment

Extension Focus BLM 8: Participation

Background

The math teacher in this high school uses class participation, in the form of question and answer, "talk-through's" on individual problem, and group work. These talk-through's require students to verbally state each step of the problem-solving process as they are trying to complete a math problem. Along with the special education teacher, the math teacher was particularly concerned with the lack of participation of five (5) students- —three (3) with math learning disabilities, one (1) with mild mental retardation, and one (1)considered at-risk for dropping out. The teachers used the ECQ (BLM 4) and ESQ (BLM 6) to determine if there were any specific gaps between the instruction and the needs of the students. The teachers identified two potential gaps that could be addressed.

Gap Analysis Questions (BLM 10)	Area of Gap
Q 6:6 Teaching - Learning Style	The teachers usually asked questions then worked toward answers; teachers did not use a lot of "Wait Time" between asking and giving the answer. Several of the targeted students need a cue to warn them of an upcoming question that they should attend to, as well as some need time to process the question before answering it. In addition, most of these students are hesitant to answer out loud for fear of being wrong.
Q14:14 Assessment	The teachers used the in-class questions and "talk-through's" as part of the students' grades in class, but for the targeted students it was not the best way to measure their current knowledge.

Extensions Identified for Differentiation
(BLM 8) – Participation

Using the gap analysis, the teachers identified several possible Extensions to address the problems. The teachers felt like the most interfering problem was a combination of the students attending to the question and their level of hesitation in answering for fear of being wrong. Given this combination problem, the teachers decided to try changing the level of participation (Teaching – Learning Style) required and giving the students a cue when critical questions were going to be asked. To accomplish this, they chose the Pass Strategy.

The Pass Strategy is not used for initial discussion or brainstorming, but for processing ideas and reviewing information. Using the Pass Strategy students are allowed to "pass" on answering a question the first time around, but must attempt an answer the second time the question comes around to them. If one student passes, the teacher calls on another student who likely knows the answer. Once the correct answer has been given, the teacher repeats it, and then re-calls on the student who passed initially.

The teachers decided that the strategy needed to be modified some for their targeted students, believing that for several of them hearing the answer only once or twice might not be enough. They formulated their strategy to allow up to 3 passes before the student got no credit for answering, with the intention of reducing the number of passes allowed after the students became more comfortable with the technique.

Implementation and Results

The teachers introduced the Pass Strategy to the entire class, explaining that they valued the students' ability to verbally express their answers but understood that sometimes it may be difficult to answer a question the first time around. The teachers also indicated that passes could only be used during certain parts of class (e.g., *not* during brainstorming) and that they would tell the students when the passes could be taken.

The Pass Strategy was used for 4 weeks every day at least once in class. The teachers tracked the number of times the five (5) targeted students answered questions or attempted a walk-through prior to using the strategy, and then counted number of times the students passed and answered correctly on the next attempt, number of times passed and answered incorrectly on the next attempt, and number of times they chose not to pass and answered correctly.

The following provides a brief summary of each student's performance before and during the use of the Pass Strategy.

<u>Student 1</u> (Mild Mental Disability) rarely answered any question out loud but would tell the special education teacher the answer by whispering it in her ear.

Student 1	Attempted to answer questions	Passed and then answered incorrectly	Passed then answered correctly	Did not pass, answered correctly
Baseline (week prior to implementation)	0%			
Week 1		30%	70%	0%
Week 2		50%	40%	10%
Week 3		10%	50%	40%
Week 4		0%	40%	60%

Student 2 (Specific Learning Disability in math) usually required up to 5 reviews before he would fully understand a concept or feel comfortable answering a question.

Student 2	Attempted to answer questions	Passed and then answered incorrectly	Passed then answered correctly	Did not pass, answered correctly
Baseline (week prior to implementation)	20%			
Week 1		10%	90%	0%
Week 2		10%	80%	10%
Week 3		10%	55%	35%
Week 4		5%	50%	50%

Student 3 (Specific Learning Disability in math) rarely could answer a question, even incorrectly, the first time it was asked and was becoming more reluctant to even attempt an answer.

Student 3	Attempted to answer questions	Passed and then answered incorrectly	Passed then answered correctly	Did not pass, answered correctly
Baseline (week prior to implementation)	25%			
Week 1		50%	50%	0%
Week 2		30%	60%	10%
Week 3		10%	50%	40%
Week 4		1%	55%	44%

Student 4 (Specific Learning Disability) typically would not attempt to answer questions. Teachers thought he seemed to "zone out" when the questioning and talk-through sessions were going on in class.

Student 4	Attempted to answer questions	Passed and then answered incorrectly	Passed then answered correctly	Did not pass, answered correctly
Baseline (week prior to implementation)	0%			
Week 1		90%	10%	0%
Week 2		30%	60%	0%
Week 3		10%	50%	0%
Week 4		10%	85%	5%

Student 5 (At-Risk for dropping out) usually did not answer in class and would offer some off hand comment to deflect his inability to answer.

Student 5	Attempted to answer questions	Passed and then answered incorrectly	Passed then answered correctly	Did not pass, answered correctly
Baseline (week prior to implementation)	0%			
Week 1		70%	30%	0%
Week 2		60%	40%	0%
Week 3		0%	95%	5%
Week 4		0%	55%	45%

It is very clear from the data that each of the five students increased their level of participation and improved their ability to provide correct answers both when using the pass strategy and choosing not to pass. The strategy did not "fix" the students – meaning that some of them were still getting incorrect answers and needing time to hear the answer more than once before they could respond correctly. However, there is a dramatic difference in their level of participation and ability to answer correctly.

While not initially focused on test scores, the teachers did notice that the test scores of these students and others in the class improved over the four-week period. The average test score for these five (5) students prior to implementing the Extension was 70% on a non-modified test. By the end of the fourth week, the average test score for these five (5) students was 81% on a non-modified test.

The teachers reported that using the Extension of changing the method of participation using the Pass Strategy did not take any additional time to prepare for and did not take any additional instructional time. It did not appear to save any instructional time, but because it did increase student performance they were comfortable with continuing to use the strategy as one way to bridge the gap between the instruction and the students' needs.

Points to Ponder about the Process and the Outcomes

There are several important points to emphasize concerning this research case.

1. The teachers used the DIGIT process to identify specific gaps and chose one Extension to bridge the gap. (No complex, high maintenance techniques were employed.)

2. The teachers did NOT change their content or their requirements for their tests. (No "dumbing down" of the curriculum. No use of tests that had been modified.)

3. The teachers changed their behaviors (by allowing students time to process questions), which in turn changed the students' performance.

4. The teachers were able to collect important data that showed them how to change their teaching (using the poster size handout to model the appropriate skill), which in turn improved student performance.

5. The students who were the target of this process improved academic scores.

6. The Extensions chosen did not cost anything and were easy to implement.

What Did You Learn?

Did you notice that in every case the teachers reported that ALL students improved their performance? Were you surprised at the significant educational growth of the students with disabilities? Were any of the strategies used by these teachers new to you? Hopefully these cases have given you strong incentive to dive in and use the DIGIT process for building your own effective differentiated instruction.

Epilogue

Hopefully, your journey through this book and the challenge of implementing differentiation in your own classroom have stretched your capacity to imagine, envision, and create effective instruction. Do not be discouraged if everything did not initially fall into place easily. Remember, this is a _process_ that will take your time, energy, and attention in the beginning - just like learning any new skill (e.g., walking). There will be some stumbling blocks, missteps, and bumps along the way. If you keep with the process you will find that soon you can walk, even run through it with great agility and speed. The process of differentiation will become second nature. Just as with learning a new skill such as walking, you and your students will reach higher, go further, and be more successful in life when you learn to differentiate instruction.

If you continue to follow the differentiation process from start to finish and take each step seriously you will soon be creating effective differentiated lesson plans that meet the unique needs of individual students, focused on content of importance, using genuine experiences and authentic assessment. These lesson plans will be focused on the most important aspects of learning, those found at the top of the Differentiated Instruction Pyramid. With your newly developed skills, you will:

- teach content in relationship to how, when, when, and where students will use it in their world, both currently and in the future,
- develop the skills and knowledge of the student, using content as the backdrop for reaching personal goals or dreams,
- provide instruction from a variety of pathways, using a mix of tools necessary for student success, and
- evaluate student progress from various perspectives to gain a complete picture of the students' capabilities in real life.

The skills required to develop and implement such lessons bear the mark of a master teacher! By learning to effectively differentiate instruction, you are giving yourself and your students knowledge, power, and promise. Good luck!

Black Line Masters

BLM 1: Process for Differentiated Instruction

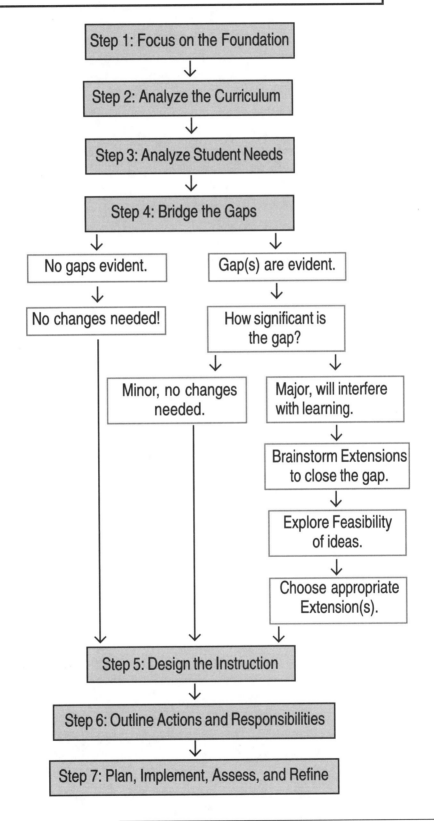

Process for Differentiated Instruction

Step 1: Focus on the Foundation
↓
Step 2: Analyze the Curriculum
↓
Step 3: Analyze Student Needs
↓
Step 4: Bridge the Gaps

No gaps evident.
↓
No changes needed!

Gap(s) are evident.
↓
How significant is the gap?

Minor, no changes needed.

Major, will interfere with learning.
↓
Brainstorm Extensions to close the gap.
↓
Explore Feasibility of ideas.
↓
Choose appropriate Extension(s).

Step 5: Design the Instruction
↓
Step 6: Outline Actions and Responsibilities
↓
Step 7: Plan, Implement, Assess, and Refine

BLM 2: Differentiated Instruction Pyramid - completed

CUT HERE

Classroom-Based Content
Grade Level Essentials
Teacher Preferences

Community-Based Curriculum
District Requirements
School Expectations

Societal-Based Curriculum
National Standards
State Standards

Cornerstones
Content Knowledge
Basic Skills

Transitions
Generalization
Problem Solving

Personal Connections
Hopes and Dreams
Adaptive Behavior

Isolated Exercises
Completing instead of comprehending

Scaffolded Instruction
Integrating and Connecting
in Context

Genuine Experiences
Relating to real life
responsibilities

Authentic Assessments
Roles in Life

Supported Performances
Personal Investigations
Approximate Applications

Situation-Specific Tests
Content Comprehension
Skill Acquisition

BLM 3: Differentiated Instruction Pyramid - blank

CUT HERE
TO HERE

BLM 4: Essential Curricular Questions (ECQ)

Name of Person Completing Form(s):_____ Date: _____

Content area(s)

Essential Curricular Questions	
Q 1 What is the content to be taught?	
Q 2 How will the student use the content in real life?	
Q 3 What background knowledge is needed for this content?	
Q 4 What is the language of instruction for this content?	
Q 5 What reading and writing skills are necessary or expected?	
Q 6 How do I normally teach this content?	
Q 7 What learning strategies are part of this content?	
Q 8 What activities will engage the learner?	
Q 9 What adaptive behaviors are expected during instruction?	
Q 10 What classroom management systems do I use?	
Q 11 What physical or sensory skills are involved in the learning?	
Q 12 What materials or services do the students use?	
Q 13 Where will the learning occur?	
Q 14 How do students show what they know during and after instruction?	

BLM 5: Essential Curricular Questions - Case Study

Name of Person Completing Form(s):_____ Date: _____

Content area(s)

Essential Curricular Questions	Initial Instructional Plan
Q 1 **What is the content to be taught?**	introduce calculating mean, median, and mode using double-digit number sets
Q 2 **How will the student use the content in real life?**	statistics; stock market; sports scores (aka batting averages); voting outcomes; weather patterns; shopping
Q 3 **What background knowledge is needed for this content?**	addition of double-digit numbers; rank ordering number sets; numbers up to 1,000; use of calculator
Q 4 **What is the language of instruction for this content?**	order, rank, add, subtract, sum, count, graph, categorize, average, show work, divide
Q 5 **What reading and writing skills are necessary or expected?**	read directions; read numeric symbols for meaning (worth); decipher word problems; 7th grade level terms; write numbers 0 - 1000; write short answers using vocabulary
Q 6 **How do I normally teach this content?**	mini-lecture; demonstrate with overhead calculators; demonstration of steps for each concept on board or overhead
Q 7 **What learning strategies are part of this content?**	graphing in order highest to lowest; manipulate data; calculator input; reading numbers; check for accuracy; note taking; discovery
Q 8 **What activities will engage the learner?**	7th graders are interested in social issues, fairness, consumerism so activities like graphing income levels of different jobs, collecting personal data for comparison; comparing items at different shops or restaurants by using mean, median, mode might get them more interested in the topic.
Q 9 **What adaptive behaviors are expected during instruction?**	independent work; small group cooperative learning; movement around the room and to the library to collect data; change from teacher demonstration to student work every 10 minutes; raise hand to ask for help
Q 10 **What classroom management systems do I use?**	at beginning of class pick up math packet with calculator; bring book, paper and pencil to class; check in at the door using chart; raise hand to answer questions; one student collects and distributes; turn lights off for attention
Q 11 **What physical or sensory skills are involved in the learning?**	punching numbers on a calculator; viewing information from paper, board, books; listening to directions; writing using a pencil; talking with peers; standing to write on the board
Q 12 **What materials or services do the students use?**	calculator, paper and pencil
Q 13 **Where will the learning occur?**	classroom and computer lab for input of data
Q 14 **How do students show what they know during and after instruction?**	vocabulary test; worksheets with 5 problems for each concept; graphing information accurately; group presentation using rubric

BLM 6: Essential Student Questions (ESQ)

Name of Person Completing Form(s): _____ Date: _____

Content area(s)

		Essential Student Questions
	Q 1	What does the student know about the content?
	Q 2	What are the interests of the student?
	Q 3	What background knowledge does the student have for this instruction?
	Q 4	To what degree does the student understand the language of instruction?
	Q 5	What reading and writing skills does the student have that impact using written materials?
	Q 6	How does the student learn?
	Q 7	What strategies does the student use to approach new learning?
	Q 8	What activities will engage the student in learning?
	Q 9	What adaptive skills does the student have that impact learning?
	Q 10	What procedures and routines does the student use or have trouble with that impact learning?
	Q 11	What physical or sensory issues does the student have that impact learning?
	Q 12	What materials or services will the student need to be successful?
	Q 13	What learning environment will allow the student to acquire, maintain, and generalize content knowledge?
	Q 14	How does the student best show what he knows and can do?

BLM 7: Essential Student Questions - Case Study

Name of Person Completing Form(s): _____ Date: _____

Content area(s)

Student Information: Nicholas		Essential Student Questions
no exposure to mean, median, mode, but knows how to average	Q 1	What does the student know about the content?
likes sports, particularly football, wrestling and baseball; keeps scores; knows batting and football data	Q 2	What are the interests of the student?
uses a calculator to input a series of up to 10 numbers; add up to 1,000	Q 3	What background knowledge does the student have for this instruction?
has difficulty with directional words such as list, order, and show your work; does not provide in-depth answers when asked to show or explain	Q 4	To what degree does the student understand the language of instruction?
reads two grade levels below his peers; word attack, skimming and reading for meaning are poor; understands pictures with simple directions better than text; no writing issues here	Q 5	What reading and writing skills does the student have that impact using written materials?
learns best by seeing and doing; learns quickly if he can physically manipulate information and see it modeled visually; auditory is his least effective learning mode	Q 6	How does the student learn?
has no specific strategies for learning; randomly approaches tasks; does not ask questions at the beginning for clarification; is not sure what is important in note taking; difficulty following more than 3 step directions	Q 7	What strategies does the student use to approach new learning?
enjoys competitive events; pays attention to activities that relate to earning points, scores; likes games; loves talking about sports scores	Q 8	What activities will engage the student in learning?
needs signals for transitioning from one activity to another; has good work-related skills, except forgets homework; trouble taking turns in some situations; acts as leader; likes independent work; respectful of others	Q 9	What adaptive skills does the student have that impact learning?
needs specific directions on how to get ready for every class; needs visual cue to get his attention; follows other typical classroom directions like raising hand, taking turns	Q 10	What procedures and routines does the student use or have trouble with that impact learning?
wears glasses consistently; no major issues in this area	Q 11	What physical or sensory issues does the student have that impact learning?
use a calculator for math; will need support from adult to redirect his attention, when trying activities with more than 3 steps	Q 12	What materials or services will the student need to be successful?
ok in classroom; can use library and science lab for research	Q 13	What learning environment will allow the student to acquire, maintain, and generalize content knowledge?
can take short paper and pencil tests; may need to explain his written answers after an essay, to better show what he knows	Q 14	How does the student best show what he knows and can do?

BLM 8: Extensions for Learning (page 1 of 2)

Extension	Description	Example
Application and Demonstration of Knowledge	The ways to demonstrate in measurable terms what has been learned or mastered; representation, delivery, product, conduct, or performance by the student.	learning logs; brochures; cartoons; diagram; dance; poster; oral reports
Complexity of Task	Level of sophistication of task; challenge or difficulty of skill; approach to problem; process for solving problem	use one research tool instead of three; apply 5-step problem solving process instead of 2-step process; research the impact of acid rain while others research simple soil erosion
Environment	The variety of settings, situations or domains necessary for learning; access and need for specialized resources; physical characteristics	specialized lighting; adapted desks; learning in the community; access to internet within learning environment
Independence Level	The degree of dependence/independence; need for direct or indirect guidance, encouragement, backing, authorization	pairs learning; job coach; contracts; one-on-one instruction
Langauge of Learning	The words used to explain, demonstrate, or demand action during instruction or independent work	use "find similarities or differences" instead of "compare" for instructions; model what "show your work" means in a math class; use pictures of the action or the person doing the action along with words
Motivation	Incentive, reward, bonus - extrinsic or intrinsic that connect to the student's needs, interests and abilities.	student-teacher partners; goal setting; menu of reinforcers; self selection and design of projects
Order of Learning	Attention to prior knowledge to determine the appropriate articulation, sequence, priority, progression, or pattern	teach/review prerequisite skills; use pretest to determine starting point; learn history from issues and patterns rather than chronological approach

BLM 8: Extensions for Learning (page 2 of 2)

Category	Description	Examples
Pace	Rate, velocity, speed, acceleration of learning	pretest and begin student at readiness point instead of lock step progression through a chapter;
Participation	The purpose of participation, degree of interaction for optimum learning	active learning; socialization and communication; research - independent or group
Procedures and Routines	The variety of methods to facilitate and communicate the learning process (e.g., direct instruction, mentorships, contracts)	flexible grouping routines; write problems on overhead; use content enhancements in delivery of instruction (e.g., mapping, mnemonics)
Purpose and Appropriateness	Matching the interests, needs and abilities of the student to the intent, goal or reason for the task	match math activities to after school employment; learn to make healthy food choices in a natural environment
Resources and Materials	The software, equipment, fixtures, gear, supplies, and furnishings appropriate for learning.	dark colored markers; large print books; audio tapes; dividers in notebooks; on-line internet connections
Size	Dimensions, quantity, scope, size, proportions of the task; Degree of decision making required; Level of challenge	complete 5 math problems while others complete 10; write a three paragraph story instead of a 10 page report
Strategies for Learning and Presentation Styles	The way information is organized, manipulated, and presented within the instruction and independent work	visual pictures for abstract concepts; listen to book on tape while class reads along; use dancing definitions to allow student movement while learning
Time	Duration, cycle, length or intervals for learning and demonstrating knowledge	take a course over a full year instead of one semester; decrease amount of time spent on a course; allow 1 additional day for work completion

BLM 9: Feasibility Worksheet

Directions: Use this sheet to document discussions on the feasibility of Extensions to support student learning. An examples is provided for you:

Rapid Results	Will the Extension quickly create visible results in student performance?	Reading program will take time, but word cards with pictures will create immediate improvement. Use both?

Feasibility Issue	Questions to Ask	Commentary/Decisions
Rapid Results	Will the Extension quickly create visible results in student performance?	
Disturbance Level	Will the Extension create significant disruption to the routines and procedures of the classroom?	
Access	Is the resource, service, or material readily available to the teacher?	
Ease of Implementation	Can the Extension be implemented without an extraordinary amount of work or training for the adults involved?	
Age Appropriateness	Does the idea fit the age of the student or will it use materials, methods, or situations that are not appropriate?	
Useable by Others	Is this an Extension that might be beneficial to other students in the room?	
Length of Time	How long will this particular Extension be needed?	
Person Implementing	Who will be the primary implementer of this Extension?	

BLM 10: Gap Analysis

Person(s) completing form_____ Date completed_____

Content Area(s)

Is there a gap?	Yes, No, Maybe with Description	Ideas for Differentiation	Try First
Q1:1 Content			
Q2:2 Real Life/ Interests			
Q3:3 Background			
Q4:4 Language of Instruction			
Q5:5 Reading and/or Writing Skills			
Q6:6 Teaching-Learning Style			
Q7:7 Learning Strategies			
Q8:8 Engaging Activities			
Q9:9 Adaptive Behaviors			
Q10:10 Management Systems			
Q11:11 Physical or Sensory Skills			
Q12:12 Materials or Services			
Q13:13 Location or Setting			
Q14:14 Assessment			

BLM 11: Gap Analysis - Case Study

Person(s) completing form_____ Date completed_____

Content Area(s)

Is there a gap?	Yes, No, Maybe with Description	Ideas for Differentiation	Try First
Q1:1 **Content**	NO		
Q2:2 **Real Life/ Interests**	NO	BE SURE TO USE SPORTS IDEAS	
Q3:3 **Background**	NO		
Q4:4 **Language of Instruction**	YES - DIRECTIONAL WORDS	MODEL AND EXPLAIN SPECIFIC WORDS, PERHAPS PROVIDE A PICTURE OF EACH WORD'S MEANING/PROCESS	both
Q5:5 **Reading and/or Writing Skills**	YES - 2 YEARS BELOW GRADE	CHANGE WORD PROBLEMS TO LOWER LEVEL BECAUSE WE ARE MEASURING THE MATH PROCEDURES, NOT THE VOCAB.; MAKE SURE DIRECTIONS ARE ON READING LEVEL	both
Q6:6 **Teaching- Learning Style**	NO	BE SURE TO USE VISUAL THOUGH	
Q7:7 **Learning Strategies**	YES - RANDOM APPROACH, NOT SELF ADVOCATE	(1) TEACH - MODEL; (2) GIVE LAMINATED EXAMPLES OF PROCESSES TAUGHT FOR PROBLEM SOLVING; (3) REINFORCE ASKING QUESTIONS WITH TICKETS AND VERBAL PRAISE	#2
Q8:8 **Engaging Activities**	NO, BUT..	BE SURE TO USE SPORTS EXAMPLES/ PROBLEMS	
Q9:9 **Adaptive Behaviors**	YES - INDEPENDENT WORK AND SOME TRANSITIONING	(1) USE TIMER TO SIGNAL CHANGE IN ACTIVITY; (2) PEER OR ADULT TO CHECK WORK AFTER 5 MINUTES OF INDEPENDENT WORK; (3) WALK BY TO REMIND HIM TO STAY ON TASK	#1
Q10:10 **Management Systems**	YES - READINESS FOR CLASS	(1) TRY LIST ON LOCKER FIRST, THEN LAMINATED CARD, MAYBE PHOTO OF ITEMS; (2) USE VERBAL REMINDERS; (3) IF UNSUCCESSFUL HAVE HIM CREATE AN EMERGENCY BAG WITH EXTRA MATERIALS TO KEEP IN ROOM AND ONE FOR HOME	#1 and 2
Q11:11 **Physical or Sensory Skills**	NO		
Q12:12 **Materials or Services**	MAYBE - DIRECTIONS WITH MORE THAN 4 STEPS	(1) MARK OFF STEPS IN INCREMENTS OF 3; (2) COLOR CODE STEPS; (3) PROVIDE DIRECT SUPPORT IN THE BEGINNING	#3 and 1
Q13:13 **Location or Setting**	NO		
Q14:14 **Assessment**	MAYBE - EXPLANATIONS OF VOCABULARY OR LONGER TESTS	MAY NEED TO VERBALLY EXPLAIN INFORMATION; MORE TIME IF TESTS ARE LONG	both

BLM 12: Lesson Plan - Part 1

Learning Principle

Student Priorities

Context

Objective(s)

Assessment

Skills

Strategies

Vocabulary

Resources

Content Connections

Materials

BLM 13: Lesson Plan - Part 1 Case Study

Learning Principle

Students solve real life problems using mathematics

Context

Been working on averaging, rank order, analyzing data for graphs - single-digit

Objective(s)

Using word problems, notebook formulas and calculators, students will:
1) identify the <u>mode</u> for a series of 2-digit numbers;
2) calculate the <u>median</u> for a series of 2-digit numbers;
3) calculate the <u>mean</u> for a series of 2-digit numbers
by writing or verbally describing the process and giving the correct answer with no less than 90% accuracy

Assessment

Daily assignments; anecdotal records for verbal responses; mini tests; large test (audio taped responses allowed)

Skills ✓

grade level reading; calculator use; listen & discuss; rank order; workbook use/organization; independent work

Strategies ✓

step-by-step process; pictures with words; verbal repetition of process/steps; attention routine to keep student focused

Vocabulary

order, rank, calculate, average, divide, mean, median, mode digits, series

Resources

manipulatives, overhead calculator, and sports statistics from web page, provided by special education teacher

Content Connections

science
economics
social studies
vocational - construction

Materials

laminated cards with steps, calculators, word problems; chart paper and markers; overhead & markers

Student Priorities

Be sure to use sports examples to keep N. involved in examples

N. will need word problems that are on third grade reading level so check the sheets and the tests

N. needs to learn step-by-step process and use it each time he solves a problem. Have him draw pictures and verbally repeat information. Post process on wall for reference. Laminate a small card for him and others to use. Color code the steps?

Get N.'s attention when teaching each new concept. Help him organize the information in his workbook.

BLM 14: Lesson Plan - Part 2

Instructional Actions

Advanced Organizer or Introduction

Explicit (Direct) Teaching

Practice

Generalization and Application

Closure

Teacher Responsibilities

BLM 15: Lesson Plan - Part 2 Case Study

Instructional Actions	Teacher Responsibilities		
Advanced Organizer or Introduction	**Mrs. M. (Gen. Ed)**	**Mr. E. (Spec Ed)**	
Discuss sports scores and their meanings; tests %s; gallop polls; why we use certain types of numbers to report data.	Walk around & check notetaking and comprehension; check N. to see if he has materials at beginning of class	Open lesson with whole group - show how to use workbooks to collect notes; get discussion going on how we use 's in sports, shopping, etc.	
Explicit (Direct) Teaching			
On overhead, as each concept is introduced, MODEL 5 problems of each: mode, median, mean - in that order. Go to practice after introducing each concept.	Model mode 1st: use step-by-step process; have Brittany make a poster of the process to hang up; Call on N. and S. to come to overhead to demo mode. B & S for median; T & R for mean.	Write verbal description of each method on chart paper next to step-by-step charts; add pictures of each step as it is explained; hand out laminated cards to those who want/need them.	
Practice			
Word problems - sheets with 5 more problems of each concept. Pair up for checking answers; Practice mode - after mastery move to median, then mean.	Prior to this activity make sure to have rewritten word problems on appropriate reading level if needed! Check for understanding at individual desks; pose questions as students work.	Hand out papers and go over vocabulary words and directions for practice; add timer to signal how much time to work and when to stop; assign pairs before class and tell students when it is time to pair-check.	
Generalization and Application			
Will lead to M&M lesson using 3 concepts for colors in bags and how M&M company uses that data to sell M&M's.		Stay close to N, S, B, & T to check for accuracy and provide assistance.	
Closure			
Ask them to journal, then share how they will use the mean, median, mode in the future. Draw examples.	At end of each class remind them to put materials away; prepare their journals for next day, etc.	Close first lessons by discussion on how we will be using this information in the M & M lessons to come.	

BLM 16: On-the-Spot Data

Lesson _____   People Involved: _____

Date(s) Taught: _____

Student Impact.

Questions to ask while instruction is in progress:

- Are all students making progress toward the goals? If not, identify who and with what they seem to be struggling.
- Are the appropriate students using the differentiations? If not, describe what seems to be interfering with their use.
- Does the differentiation seem to be making a difference in student performance? If so, what changes are evident?

Items to collect:

work samples - anecdotal notes   - notes from interviews with students - video

Teacher Responsibilities.

Questions to ask while instruction is in progress:

- Did I/We complete each instructional action as planned? If not, what happened?
- Did I/We implement the differentiation as planned? If not, what happened to prevent the implementation and what was the outcome of not having the differentiation?

Items to collect:

anecdotal notes - discussion notes - video - observations by others

Instructional Effectiveness.

Questions to ask while instruction is in progress:

- Is the instruction producing the desired results? If not, what seems to be happening?
- Is the instruction efficient? If not, what areas seem inefficient and what appears to be the cause? (e.g., amount of time, number of changes)
- Is this a lesson or differentiation I/We would use again under similar situations?

Items to collect:

anecdotal notes - student outcomes - video - student interviews

BLM 17: Data Analysis Notetaking Sheet

Lesson: _____ People Involved: _____

Date(s) _____

Review the data collected and take notes concerning each question below:

To what degree did all students make progress toward the intended goals using the differentiations provided?

Positive Results   Problem Areas

To what degree did I/We complete the instructional actions as planned?

Positive Results   Problem Areas

To what degree did the instructional actions and differentiation facilitate the intended results?

Positive Results   Problem Areas

Overall, was this an efficient and effective way to deliver this instruction given the content and students in this classroom?

Positive Results   Problem Areas

Based upon this information, what refinement should be made for the next instructional plan?

Appendices

Appendix A

Models of Collaborative Teaching

Prepared by Anne M. Moll, Ed.D.

A look at the different models for Collaborative Teaching might be helpful here. There are at least three different models of collaborative teaching commonly used in schools (Moll, 96). These models are defined below with specific examples from elementary, middle and high school. The term *Strategic Teacher* is used in the descriptions to refer to any professional who works with the general education teacher to serve students with disabilities. The most common Strategic teachers include special education, speech language pathologists, physical therapists, occupational therapists, instructional assistants, interpreters, and specialists in vision and hearing.

Model 1: Collaborative Partner Model

The General and Strategic teachers plan, implement, and evaluate instruction together in the general education setting for a specific amount of time on a consistent basis. The key factor in this model is that the teachers have a guaranteed amount of time together for particular classes or days (e.g., all 5th period; Monday, Wednesday and Friday from 9:00 - 11:00 am). Research suggests there are two different ways teachers interact using a partner model. This model is used when the students with disabilities have the capacity, when appropriate differentiation is provided, to participate in the instruction. There are two ways teachers make this model work: Role Exchange or Content/Skill Development.

Role Exchange

Each teacher assumes responsibilities for delivery of instruction and evaluation based upon their strengths and preferences. Teachers swap roles during instruction. The general education teacher is responsible for determining content and ensuring quality, but the strategic teacher may be the person who delivers the instruction to the class. The strategic teacher is responsible for ensuring specialized services are provided, but the general education teacher may be providing the services while the special teacher provides total class instruction.

Elementary Example: Ms. Sachleben is the "strategic" teacher. Her overall responsibility is to ensure that 7 students in the class receive support in reading comprehension, communication, and writing skills. Mr. Burrow is the fourth grade teacher. His overall responsibility is to ensure that students have opportunities to explore and learn the appropriate content for fourth graders according to his district and state guidelines. The class is preparing to learn about the state of Kentucky. Ms. Sachleben has extensive knowledge of Kentucky, many artifacts, pictures, books and videos from various parts of the state, and has previously taught this topic using a unit format. The two teachers ensure that the unit aligns with the core curriculum and national standards for social studies. In teaching the unit Ms. Sachleben assumes the role of "content" teacher and Mr. Burrow assumes the role of "strategic" teacher, ensuring that the students who need specialized assistance receive the appropriate services. This gives Mr. Burrow a chance to work with the 7 students in a more intense manner and to discover what methods are effective so that he can use them when he is teaching content.

Middle - High School Example: Ms. Klapheke is the "strategic" teacher. Her overall responsibility is to ensure that 5 students in the class receive support in reading comprehension, study skills and writing skills. Mr. Lampert is the "social studies" teacher. His overall responsibility is to ensure that students have opportunities to explore and learn the appropriate social studies content. The class is preparing to learn about World War II. Ms. Klapheke has extensive knowledge on WWII, many artifacts from her father's participation in the war, and has previously taught this topic using a unit format. The two teachers ensure that the unit aligns with the core curriculum and national standards for social studies. In teaching the unit Ms. Klapheke assumes the role of "content" teacher during their studies of WWII and Mr. Lampert assumes the role of "strategic" teacher, ensuring that the students who need specialized assistance receive the appropriate services.

Content/Skill Development

The general education teacher is responsible for and provides instruction on the content consistently. The strategic teacher, on a consistent basis, is responsible for and provides strategies, reteaching, reinforcing, or restating instruction to enhance learning and connections to content. The strategic teacher provides those services to both the students with disabilities and their non-disabled peers.

Elementary Example: Ms. Combs is the "strategic" teacher. Her overall responsibility is to provide services to 8 students in the language arts class who have difficulty with writing and reading comprehension. Ms. Hito is the "content" teacher. Her overall responsibility is to provide instruction in language arts based upon the school's curriculum. Each week, Ms. Combs begins the first class with a review of the previous week's learning. She then uses a reading and writing jump start to prepare the class for the week's focus including vocabulary, literature themes and writing guides. Throughout the week she continues to support student learning by emphasizing vocabulary, checking writing, following up on comprehension in small groups. Ms. Hito guides the students through the content of the class using the writing guide as an outline for the teaching. She reinforces vocabulary, comprehension and writing skills for all students.

Middle - High School Example: Ms. Bronger is the "strategic" teacher. Her overall responsibility is to provide services to 8 students in the English/literature class who have difficulty with note taking, study skills, and reading comprehension. Ms. Juarez is the "content" teacher. Her overall responsibility is to provide instruction in literature/ English based upon the school's curriculum. Each week, Ms. Bronger begins the first class with a review of the previous week's learning. She then uses a study skills jump start to prepare the class for the week's focus including vocabulary, literature themes and study guides. Throughout the week she continues to support student learning by emphasizing vocabulary, checking study guides, following up on comprehension in small groups. Ms. Juarez guides the students through the content of the class using the study guide as an outline for the teaching. She reinforces vocabulary, comprehension and notetaking skills for all students.

Model 2: Supportive Teaching Services

The General and Strategic teachers plan, implement, and evaluate instruction together in the general education setting. The strategic teacher spends a limited amount time in the general education setting and but works with the students in a separate environment. The general education teacher is responsible for essential content as well as specialized services when the strategic teacher is not present. The strategic teacher is responsible for focusing on the special needs of individual students as well as content instruction using materials and experiences directly related to the content that students miss while out of the general education setting. There are two common ways this model is used: In-Class with Dedicated Support, and Parallel Dedicated Support. The phrase *dedicated support* is used to refer to times when a student needs time apart from the normal classroom routine to work on skills, knowledge, or processes and usually infers that the student is receiving support in an environment other than the general classroom.

In-Class with Dedicated Support

The general education teacher drives content and ensures that specially designed instruction, such as in-class extensions, are provided when the strategic teacher is not in the room. The general education teacher provides guidance to the strategic teacher on activities and materials for use during dedicated support time. The strategic teacher spends a specific amount of time in the general education setting, but typically not a full day or class period. She provides materials, conducts activities to support content/skill development in general class and uses materials and activities in a separate setting to enhance students' comprehension and skills for application in the classroom.

Elementary example: Ms. Kennedy is the math content teacher in 6th grade. National standards for the 6th grade suggest that students work on number sense and operations for real world problem solving. Ms. Stashky is the "strategic" teacher. In one 6th grade class there are 9 students who have difficulty with math reasoning and calculations. These students can get the material if they learn it in smaller increments, use manipulatives, and have extended time to learn and practice the content. Ms. Stashky meets each morning for 30 minutes with the 9 students during first period (which is study skills block for all students). She uses manipulatives, specific study maps to review the material from the day before, checks for understanding, and introduces material that will be covered in the day's class using similar study guides. This time provides the students additional opportunities to practice and comprehend content that has and will be covered in class. Ms. Stashky also works in the 6th grade class 3 days out of the week to support the students' in-class performance. Ms. Kennedy uses the maps in class to help students frame their learning and prepare them for exams on the content.

Middle - High School Example: Mr. Leffler is the "content" teacher in Algebra 1. Ms. Aubrey is the "strategic" teacher. In the Algebra 1 class there are 9 students who have difficulty with math reasoning and higher level calculations. These students can get the material if they have extended time to learn and practice the content. Ms. Aubrey meets each morning for 30 minutes with the 9 students during first period (which is study skills block for all students). She uses specific study guides to review the material from the day before, checks for understanding, and introduces material that will be covered in the day's class, using similar study guides. This 30 minute period provides the students additional time to practice and comprehend content that has and will be covered in Algebra 1 class. Ms. Aubrey also works in the Algebra 1 class 2 days out of the week to support the students' in-class performance. Mr. Leffler uses the same study guides in class to help students frame their learning and prepare them for exams on content.

Parallel Dedicated Support

The general education teacher drives content and ensures that differentiations are provided and consistent, with dedicated support learning activities. The Strategic teacher spends very little time in the general education setting but the two teachers plan together and communicate regularly on student progress. The Strategic teacher builds on student skills in a different setting using materials/content consistent with general class instruction. The student is working on the same content, with at least similar activities in both environments.

Elementary Example: Mr. Underwood is the 3rd grade teacher. He plans his 3rd grade lessons in conjunction with Ms. Hill, the "strategic" teacher. The two teachers meet once per week to discuss issues, problem solve, and plan. Mr. Underwood teaches a 3rd grade class that has 26 students including 8 students with reading comprehension problems and 4 with attention deficits. Ms. Hill provides Mr. Underwood with reading comprehension strategies and web outlines which he uses to help the students comprehend new information and stay on task. Ms. Hill works with the students during study skills period to reinforce comprehension of learning in 3rd grade content, keep up-to-date on assignments and prepare for exams. Once a week Ms. Hill comes to the class to observe and assist students. This helps her know what to focus on when she works with the students in her room.

Middle - High School Example: Mr. O'Bryan is the science teacher. He plans his science lessons in conjunction with Ms. Herner, the "strategic" teacher. The two teachers meet once per week to discuss issues, problem solve and plan. Mr. O'Bryan teaches a science class that has 28 students including 9 students with reading comprehension problems, 2 with attention deficits, 1 with Aspergers and 3 who need remedial work in writing but do not qualify for special education services. Ms. Herner provides Mr. O'Bryan with content enhancement strategies, notetaking outlines, and writing formats which he uses to help the students comprehend new information and stay on task. Ms. Herner works with the students during study skills period to reinforce writing, comprehension of learning in science class, focus on most important features of a learning activity, keep up to date on assignments, and prepare for exams.

Model 3: Consultative Services

In the third model type, the general and strategic teachers discuss individual student needs in relationship to performance in the general education setting. The teachers do not work in the same classroom at any time, but confer to ensure students are making progress toward their goals. The Consultative model is used when one of two situations arise.

There are times when the general education teacher can implement differentiated instruction without any direct help from other professionals. However, the teacher feels that is is necessary to confer with the strategic teacher to acquire strategies or materials for differentiation. In this model the strategic teacher may or may not have interaction with student.

The other situation that calls for this model is when a special education teacher is serving a student or group of students with disabilities in a self contained environment for most or all of the day. In these cases, the students with disabilities are typically not able to participate in the general classroom (e.g., violent behaviors). The special education teacher confers with the general education teacher to ensure that the students are making progress in the general education curriculum while they are working on the skills which prevent them from participating in the general classroom. In this instance the special education teacher works with other strategic teachers and the general education teacher to provide differentiated instruction to the student(s). The general education teacher provides content, materials, and ideas, for the special education teacher and other strategic teacher to implement in a different setting.

Elementary Example: Mr. Bryant is the general education teacher in the first grade. He has 4 students who have difficulty organizing information and therefore do not always get their work done on time. In addition, there are four students who have attention problems that interfere with them participating in large group activities. Mr. Bryant meets once a week for 30 minutes with Mrs. Cox, the special education teacher at the school. During that time, they discuss methods that Mr. Bryant can use to help the students organize information and stay on task, or the results of what he is using to help those students. Mrs. Cox provides him with ideas, materials; he models techniques to use that will help the students. She does not work directly with the students.

In addition, during that time frame, Mr. Bryant helps Mrs. Cox. She currently has two students in her room who cannot thrive in the general education setting at this time because of specific behavior problems. She is working on improving their behavior and eventually plans to integrate them into Mr. Bryant's class. However, until the behaviors are under some level of control, she is responsible for making sure that they have access to the content that is typical for 1st graders. Mr. Bryant provides her with lessons, activity ideas and materials that can be used to keep the students up to date on the class content. She uses his notes, materials and ideas to tackle content and their behaviors so that eventually they can return to the classroom and be on track academically.

Middle - High School Example: Mr. Spence is the general education teacher. He teaches Biology this semester. In his second block, there are 4 students who have difficulty organizing information and therefore do not always get notes taken, homework completed, or steps for lab accomplished. Mr. Spence meets once a week for 20 minutes with Mrs. Hawkins, the special education teacher at the school. During that time, they discuss methods that Mr. Spence can use, or the results of what he is using to help those students. Mrs. Hawkins provides him with ideas, materials and general support on implementing services that will help the students. She does not work directly with the students.

During that time frame, Mr. Spence also helps Mrs. Hawkins. She currently has two students in her room who cannot thrive in the general education setting at this time because of specific behavior problems. She is working on improving their behavior and eventually plans to integrate them into Mr. Spence's class. However, until the behaviors are under some level of control, she is responsible for making sure that they have access to the content in Biology and other classes. Mr. Spence provides her with lecture notes, lab ideas and materials that can be used to keep the students up to date on the Biology class. She uses his notes, materials and lab ideas to tackle content and their behaviors.

Appendix B

Defining Management Styles

Prepared by Anne M. Moll, Ed.D.

Directions: Write your response to the following statements. Base your response on the way you normally operate your classroom. Share and compare your responses to other individuals in your team.

Routines and Procedures

Before and After

1. I usually arrive at school by:

2. I like to leave school no later than:

3. In the morning before the students arrive I usually:

4. Committees and other responsibilities I typically have before and after school that impact my time include:

During School Time

1. The first thing I expect/have the students do in the morning, or at the beginning of class is:

2. I collect work/homework by:

3. When it comes to restroom breaks and the getting a drink of water, I:

4. During class, when students need materials or to sharpen their pencils, I:

5. When there are papers, reports or activities to be collected and evaluated, I:

6. Other routine procedures that are important to me:

Room Arrangement

1. My classroom has (desks, tables, work centers) for students to sit/work:

2. I like my desk to be located:

3. I like to keep and organize the materials used for instruction in the following ways:

4. I use the bulletin boards for:

5. Clutter and disorganization of my desk and the areas of the classroom are some thing that I:

6. The typical room arrangement I use for instructional purposes looks like this: (Draw it!)

7. The types of distracters I can tolerate in my room include (e.g., mobiles hanging, noise, background music)

8. Other organization preferences I have about my room:

Student Supervision

1. Typical Rules of the Room and expected behaviors are:

2. The type of positive reinforcement I use is:

3. Consequences for not following rules are:

4. I prefer that students keep their materials:

5. Other student supervision issues are:

Instructional Planning, Implementation and Evaluation

Planning

1. I like to have my instructional planning completed for the next week no later than:

2. When I plan for instruction, I usually:

3. Some of the issues I must contend with when I plan instruction are:

4. I like to design my lesson plans like: (e.g., in writing, on computer, in book)

Implementation

1. My preferred teaching style is:

2. When I provide direct instruction, I typically deliver it using the following: (e.g., over head, board, computer; lecture, print)

3. Some of the materials I use to help with instruction are: (e.g., manipulatives, notes)

4. I use these strategies to help students focus on important information in class:

5. I use textbooks as :

6. Grouping strategies I am comfortable using include:

7. The majority of the classroom work is designed so that students are engaged: (e.g., independent, small group, large group)

8. For variations in ability and performance, I make these modifications:

9. The primary type of teaching I use is: (e.g., hands-on, lecture, discovery)

10. When coteaching with another person, I would prefer that my role be:

11. When it comes to students leaving the classroom for other purposes (e.g., therapy) I would prefer that:

Evaluation

1. My preferred style for student evaluation is: (e.g., paper and pencil tests, projects)

2. Typically I assess my students as often as:

3. My grading scale or rubric is typically:

4. For variations in ability and performance, I make these considerations when grading:

5. I keep a record of evaluation and performance using: (e.g., grade book, portfolio)

6. If a student misses a test or an assignment (with legitimate reasons) I allow the student to:

7. If students are chronically late with assignments or never turn them in, I usually:

8. I use my assessment information in the following ways to communicate to students and parents:

Communication and Working with Paraeducators

1. I see the paraeducator's primary role and responsibilities in my classroom as:

2. My responsibility for the work of the paraeducator includes:

3. The degree to which I like to include the paraeducator in planning, instruction and assessment is:

4. If the paraeducator has ideas, concerns or questions, I would like for him or her to:

Communication and Interaction with Parents

1. I like to communicate to the parents as often as:

2. The way(s) in which I encourage parental support include:

3. I include my parents in short and long range planning in this way:

4. My preference(s) for communicating with parents include:

5. If parents have concerns and want to talk or meet with me, I usually:

Once you have completed this on your own, discuss your responses openly with your potential partner.

In what areas are your management styles similar? In which areas do your styles differ? Is the difference small or great?

Write out your major differences and similarities that will create smooth and/or difficult collaborative work.

Appendix C

Creative Ways to Make Time

for Collaborative Planning when the System Doesn't Adapt Appropriately

Prepared by Anne M. Moll, Ed.D.

1. Schedule lunch and planning back to back. Schedule your lunch at the same time.

2. Schedule early and late duties on the same weeks so that other weeks are open.

3. Bring large groups of students together for independent or group projects.

4. Train volunteers to work with students on individual projects which are overseen by the teachers.

5. Invite community leaders in all professions to come and work with students.

6. Hire a permanent floating teacher to work in classes on a regular basis.

7. Have the principal or counselor take over instruction for a class once every two weeks.

8. Set aside time everyday with no interruptions, such as fifteen minutes before school starts.

9. Extend the school day and prorate teacher salaries.

10. Chose one day per month as collaborative planning day. Have large group activities planned. Teachers "swap" half days for collaborative work and large group instruction.

11. Relieve teachers of other duties.

12. Hire a substitute once per month for teachers.

13. Change to block scheduling and create an "additional" block of time; use enrichment course activities.

Appendix D

Sample Lesson Plan

Annsley Frasier Thornton School of Education/Bellarmine University

---

Lesson Plan Format - Following KTIP Structures

Demographic information recorded prior to observation should include:

Name: _____ Date: _____ Lesson Length: _____

School: _____ Age/Grade Level: _____ # of Students: _____

Subject: _____ Topic: _____ # of IEP's: _____

Actions written prior to the observation should include:

Objectives - Clearly state your broad goals and specific objectives for learning (e.g., concepts, procedures, skills, etc. you want students to learn).

Student Assessment - Clearly state how you will assess student progress including performance criteria. Attach written assessment measures used in relation to the lesson. You should make clear how you will assess each of the objectives outlined above.

Connections - Explain how your objectives relate to Kentucky Learner Goals and standards for learning content established by professional organizations.

Context - Clearly describe how these objectives and this lesson relate to your broad goals for teaching about the topic. Explain what you have done previously which relates to this lesson.

Materials/Technology - List materials used during the lesson. Attach print material to be used with students.

Procedures - Describe the strategies and activities you will use to involve students and accomplish your objectives including how you will trigger knowledge and adapt strategies to meet individual student needs. *You should particularly address how you will attend to the learning needs of IEP students.*

Impact and refinement written after the lesson and conference and reviewed during the committee meeting should include:

Impact—Reflection/Analysis of Teaching and Learning - Discuss student progress in relation to the stated objective (i.e., what they learned with indicators of achievement). Discuss success of instruction as it relates to assessment of student progress. It is particularly important to include an analysis of student work which was not satisfactory and samples of student work analyzed.

Refinement—Lesson Extension/Follow-up - Based on the reflection, discuss plans for subsequent lessons to reinforce and extend understanding particularly for students who did not make satisfactory progress.

Bibliography

Algozzine, B., Christenson, S. & Ysseldyke, J. E. "An analysis of the incidence of special class placement: The masses are burgeoning." *The Journal of Special Education*, 17, 141-147, 1982.

Allington, R. L. & McGill-Franzen, A. "Different programs, indifferent instruction." In D. K. Lipsky & A. Gartner (Eds), *Beyond separate education: Quality education for all.* (pp75-79). Baltimore, MD: Paul Brooks, 1989.

Baker, E. T. *Meta-analytic evidence for non-inclusive educational practices: Does educational research support current practice for special needs students?* [CD-ROM]. Abstract from: ProQuest File: Dissertation Abstracts Item: 9434644, 1994.

Baker, E. T., Wang, M. C., & Walberg, H. J. "The effects of inclusion on learning." *Educational Leadership,* 52, 33 - 35, 1995.

Bellarmine University. Bellarmine University lesson plan format. 2001 Newburg Road, Louisville, Ky. 40205, 2002.

Bigge, J. L. and Stump, C. S. *Curriculum, Assessment and Instruction for students with disabilities.* Wadsworth Publishing, Belmont: CA, 1999.

Brown v. Topeka Board of Education. 347 U.S. 483, 1954.

Bulgren, J.A., Schumaker, J.B., & Deshler, D.D. The Concept Mastery Routine, *The Content Enhancement Series*, Edge Enterprises, Inc.: Lawrence, KS , 1993.

Carlberg C., & Kavale, K. "The efficacy of special versus regular class placement for exceptional children: A meta-analysis." *Journal of Special Education,* 14, 295 - 309, 1980.

Gartner, A. & Lipsky, D.K. *The yoke of special education: How to break it.* Rochester, NY: National Center on Educational Restructuring and Inclusion, 1989.

Gartner & Lipsky. *Inclusion: a service, not a place. A whole school approach.* Dude Publishing: Port Chester, NY, 2002.

Gronlund, Norman E. *How to write and use instructional objectives, 5th edition.* Englewood Cliffs, NJ: Prentice Hall, Inc., 1995.

KDE CATS Research Files, Spring 2002 - *Kentucky Performance Report: Disaggregated Data*, Kentucky Department of Education, Frankfort, KY, 2002.

Lipsky, D. K. & Gartner, A. *National study of inclusive education.* New York: National Center on Educational Restructuring and Inclusion, 1994.

Mager, Robert F. *Preparing instructional objectives: A critical tool in the development of effective instruction, 3rd edition,* The Center for Effective Performance, Inc., Atalnta, GA, 1997.

Moll, A. M. *Creating a single service delivery system in education: The impact of the Collaborative Teaching Model Training Project on Kentucky schools.* UMI Dissertation Abstracts Item: 9632299, 1996.

National Skills Standard Board, 1441 L Street, Suite 9000, Washington, DC 20005-3512

O'Connor, Ken. *How to grade for learning.* Arlington Heights, IL: Skylight Publishing, 1999.

Pike, Bob. *Creative Teaching Techniques.* The Bob Pike Group: Minneapolis, MN, 2000.

Price, K.M. and Nelson, K. L. *Daily planning for today's classroom: A guide for writing lesson and action plans.* 2nd Ed. Boston: Wadsworth Publishing, 2003.

Pugach, M. C. & Johnson, L. J. "Pre referral interventions: Progress, problems, and challenges." *Exceptional Children,* 56, 217 - 235, 1989.

Sprick, R., Garrison, M., & Howard, L. CHAMPS: *A proactive and positive approach to classroom management.* Sopris West: Longmont, CO, 1998.

Wang, M. C. & Baker, E. T. "Mainstreaming programs: Design features and effects." *The Journal of Special Education,* 19, 503-521, 1986.

Wang, M. C., Reynolds, M. C. & Walberg, H. J. "Rethinking special education." *Educational Leadership,* 44, 26 - 31, 1986.

Resources: Print and Video Materials

Available from National Professional Resources, Inc.
1-800 453-7461 • www.nprinc.com

Allington, Richard L. & Patricia M. Cunningham. *Schools That Work: Where all Children Read and Write*. New York: NY, Harper Collins, 1996.

Anderson, Winifred, Stephen Chitwood, & Diedre Hayden. *Negotiating the Special Education Maze*. Bethesda, MD: Woodbine House, 1997.

Armstrong, Thomas. *The Myth of the A.D.D. Child*. New York, NY: Penguin Putnam Inc., 1997.

Armstrong, Thomas. *Beyond the ADD Myth: Classroom Strategies & Techniques* (Video). Port Chester, NY: National Professional Resources, Inc, 1996.

Bateman, Barbara & Annemieke Golly. *Why Johnny Doesn't Behave: Twenty Tips for Measurable BIPs*. Verona, WI: Attainment Company, Inc., 2003.

Bateman, Barbara & Cynthia Herr. *Writing Measurable IEP Goals & Objectives*. Verona, WI: Attainment Company, Inc., 2003.

Batshaw, Mark L. *Children with Disabilities, 4th Edition*. Baltimore, MD: Paul H. Brookes Publishing, 1997.

Beecher, Margaret. *Developing the Gifts & Talents of All Students in the Regular Classroom*. Mansfield Center, CT: Creative Learning Press, Inc., 1995.

Bender, William. *Differentiating Instruction for Students with Learning Disabilities*. Thousand Oaks, CA: Corwin Press, 2002.

Block, Martin E. *A Teacher's Guide to Including Students With Disabilities in Regular Physical Education*. Baltimore, MD: Paul H. Brookes Publishing, 1994.

Bocchino, Rob. *Emotional Literacy: To Be a Different Kind of Smart*. Thousand Oaks, CA: Corwin Press, 1999.

Buehler, Bruce. *What We Know...How We Teach – Linking Medicine & Education for the Child with Special Needs* (Video). Port Chester, NY: National Professional Resources, Inc., 1998.

Burrello, Leonard, Carol Lashly, Edith E. Beaty. *Educating All Students Together: How School Leaders Create Unified Systems*. Thousand Oaks, CA: Corwin Press, Inc., 2001.

Bunch, Gary. *Inclusion: How To*. Toronto, Canada: Inclusion Press, 1999.

Cohen, Jonathan. *Educating Minds and Hearts: Social Emotional Learning and the Passage into Adolescence*. New York, NY: Teachers College Press, 1999.

Darling-Hammond, Linda. *The New Teacher: Meeting the Challenges* (Video). Port Chester, NY: National Professional Resources, Inc., 2000.

Darling-Hammond, Linda. *The Right To Learn: A Blueprint for Creating Schools That Work.* San Francisco, CA: Jossey-Bass Publishers, 1997.

Dover, Wendy. *The Personal Planner & Training Guide for the Para Professional* (3-ring binder). Manhattan, KS: MASTER Teacher, 1996.

Dover, Wendy. *Inclusion: The Next Step* (3-ring binder). Manhattan, KS: MASTER Teacher, 1999.

Doyle, Denis P., & Susan Dimentel. *Raising The Standard, 2nd Edition.* Thousand Oaks, CA: Corwin Press, Inc., 1999.

Downing, June E. *Including Students with Severe and Multiple Disabilities in Typical Classrooms.* Baltimore, MD: Paul H. Brookes Publishing, 1996.

Elias, Maurice, Brian Friedlander & Steven Tobias. *Engaging the Resistant Child Through Computers: A Manual to Facilitate Social & Emotional Learning.* Port Chester, NY: Dude Publishing, 2001.

Falvey, Mary A. *Inclusive and Heterogeneous Schooling: Assessment, Curriculum, and Instruction.* Baltimore, MD: Paul H Brookes Publishing, 1995.

Fisher, Douglas, Caren Sax, & Ian Pumpian. *Inclusive High Schools.* Baltimore, MD: Paul H. Brookes Publishing, 1999.

Flick, Grad L. *ADD/ADHD Behavior-Change Resource Kit.* West Nyack, NY: Center for Applied Research in Education, 1998.

Friend, Marilyn. *Complexities of Collaboration* (Video). Bloomington, IN: Forum on Education, 2000.

Friend, Marilyn. *The Power of Two: Making a Difference Through Co-Teaching, 2nd Edition* (Video). Bloomington, IN: Forum on Education, 2004.

Friend, Marilyn. *Succerssful High School Inclusion: Making Access a Reality for All Students* (Video). Bloomington, IN: Forum on Education, 2001.

Forum on Education (Producer). *Adapting Curriculum & Instruction in Inclusive Classrooms* (Video). Bloomington, IN: 1999.

Gardner, Howard. *The Disciplined Mind: What All Students Should Understand.* New York, NY: Simon & Schuster, 1999.

Gardner, Howard. *How Are Kids Smart?* (Video) Port Chester, NY: National Professional Resources, Inc., 1996.

Giangreco, Michael F. *Quick-Guides to Inclusion: Ideas for Educating Students with Disabilities.* Baltimore, MD: Paul H. Brookes Publishing, 1997.

Giangreco, Michael F. *Quick-Guides to Inclusion 2.* Baltimore, MD: Paul H. Brookes Publishing, 1998.

Giangreco, Michael, Chigee J. Cloninger, & Virginia Salce Iverson. *Choosing Outcomes & Accommodations for Children (COACH), 2nd Edition.* Baltimore, MD: Paul H. Brookes Publishing, 1998.

Glasser, William. *Alternative Strategies to Social Promotion* (Video). Port Chester, NY: National Professional Resources, Inc., 1998.

Glasser, William. *Choice Theory: A New Psychology of Personal Freedom.* New York, NY: HarperCollins, 1998.

Goleman, Daniel. *Emotional Intelligence: Why it Can Matter More Than IQ.* New York, NY: Bantam Books, 1995.

Goleman, Daniel. *Emotional Intelligence: A New Vision for Educators* (Video). Port Chester, NY: National Professional Resources, Inc., 1996.

Goodman, Gretchen. *Inclusive Classrooms from A to Z: A Handbook for Educators.* Columbus, OH: Teachers' Publishing Group, 1996.

Gore, M.C. *Successful Inclusion Strategies for Secondary and Middle School Teachers: Keys to Help Struggling Learners Access the Curriculum.* Thousand Oaks, CA: Corwin Press, 2003.

Gregory, Gale and Chapman, Carolyn. *Differentiated Instructional Strategies: One Size Doesn't Fit All.* Thousand Oaks, CA: Corwin Press, 2002.

Guilford Press (Producer). *Assessing ADHD in the Schools* (Video). New York, NY: 1999.

Guilford Press (Producer). *Classroom Interventions for ADHD* (Video). New York, NY: 1999.

Gusman, Jo. *Multiple Intelligences and the 2nd Language Learner* (Video). Port Chester, NY: National Professional Resources, Inc., 1998.

Halvorsen, Ann T. & Thomas Neary. *Building Inclusive Schools: Tools and Strategies for Success.* Needham Heights, MA: 2001.

Hammeken, Peggy A. *Inclusion: An Essential Guide for the Para Professional.* Minnetonka, MN: Peytral Publications, 1996.

Hammeken, Peggy A. *Inclusion: 450 Strategies for Success.* Minnetonka, MN: Peytral Publications, 2000.

Harwell, Joan M. *Ready-to-Use Information & Materials for Assessing Specific Learning Disabilities, Volume I.* West Nyack, NY: Center for Applied Research in Education, 1995.

Harwell, Joan M. *Ready-to-Use Tools & Materials for Remediating Specific Learning Disabilities, Volume II*. West Nyack, NY: Center for Applied Research in Education, 1995.

HBO (Producer). *Educating Peter* (Video). New York, NY: 1993.

Heacox, Diane. *Differentiated Instruction: How to Reach and Teach All Learners (Grades 3-12)*. Minneapolis, MN: Free Spirit Press, 2002.

Iervolino, Constance, & Helene Hanson. *Differentiated Instructional Practice Video Series: A Focus on Inclusion (Tape 1), A Focus on the Gifted (Tape 2)*. Port Chester, NY: National Professional Resources, Inc. 2003.

Janney, Rachel, Martha E. Snell. *Behavioral Support*. Baltimore, MD: Paul H. Brookes Publishing Co., Inc., 2000.

Janney, Rachel, Martha E. Snell. *Modifying Schoolwork*. Baltimore, MD: Paul H. Brookes Publishing Co., Inc., 2000.

Jensen, Eric. *The Fragile Brain: What Impairs Learning and What We Can Do About It*. Port Chester, NY: National Professional Resources, Inc., 2000.

Jensen, Eric. *Practical Applications of Brain-Based Learning*. Port Chester, NY: National Professional Resources, Inc., 2000.

Jorgensen, Cheryl M. *Restructuring High Schools for All Students*. Baltimore, MD: Paul H. Brookes Publishing, 1998.

Kagan, Spencer, & Miguel. *Multiple Intelligences: The Complete MI Book*. SanClemente, CA: Kagan Cooperative Learning, 1998.

Kagan, Spencer, & Laurie. *Reaching Standards Through Cooperative Learning: Providing for ALL Learners in General Education Classrooms* (4-video series). Port Chester, NY: National Professional Resources, Inc., 1999.

Kame'enui, Edward J., & Deborah C. Simmons. *Adapting Curricular Materials, Volume 1: An Overview of Materials Adaptations – Toward Successful Inclusion of Students with Disabilities: The Architecture of Instruction*. Reston, VA: Council for Exceptional Children, 1999.

Kennedy, Craig H. & Douglas Fisher. *Inclusive Middle Schools*. Baltimore, MD: Paul H. Brookes Publishing, 2001.

Kennedy, Eileen. *Ready-to-Use Lessons & Activities for the Inclusive Primary Classroom*. West Nyack, NY: Center for Applied Research in Education, 1997.

Kliewer, Christopher. *Schooling Children with Down Syndrome*. New York, NY: Teachers College Press, 1998.

Kluth, Paula, Diana Straut, & Douglas Biklen. *Access to Academics for All Students*. Mahwah, NJ: Lawrence Erlbaum Associates, Inc., 2003.

Kohn, Alfie. *The Schools Our Children Deserve.* New York, NY: Houghton Mifflin Company. 1999.

Lang, Greg, & Chirs Berberich. *All Children are Special: Creating an Inclusive Classroom.* York, ME: Stenhouse Publishers, 1995.

Lavoie, Richard. *F.A.T. City: How Difficult Can This Be?* (Video). Charlotte, NC: PBS Video, 1989.

Lavoie, Richard. *Beyond F.A.T. City* (Video). Charlotte, NC: PBS Video, 2005.

Levine, Mel. *A Mind at a Time.* New York, NY: Simon & Schuster, 2002.

Lipsky, Dorothy K., & Alan Gartner. *Inclusion and School Reform.* Baltimore, MD: Paul H. Brookes Publishing, 1997.

Lipsky, Dorothy K., & Alan Gartner. *Inclusion: A Service, Not A Place – A Whole School Approach* (Video). Port Chester, NY: National Professional Resources, Inc., 2002.

Lipsky, Dorothy K., & Alan Gartner. *Standards & Inclusion: Can We Have Both?* (Video). Port Chester, NY: National Professional Resources, Inc., 1998.

Maanum, Jody L. *General Educator's Guide to Special Education: A Resource Handbook for All Who Teach Students with Special Needs.* Minnetonka, MN: Peytral Publications, Inc., 2000.

MASTER Teacher (Producer). *Lesson Plans & Modifications for Inclusion and Collaborative Classrooms* (4-video series). Manhattan, KS: 1995.

MASTER Teacher (Producer). *Inclusion: The Next Step* (4-video series). Manhattan, KS: 1999.

MASTER Teacher (Producer). *Inclusion Video Series* (4-video series). Manhattan, KS: 1994.

MASTER Teacher (Publisher). *Lesson Plans and Modifications for Inclusion and Collaborative Classrooms, Book 1 & 2* (3-ring binder). Manhattan, KS: 1996.

McGregor, Gail, R. Tumm Vogelsberg. *Inclusive Schooling Practices: Pedagogical and Research Foundations.* Baltimore, MD: Paul H. Brooks Publishing Co., Inc. 1998.

Meyen, Edward L., Glenn A. Vergason, & Richard J. Whelan. *Strategies for Teaching Exceptional Children in Inclusive Settings.* Denver, CO: Love Publishing, 1996.

Minskoff, Esther & David Allsop. *Academic Success Strategies for Adolescents with Learning Disabilities & ADHD.* Baltimore, MD: Paul H. Brookes Publishing, 2002.

Moore, Lorraine O. *Inclusion: Strategies for Working with Young Children.* Minnetonka, MN: Peytral Publications, 1997.

Nolet, Victor & Margaret McLaughlin. *Accessing General Curriculum: Including Students with Disabilities in Standards-Based Reform.* Thousand Oaks, CA: Corwin Press, 2000.

Pierangelo, Roger. *The Special Education Teacher's Book of Lists, 2nd Edition.* West Nyack, NY: Center for Applied Research in Education, 2003.

Porter, Stephanie, et al. *Children and Youth – Assisted by Medical Technology in Educational Settings: Guidelines for Care.* Baltimore, MD: Paul H. Brookes Publishing, 1997.

Putnam, Joanne W. *Cooperative Learning and Strategies for Inclusion.* Baltimore, MD: Paul H. Brookes Publishing, 1998.

Renzulli, Joseph S. *Developing the Gifts and Talents of ALL Students: The Schoolwide Enrichment Model* (Video). Port Chester, NY: National Professional Resources, Inc., 1999.

Rief, Sandra F. *The ADD/ADHD Checklist.* Paramus, NJ: Prentice Hall, 1998.

Rief, Sandra F. *How to Reach and Teach ADD/ADHD Children.* West Nyack, NY: Center for Applied Research in Education, 1993.

Rief, Sandra F., & Julie A. Heimburge. *How to Reach & Teach All Students in the Inclusive Classroom.* West Nyack, NY: Center for Applied Research in Education, 1996.

Rief, Sandra. *ADHD & LD: Powerful Teaching Strategies & Accommodations* (Video). Port Chester, NY: National Professional Resources, Inc., 2004.

Rief, Sandra. *How to Help Your Child Succeed in School: Strategies and Guidance for Parents of Children with ADHD and/or Learning Disabilities* (Video). Port Chester, NY: National Professional Resources, Inc., 1997.

Sailor, Wayne. *Creating A Unified System: Integrating General and Special Education for the Benefit of All Students* (Video). Bloomington, IN: Forum on Education, 2004.

Salovey, Peter. *Optimizing Intelligences: Thinking, Emotion, and Creativity* (Video). Port Chester, NY: National Professional Resources, Inc., 1998.

Sapon-Shevin, Mara. *Because We Can Change the World.* Boston, MA: Allyn & Bacon, 1999.

Schumaker, Jean, & Keith Lenz. *Adapting Curricular Materials, Volume 3: Grades Six* Through Eight – Adapting Language Arts, Social Studies, and Science Materials *for the Inclusive Classroom.* Reston, VA: Council for Exceptional Children, 1999.

Schumm, Jeanne Shay and Schumm, Gerald. *The Reading Tutor's Handbook.* Minneapolis, MN: Free Spirit Publishing, 1999.

Scully, Jennifer L. *The Power of Social Skills in Character Development: Helping Diverse Learners Succeed.* Port Chester, NY: Dude Publishing, 2000.

Stirling, Diane, G. Archibald, L. McKay, S. Berg. *Character Education Connections for School, Home and Community: A Guide for Integrating Character Education.* Port Chester, NY: National Professional Resources, Inc., 2001.

Shum, Jeanne Shay. *Adapting Curricular Materials, Volume 2: Kindergarten Through* Grade Five – Adapting Reading & Math Materials for the Inclusive Classroom. Reston, VA: Council for Exceptional Children, 1999.

Snell, Martha E., Rachel Janney. *Collaborative Teaming*. Baltimore, MD: Paul H. Brookes Publishing Co., Inc., 2000.

Snell, Martha E., Rachel Janney. *Social Relationships & Peer Support*. Baltimore, MD: Paul H. Brookes Publishing Co., Inc., 2000.

Stainback, Susan, & William. *Inclusion: A Guide for Educators*. Baltimore, MD: Paul H. Brookes Publishing, 1996.

Strichart, Stephen S., Charles T. Mangrum II, & Patricia Iannuzzi. *Teaching Study Skills* and Strategies to Students with Learning Disabilities, Attention Deficit Disorders, *or Special Needs, 2nd Edition*. Boston, MA: Allyn & Bacon, 1998.

Teele, Sue. *Rainbows of Intelligence: Raising Student Performance Through Multiple Intelligences* (Video). Port Chester, NY: National Professional Resources, Inc., 2000.

Thousand, Jacqueline S., Richard A. Villa, & Ann I. Nevin. *Creating Collaborative Learning: A Practical Guide to Empowering Students & Teachers*. Baltimore, MD: Paul H. Brookes Publishing, 1994.

Thurlow, Martha L., Judy L. Elliott, & James E. Ysseldyke. *Testing Students with Disabilities*. Thousand Oaks, CA: Corwin Press, 1998.

Tilton, Linda. *Teacher's Toolbox for Differentiating Instruction: 700 Strategies, Tips, Tools, & Techniques*. Shorewood, MN: Covington Cove Publications, 2003.

Tomlinson, Carol Ann. *How to Differentiate Instruction in Mixed-Ability Classroooms, 2nd Edition*. Alexandria, VA: ASCD, 2001.

U.S. Department of Education (Publisher). *To Assure the Free Appropriate Public Education of All Children with Disabilities*. Washington, DC: 1998.

VanDover, Theresa. *A Principal's Guide to Creating a Building Climate for Inclusion* (3-ring binder). Manhattan, KS: MASTER Teacher, 1995.

Villa, Richard A., & Jacqueline S. Thousand. *Restructuring for Caring and Effective Education*. Baltimore, MD: Paul H. Brookes Publishing, 2000.

Villa, Richard A. *Collaboration for Inclusion Video Series* (Video Set). Port Chester, NY: National Professional Resources, Inc. 2002.

Villa, Richard S. & Jacqueline S. Thousand. *Creating An Inclusive School, 2nd Edition*. Alexandria, VA: Association for Supervision & Curriculum Development, 2005.